NORMAN CONQUEST

One man's tale of high-flying
adventures and a life in the fast lane

VIC NORMAN

© **Porter Press International/Vic Norman**

All rights reserved. No part of this publication may be reproduced, stored in a retrieval system or transmitted, in any form or by any means, electronic, mechanical, photocopying, recording or otherwise, without prior permission in writing from the publisher.

First published April 2021

ISBN 978-1-913089-24-5

Published by Porter Press International Ltd
Hilltop Farm, Knighton-on-Teme,
Tenbury Wells, WR15 8LY, UK
Tel: +44 (0)1584 781588
sales@porterpress.co.uk
www.porterpress.co.uk

Edited by Octavia Stocker
Editorial consultant James Page
Design by Martin Port
Printed by Gomer Press Ltd
Front cover photograph by Rhody Sims
Additional images supplied by Clive Richardson, Alain Ernoult, Getty Images,
Alamy, James Page, Jake Syratt and Jill Furmanovsky.

COPYRIGHT

We have made every effort to trace and acknowledge copyright holders and apologise in advance for any unintentional omission. We would be pleased to insert the appropriate acknowledgement in any subsequent edition.

ACKNOWLEDGEMENTS

Firstly, let me thank all past and present AeroSuperBatics team members, all my sponsors and those involved in keeping them, many who have become close friends. Thank you to all the photographers, film crew and media teams for capturing all the magic. For those who joined me in making Rendcomb happen, with a special thanks to Sir Torquil Norman and Nick Mason.

The following doctors for keeping me in one piece: David Mitchell, Ian Davis, Eleanor Ivory. To Dr Robert Marcus for helping me to sort out my cancer and Professor Ian Craft for helping deliver various Norman babies of all generations.

For being blessed with wonderful children and grandchildren who have added enormously to my life and time spent on this planet.

To my mother, father and nanny for looking after me during my early years, and particularly to my father, who gave me the passion for everything that has an internal combustion engine.

To my friends who have given me laughs, adventures and some damn good memories.

The team who have got this book out of my head and into print.

And lastly to Anne, who has supported me when we first met as teenagers and has always encouraged me to chase my dream, and given me love and care all of my life.

NORMAN CONQUEST

One man's tale of high-flying adventures and a life in the fast lane

PORTER PRESS INTERNATIONAL

CONTENTS

	DEDICATION	6
	INTRODUCTION	7
	FOREWORD by ALAIN DE CADENET	8
1	FAMILY LIFE	10
2	SCHOOL YEARS	42
3	ANNE	48
4	A NEW DIRECTION	64
5	MY CARS	70
6	ROSSO RACING	96
7	TAKING TO THE AIR	104
8	WINGWALKING AND BEYOND	126
9	FROM CADBURY TO UTTERLY BUTTERLY	136
10	CHINESE ADVENTURE	160
11	HEROES	182
12	A DAY IN THE LIFE	196
13	AIRFIELDS AND HOUSES	208
14	MOTORBIKES	218
15	INTO THE FUTURE	236
	AFTERWORDS by JEREMY CLARKSON, NICK MASON & ANDY OFFER	262
	APPENDICES	268

TO ANNE

My dearest person, who has loved and supported me all of my adult life. On her 70th birthday we asked 40 friends to have lunch at Le Manoir aux Quat'Saisons and I made a short speech that I repeat for you here...

I have known Anne all our adult lives. She is a totally selfless person, only thinking of others rather than herself. She is sharp as a razor, brave as a lion and a qualified pilot. She had ridden on the back of my bike across the Sahara desert and rallied with me in South Africa in our old Porsche 356C.

In the 1960s, Anne was a Lucie Clayton fashion model. She was in adverts on the TV and was pictured in *Vogue* and in numerous other magazines and carried on modelling with hand shots when she was eight months pregnant. She was then, and is still now, stunningly beautiful.

She drove a Ford GT40 on the road with Zoe, our first child, in a carrycot on the passenger seat, and likewise in our AC Cobra. After Sam, the last of our three children, reached 18 years of age, Anne obtained her pilot's licence and we have had many adventures flying together, including one engine failure with a fire, landing in a small field in the middle of France, and on another occasion having to carry out a deadstick landing in Texas.

She is a wonderful homemaker and great cook, and has been the most kind, caring person, especially during my cancer treatment. She is very special and, when I was at Le Mans in 1972, I wrote a poem and had it put on a dog tag:

The wearer is not only beautiful in body and kind in heart but also thankfully my wife.

This is still so true today.

INTRODUCTION

The whole idea of writing a book started with me wanting my grandchildren to know something about my upbringing and side of their family. It was meant to be just a few pages long and I was planning on having a dozen copies put together by our local printers.

I started making notes 12 years ago when I took our whole family to Barbados around Christmas time. It ground to a halt when I got back to the UK as flying and work took over and, of course, I also lost my notes. During moments of spare time, I started the whole process again on several occasions. At first, I wrote long hand, which only I could read since I have such bad handwriting. I then decided to try typing myself and, slowly but surely, I did get quicker with my two-finger tapping.

Then the dreaded coronavirus pandemic struck and, after being told that I was a highly vulnerable and at risk, I decided that I would get on with it and finish my notes. Those first few pages grew into around 85,000 words and it was at that point that I decided I'd had enough of being a writer. There is so much left to tell, but it will just have to do.

Several friends are mentioned in my book, but there are several more who have not featured. To those absent friends, I apologise – though they might be rather relieved.

I've been so very lucky because I feel that I have never had a job and have never had anyone telling me what to do. One could become big-headed, but I've learnt that there are many who know much more than me, and that the real trick is to learn what you can from people whose opinions you respect.

What do I hope to be remembered for in years to come? Well, hopefully for being a family man who loved and enjoyed spending time with our offspring.

Enjoy the book and maybe it will bring a smile to your face, as it certainly has to mine.

Vic Norman

FOREWORD
ALAIN DE CADENET

If you happen to grow up somewhat surrounded by active people doing interesting things, there are no surprises if some of them influence how your own life shapes up. Spend time in private aircraft, tasty automobiles and riding on motorcycles; soon you may want to be in control of them yourself. Certainly you can see that Vic Norman was well bitten by this need at an early age.

Fortunately he possessed an incredible determination to get on with it. Add in perseverance, respect for those who came before him, and endowed with an ability to discipline himself for the time in hand and we can see that he developed the ingredients for a really worthwhile life. Couple this up with a congenital love of all forms of transport on water, on earth and in the air, and what had been merely a fortuitous choice rapidly became a way of life.

Oh yes, there was plenty of luck involved. But it was tempered by sound judgement too. How many people sadly miss the best opportunity that they might have had in life? Turn down just what they should be grasping with both hands by way of work or a relationship? Not that he always got it right, of course, but he had the knack of being able to pick himself up, start all over again if needs be, and then 'deliver the goods' as promised.

Those of us who were present when he announced that he was embarking on a fresh business operating a wingwalking flying circus using 1940s biplanes looked at each other in disbelief. He ran it continuously for 35 years, providing entertainment to countless tens of thousands of people in Europe and as far afield as China. The most successful such undertaking ever, outside the USA.

He needed to have an excellent sense of humour to get on with what life threw up at him. An innate ability to deal with matters of a moment – including making decisions that would save his life if he got them right, but might kill him if he didn't. Discovering and resurrecting the long-forgotten Royal Flying Corps training airfield at Rendcomb, for instance, was a masterstroke. I wonder how many thousands of visitors have benefited from airshows there.

Strange to see and read about the life of someone you know so well; all just laid out in front of you. His own photographs and own words to explain most of it. And all this from a family man, an Honorary Air Commodore in the RAF, who is still making a serious contribution to the joy of his own life and all those who share it with him.

This tome has certainly reaffirmed to me that with belief in our own abilities and help from kindred spirits, you can get a quart into life's pint pot.

Alain and Vic at the
Rock Café, Los Angeles

Chapter one
FAMILY LIFE

I was born on 18 February 1947, a day after my father's birthday. I was a premature arrival. My mother had done only seven months of her nine-month term, so my birth was by caesarean section and I weighed just two and a half pounds. I was told that the only reason I survived was because a nurse on the maternity ward spent hours trying to get me to suck.

Growing up in those early years I was looked after very well and, in fact, I was rather spoilt. I had a nanny called Mary, who came over from Ireland when she was only 15 to work for my father as a housemaid. We lived in a big house on Manor Road in Chigwell and Dad had all the toys that you would ever want.

My mother, Elsie, came from a middle-class family with six daughters. Their father Percy was killed during the war when a doodlebug exploded on a bus taking him home from his engineering firm. I heard from my mother that he was a very kind, gentle man and that all his daughters adored him. Gertrude, my grandmother (who I remember as being a tough old lady who played the piano very well), ended up getting four of the six sisters on the stage to bring in funds to run the family home. My mother was one of theatrical impresario CB Cochran's young ladies and she was stunningly beautiful. I'm not sure where my father met her, but I am pretty certain it must've been love at first sight. During the war she was an ambulance driver, and she was on the stage entertaining the pilots during the Battle of Britain.

I don't think I ever really bonded with my mother. She was a terribly kind person but for some reason I never felt that close to her. The person I adored was my father, Samuel Eric Norman, but the trouble was he was hardly ever at our family home; he had built up a successful engineering business called the Balfour (Marine) Engineering Company.

Dad was born in 1914 in the East End of London. His father, Sydney Edgar Norman – my grandfather, who I never met – had a small marine engineering business doing repairs and work for the London

Left: my dad giving me my first dog, Snooky. Right: getting ready to race.

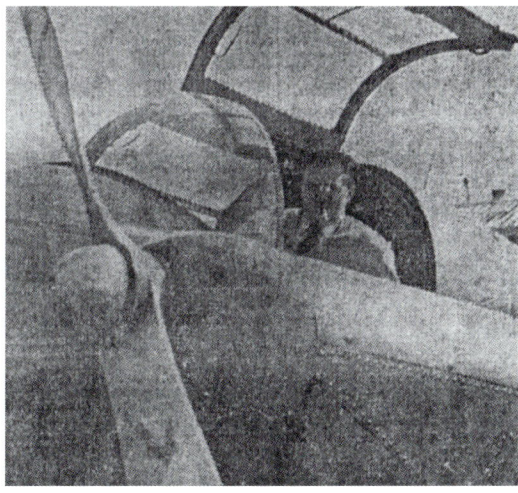

Clockwise from left: my mum when she was 15; nice hairstyle!; my first day at school; dad in his Miles Gemini aircraft.

docks, as well as other engineering jobs in the local area. My father's mother died when he was very young, just two or three years old, and I know very little (in fact nothing) about his early childhood. I know that he joined the Merchant Navy when he was 13 years old and that he obtained an engineering apprenticeship, which stood him in very good stead later on in life.

My father had an older brother called Leslie, who trained to be an accountant and joined the family business, Balfour (Marine) Engineering, which had by then moved to Balfour Road in Ilford. My father inherited the business when his father died. It started off as a workshop behind the house and my father steadily built the business up, building an office block five stories high with a large engineering workshop behind the offices. The workshop took up two floors – the ground floor was for heavy machinery (large turning lathes, milling machines, grinding machines, and jig borers), while the upper engineering floor was for the more lightweight work and assemblies. He ended up employing more than 300 people, all working on high-precision engineering jobs for most of the aircraft industry within the UK, namely Rolls-Royce, the Bristol Aeroplane Company, and English Electric.

This all gave him and our family a high-powered lifestyle, and he was also a very strong and determined man and very straight-talking, and called a spade a spade. He learnt to fly and obtained his pilot's licence in 1945. During the war, his factory worked flat-out and I know he received the best machine tools and re-equipped his factory with equipment from America, which was all part of the war effort and our government's arrangements. He was the first person to land at London Southend Airport after the war and, although with his lighter, smaller aircraft he operated from the Herts & Essex Aero Club, he was later based at Stapleford Airfield.

Stapleford was owned by Roger and Buster Frogley. Roger was a famous grasstrack speedway rider, which was a big spectator sport after the war and I've been told a lot of gambling used to take place on who would win. I've also heard that the riders used to fix some of the races and that Roger made enough money during one season to buy the land at Stapleford and obtain planning permission to turn it into an airfield.

My dad had several aircraft, all of which got steadily bigger as his business became more and more successful – starting with the Proctor, several Geminis, a few Doves, a four-engined Heron and a Miles Marathon, which was the largest aeroplane he had and was converted into a flying showroom when his jukebox business, BAL-AMi, really took off.

He had been to New York, on either the *RMS Queen Elizabeth* or the *RMS Queen Mary*, and negotiated a deal with Automatic Musical Instruments Company (AMI) to manufacture jukeboxes for the whole of the UK and Europe

Left: aged 17, my mum joined Mr Cochran's Young Ladies – a musical theatre revue act.
Right: I might be sitting down here, but the shot marks the day that I took my first steps.

Having flown it from Stuttgart, dad presented me with my first racing car in 1951. I was just four years old, but it was a moment that kick-started my appetite for anything mechanical – something that my dad always encouraged.

16 NORMAN CONQUEST

under licence. This, of course, was the start of the '45' record and rock 'n' roll as we know it. My father started manufacturing jukeboxes at his factory in Ilford but he couldn't keep up with demand, so he set up a very large factory in Harlow (Essex) and a small subsidiary factory in Le Touquet. I know that he built the factory in France because there were some tax benefits that had something to do with the percentage of parts made in the UK.

The operators of jukeboxes couldn't buy them fast enough because every cafe and pub was keen to have a jukebox on-site blaring out all those wonderful records. My mother was keen to earn some pocket money so she ended up having about 20 of her own jukeboxes and used to be driven by her chauffeur from pub to cafe making her collections.

My father was living a real playboy lifestyle – working hard, earning lots of money and spending it on his passions (cars, planes and boats) and spoiling his family with fantastic holidays in the south of France, staying in the Carlton Hotel. We went to Cannes for nine weeks every summer and in the winter we went skiing in St Moritz, Switzerland. My mother had an SL Mercedes and, at one point, a Powder Blue Rolls-Royce. He bought a new Bentley every year from Jack Barclay (the oldest and largest Bentley dealer in the country), who he was very friendly with, as well as a new Ferrari, which he bought directly from the factory in Maranello. He had an arrangement with Mr Ferrari to get a car delivered straight from the factory to the Carlton Hotel and placed in the number-one slot right outside the entrance.

The Miles Marathon was the largest of my dad's aeroplanes and became a flying showroom for his BAL-AMi jukebox business.

I remember very well when he brought his first Ferrari over to our house in England. It was a 410 Superamerica painted a wonderful metallic blue, but the thing that really impressed me was seeing the speedometer showing 300kph. I was only around eight years old, and of course I thought it meant 300mph. My father taught me how to start the car and gently warm it up ready for him to drive, and I still remember the fantastic noise and high-speed sound of the starter motor as the engine burst into life. But I did have to be careful not to flood the engine during that cold start.

Clockwise, from right: first day skiing with my brother in St Moritz; dad and friend Bill Larkin, delivering Christmas presents to a Dr Barnardo's home; my dad's Ferrari parked outside the Carlton Hotel in Cannes, next to my mother's Rolls-Royce.

Skiing again – getting better, but still using wooden skis and sporting lace-up leather boots!

Manor House

The house that I was brought up in, Manor House in Chigwell, ended up being the largest house on the road after my father added a very large extension. The whole thing had this magnificent green-tiled roof and I remember being told when it was being put on that the cost of each tile was two shillings and sixpence, which, in the 1950s, was an enormous amount of cash when you consider how big the house was.

My father employed a really skilful carpenter called Frank and he was always at our house either building a large staircase or oak-panelling the sitting room, as well as building all the fitted cupboards in the bedrooms and rather flash bathrooms.

The house had a billiard room and ballroom, and it was a great place to play as a child. We used to play ice hockey in the ballroom using proper ice-hockey sticks and a very hard chuck; with the highly polished wooden floor the game was very like the real thing! The billiard room had a full-size snooker table with overhead lighting and a whole range of cues and rests, as well as solid ivory balls. However, what really made the room special for me and my friends was that we had one of my father's hidden-away jukeboxes full of '45' records, with all the latest singles by the latest pop groups.

After my father died, my mother sometimes held very large parties at the house and celebrities such as Bobby Moore, Sean Connery, Kathy Kirby and Bruce Forsyth would turn up. I guess it was the free food: lobsters, oysters and Meringue Glacé delivered from the Coq d'Or in Mayfair, which was one of my mum and dad's favourite restaurants.

When I got married, my mother moved out of the family home and bought a cottage near Ongar in Essex (she had a mews house around the corner from Harrods in Kinnerton Street, too), so Anne and I moved into Manor House, which at that point was the only house I'd ever lived in.

'After my father died, my mother sometimes held very large parties at the house and celebrities such as Bobby Moore, Sean Connery, Kathy Kirby and Bruce Forsyth would turn up.'

Putting the grounds of Manor House to good use with my first go-kart (left) and motorcycle.

During my younger days spent in the south of France, my dad would commute each week from his work in his de Havilland Dove. I knew when he was coming back because he used to fly low over the beach, which was a signal for Vincent, his Boat Captain, to drive his Ferrari from the hotel to Cannes Airport to collect him. He had a 57ft Chris-Craft Constellation yacht named *BAL-AMi* and a twin-engined Riva that was used for fast trips to St Tropez and both day- and night-time trips to his favourite restaurants.

I used to do a lot of waterskiing and became quite good at it. I had a friend called Simon Sherman whose family were in the fashion business (Sambo fashions) and he had this little speedboat called an Albatross and we would waterski all day long. Before getting the Riva, my father had a boat called a Chris-Craft Cobra – only a very small number were manufactured in 1955. They were incredibly fast and there were just two of them in the south of France: my father's and the Aga Khan's. Sometimes they would meet up and have a bit of a race. My father bought the boat when he was in New York and it was in a showroom on Fifth Avenue. He had it brought back on one of 'the Queens' and then sent down to the south of France. He soon got fed up with it, though, and gave it to his best friend, Bill Larkin, and then replaced it with the twin-engined Riva and his 57ft Chris-Craft cruiser.

On one holiday, Donald Campbell, the speed

Clockwise from right: waterskiing in the bay at Cannes; strolling on the beach with my parents; the whole family in my dad's twin-engined Riva speedboat.

Posing in the 1955 Chris-Craft Cobra — one of only 56 Cobra 21s built and powered by a Chrysler Hemi V8.

Right: my own BAL-AMi Model I jukebox, dating from 1958.
Far right: asking my dad if we were going flying again today...

28 NORMAN CONQUEST

Above: holding the cups awarded for the Grand Prix d'Honneur – first place for my dad's Ferrari and third for my mum's Rolls-Royce.
Right: looking wistful while on holiday in Cannes.

record-breaker, was down in Juan-les-Pins at the Hôtel la Provençal showing his films and trying to raise money for his next record attempt. I think it must have been at the same time as a Monaco Grand Prix because Stirling Moss was also there. The next day, my father invited Campbell and Moss to come on his yacht to St Tropez for lunch. We went there in convoy with the 57ft cruiser, the new Riva and the Chris-Craft Cobra. After lunch, my dad asked us whether we'd all like to waterski back to Cannes. Both Moss and Campbell said that they would, and my father bet them that I would stay up longer than them.

We started just outside the harbour in St Tropez with three ski ropes. I was in the middle, Campbell was on the right and Moss was on my left. The Riva gave a very big wake and it was the sure advantage to be in the middle; however, I was only 10 or 11 years old at the time. I remember the sea was quite rough, and after a short time Campbell fell off and was picked up by the other speedboat. That just left me and Stirling, who was very fit and at the top of his game. The distance between St Tropez and Cannes was around 31 miles and I think it must have been after about 20 miles that Stirling also fell off. I remember thinking, 'I have to hang on.' I knew that my father would be very proud of me for beating the two famous sportsmen. I made it, and there was a big celebration on the beach and in the restaurant with lots of drinking and laughing.

After a couple of hours, I saw my dad looking at me because it was coming up to seven in the evening, which was the best time, when the sea was calm, to go waterskiing. He said to me, 'What would you like to do?' and I replied that, 'Well, we normally go waterskiing at seven' – so that's exactly what we did. Dad could only do one lap around the block. He used to get very tired, and that evening all I could manage was one circuit as well. When we were getting changed, my dad grabbed one of my hands and saw that they were bleeding. He didn't need to

1954 British Grand Prix

When I was seven years old, my father took me to the British Grand Prix. I was very excited because I'd never been to a motor race before and I knew my dad drove very quickly. I loved going in his Bentley Continental, which had a sloping back and to me looked just like a race car.

We took our seats in the grandstand opposite the pits, which was a huge excitement as the Mercedes-Benz team was there and they'd pushed their cars out onto the grid with covers on so no one was sure what they would look like. Anyway, the covers were finally taken off and there were these magnificent Grand Prix cars with streamlined all-enveloping bodies. The other cars I remember were the bright-red Ferrari and lots of Maserati in different colours. I now realise that those Maseratis were the wonderful 250F racing cars. I was lucky enough to actually own one later in life and to race it at Vintage Sports-Car Club meetings and also pre-race at a European Grand Prix, but more on that later.

When the race started, the flag dropped and the noise was just fantastic to a seven-year-old boy. The smell of Castrol R oil was fantastic, too – a smell I've always loved and which always reminds me of that first time I ever experienced it. I think the Mercedes-Benz went straight into the lead from what I can remember, but there was much excitement as it kept hitting the oil drums placed on the inside of corners. I realise now that it kept happening because the driver couldn't see properly over the bonnet because the wheels were enclosed.

The race must've gone on for a long time because I remember going with my dad to the Bentley drivers' marquee. My dad was a guest of Jack Barclay, whose showroom in Berkeley Square happened to be opposite my dad's office. After lunch we went back to the grandstand. The race was still going on and Mike Hawthorn, in a Ferrari, was just about to take the lead. Both my dad and I were very excited when he finally overtook the Mercedes driven by Fangio, who I now realise was the best driver during that period in the 1950s. Our British driver, Stirling Moss, was also in the race but I can't really remember what happened or where he finished...

I was exhausted with all the excitement and from being out in the open with the noise and, most of all, from being with my dad. I think I must've fallen asleep on the way home and Mary, my nanny, would've put me to bed straight away. Thinking about this day now, I'm sure that it gave me the passion and love for all the Grand Prix cars and sports cars that took part in those races in the 1950s and meant that the car I always wanted to have, if I ever could afford it, was one of those Maserati 250Fs.

> '**I now realise that those Maseratis were the wonderful 250F racing cars. I was lucky enough to actually own one later in life and race it at Vintage Sports-Car Club meetings**'

Witnessing the Maserati 250F in action at the 1954 British Grand Prix was truly inspirational and years later I was fortunate enough to race my very own example.

say anything, but I could see how terribly proud he was of me.

I remember on one flight to France with his family friends in the back of the eight-seater plane, I was up front with him in the cockpit in the co-pilot's seat. I suppose that I was eight years old and pretty used to taking the controls and keeping the plane on a steady course. He told me to fly straight and level, and then he got up and walked to the back of the aeroplane to speak to his chums. One of them was obviously alarmed and asked who was flying and he said, 'The boy.' There were screams from my mother but to him it was a great joke.

On another occasion in the winter, I was with my dad and a whole bunch of his friends drinking and telling jokes on the terrace of the Carlton Hotel, and one of his friends told my dad that he had a hole in one of his shoes – I guess as a bit of a put-down. Dad told his pilot Jones, who would sometimes fly with him, to go and collect a new pair of shoes he had ordered – made from black crocodile skin, of course. Jones asked which shop, assuming it would be nearby in Cannes, and my dad said, 'I get my shoes made in Milan so take the aeroplane and collect them as I will need them for tonight.'

Jack Hylton, the composer and impresario, was a good friend of my dad's. He would often be on his yacht and I know we went to lots of première nights together, including *My Fair Lady*, *Gigi*, *South Pacific* and many more. Hylton arranged this for my

Clockwise from left: enjoying the sun at Carlton Beach, Cannes; my glamorous mother, in contrast to my rather stern-looking grandmother.

NORMAN CONQUEST 33

Lunch on the beach with my mum and brother — me sitting on the lap of my nanny, Mary.

'I gave a heartfelt eulogy at her funeral about what a wonderful person she was and the lifestyle she had working for my mum and dad. I still miss her.'

Mary

My nanny, Mary, was kind and caring all of my life, and was always there until the time that I went to boarding school. She would cook all our food, for my brother William and I, and also for all the friends I brought home. I'm not sure what else she did because I never really took any notice and just took her for granted.

She would always go out on a Saturday night with another housekeeper who worked for my dad's brother, Leslie Norman, and she would get driven to wherever they wanted to go by Harry the driver, and sometimes in my dad's Bentley. She had a boyfriend called Paul, who was a solicitor, and me and my friends used to give him a really hard time on the odd occasion he turned up at Manor House.

Mary married him and moved into her own house in Banbury, which was very nice and upmarket. However, several years later I heard from Mary that Paul had lost all their money and they'd sold the house to pay off various debts. They moved into a small rented two-bedroom cottage and Anne and I went to visit a few times, but Paul always went out when we went in. Paul then died of a heart attack while shopping in Banbury, and we went to visit. Mary told me how bad the gambling had been and that she did not know what she was signing on for, and that when the bank came to repossess it was a huge shock to her. Mary asked me if I would go into Paul's bedroom and sort his things out. Well, it was a disaster – he was gambling on lucky dips and anything he could get his hands on, making promises of getting money, and goodness knows what else.

Anne and I used to visit every couple of months and I gave her a small monthly payment to help her along. She always said that she could manage but it was nice to know that she had a small income. She became pretty lonely and she would love talking to Anne about old times travelling to the south of France and about Manor House. Anne arranged for her to have a rescue dog called Charlie, a sweet Cavalier King Charles Spaniel that she adored.

Mary became more and more frail over a short period of time and she was taken into hospital a few times, during which Charlie would spend time with her neighbour, but she would always come out. She became more and more ill and she asked Anne if we would have Charlie if anything happened to her; she knew that she was dying. She told me that she had made me an executor of her will and where and who her solicitors were – they were her ex-husband's old business in Banbury.

We visited her in hospital, and we were told that she would not last long and that she wanted her ashes to be put in our garden with Charlie's ashes when he passed away. We said our goodbyes and how much we loved her and a couple of days later we heard that she had passed away.

Anne got a call from Mary's neighbour asking if we could collect Charlie. He was in a bad way, very overweight because Mary had been giving him food all the time and he was not getting any exercise. He also had to be carried outside to pee because one of his hind legs didn't work. Slowly, our two Cavalier King Charles Spaniels (both girls) got Charlie's interest and he started shuffling outside with them through the dog door. He was losing weight on a proper diet and in a very short time became fully active, chasing around with our dogs. He really did have a second lease of life.

I visited Mary's solicitors and gave them everything that I could find in her house: old cheque books, bills, statements. There was nothing in her estate of value but her family in Ireland contacted me, hoping to inherit, and I put them onto the acting solicitors. I got a phone call several weeks later telling me that everything had been left to me, so I told her Irish family that they could come over before her funeral and select whatever they wanted from Mary's house, as well as her small items of jewellery, as I didn't want any of it. They seemed rather pleased but I think they were hoping for much more.

Several weeks later, the solicitor rang me again and told me that he had found another bank account with £25,000 in it, and it was of course mine. When I checked the account I saw that she had saved all the money I had given her in case of a rainy day and she had not spent a penny. God bless her.

I gave a heartfelt eulogy at her funeral about what a wonderful person she was and the lifestyle she had working for my mum and dad. I still miss her. Mary and Charlie's ashes were mixed together and she is buried in our garden by a lovely rose with their own seat, which I have found to be a very peaceful place.

dad. On one occasion, when I was about 10 years old, we were in the south of France and somehow my dad persuaded Jack to have a go at waterskiing, even though he had never skied before. I jumped in the shallow water with him to help him put on his skis, gave him the rope and helped to get him in the right position to start. He was told not to let go of the rope.

He had a very young and voluptuous Italian singer with him and I think that she was the main attraction for both Jack and my dad, and any other man she walked past – her name was Rosalina Neri. The speedboat started and Jack managed to get up for about three seconds and then fell, but he still didn't let go of the rope and, well, he nearly drowned and when he was pulled out of the sea he had lost his swimming trunks too.

Rosalina was making a huge fuss, waving her arms and shouting, 'Poor Jackie! Poor Jackie!' and she wrapped a towel around him to cover his private parts while my dad and his friend Bill Larkin were in hysterics. That night on the terrace, the men in black tie and the girls in very smart flocks had a laugh talking about it and Mr Hylton enjoyed all the fuss and attention he was receiving from Rosalina and his mates.

Another good friend of my dad's who used to visit our house on Manor Road was Steve Glander, who I think was the boss of the Flying Squad. The customs officers at Southend Airport knew that my dad was using a legal tax loophole that involved parts going in and out of the country for his jukebox business. The word got out that my dad was flying in from Le Touquet with his aircraft full of parts and that the customs police were going to impound the aircraft as soon as it landed. This next part of the story is what I have been told: Steve Glander heard this was going to happen so he arranged two police motorcyclists to be positioned on the runway threshold waiting for the aircraft arrival. Apparently my dad came in to land but just before touching down he saw the police motorcycles, opened the throttles and headed back to France. On another occasion, the boxes were unpacked mid-air and thrown out into the Channel.

One time my mother, my friend Nick Lancaster and I were waiting to go up to the West End and have dinner at the Coq d'Or. My dad was late getting back from work and we were all waiting, looking very smart with my mum in one of her beautiful Norman Hartnell or Dior dresses. We were meeting my parents' friends at 8.30pm, and at 8.00pm there was still no sign of my dad. He finally arrived with his sleeves rolled up, covered in oil. He had been repairing a machine tool at his factory. My mum was furious, shouting that we were going to be late and that he must telephone the restaurant to apologise

> 'We were meeting my parents' friends at 8.30pm and at 8.00pm there was still no sign of my dad. He finally arrived with his sleeves rolled up, covered in oil. He had been repairing a machine tool at his factory.'

My brother and I out to dinner with Mum and Dad and having to dress up in a smart suit and tie!

Above: in the garden at Manor House with our white Alsatian, Brimus, and my poodle, Dukey. Left: Mum and Dad all dressed up and on a dinner date.

to their friends. I saw him on the phone and then he rushed upstairs, washed, got changed and we all jumped into the Bentley.

My mother was not a good passenger and my dad always drove very quickly. Down the bottom of our road was Claybury Police Station and as we got near my dad hooted and two Wolseley police cars pulled out with their bells ringing, one positioned in front and the other at the rear. It was the most fantastic ride, only 12 miles from Chigwell to Mayfair but we jumped all the lights, overtook on the wrong side of the road and arrived at the restaurant right on time. Nick and I were ecstatic and Mum was a nervous wreck. My dad said, 'There you are, Elsie. We are not late.'

Dad was a very generous man and I guess 'easy come, easy go' as he would always pick up the bill at restaurants when he used to visit with his friends and family. I never spent enough time with him as he was away a lot but he nearly always came home to Manor House at weekends for a big Sunday lunch. I was taught to be well-mannered, to always open doors for ladies, to pull their chairs out for them at the dining table, to never have elbows on the table – good old East End self-made-men manners, but of course the other side was that my dad never stopped swearing, which was just how East Enders spoke.

You can't imagine how much fun it was for me as a child being with my dad. I never knew which car he would decide to go out in or where we were going, but it would often be to the airfield to fly off to Le Touquet, where he had a house opposite the Westminster Hotel and the BAL-AMi factory. He was very good at dealing with and being friendly with people from across the whole of society, and while to others he might have been a bit frightening sometimes, to me he was only ever kind and loving.

My mother ran the house very well and it was always kept immaculate, and when she knew that my father was coming home from one of his foreign trips everything was double-dusted and polished. I became very friendly with the staff, especially the chauffeur Harry Lovell, who used to play football with me against the garage doors and take me wherever I wanted to go, like roller-skating at the local town hall.

Before she met my father, my mother had married William George Chandler, an RAF officer and the oldest son of the self-made man (also called William George) who built Walthamstow Stadium, a greyhound racing track, in 1933. He was a tough and very wealthy man. Tragically, my mother's first husband died just after the war, leaving behind a two-year-old son, named after his father and grandfather, who was my half-brother. William is four years older than me.

I never really joined in any activities with William. He was always doing something inside and I loved being outside, riding my bike and playing games, as well as running around like mad, but he wasn't

The Vincent motorcycle

It must have been about 1952 when my dad arrived back from work one evening on a shiny black and polished aluminium motorcycle. I later learned that this was one of the new Vincent Black Shadows, the first road-going motorcycle to exceed 150mph. I was only five years old, but I ran outside as I heard it being revved up and to me it looked like the most amazing piece of machinery. My dad was sitting on it in one of his immaculate Savile Row suits and a silk shirt, with his tie wrapped round the back of his neck – no glass, no helmet, just a big smile.

The next morning after breakfast, I ran outside to look at the motorbike again. When Dad came out he let me sit on it and asked me if I'd like to have a ride. Well, I couldn't believe it, but he told me to go inside and get a coat on. I remember my mother coming out and saying, 'Sam, you can't take Vicki!' They always called me that, even though my name is Samuel like my dad's.

The next thing my dad did was kick-start the engine and then he lent over, picked me up and sat me in front of him on the fuel tank, and told me to hold onto the handlebars very tight. After a couple of turnings out of our drive there was a long, wide road with a gentle hill in the middle of it leading down to our local shopping area called Barkingside. When we got on that road, my dad opened the throttle and the noise and speed were absolutely intoxicating to me as a young boy. He slowed down once we reached a built-up area and we eventually ended up at his factory in Ilford. One of my dad's drivers gave me a lift back home in a Bedford van but I think I was hooked on motorcycles for life after that first fast, shiny, black machine.

The motorcycle didn't hang around that long. For my dad, it was just another toy he had to have – the latest bit of kit. Around the same time there were twin brothers working at the factory. They were called the Barker brothers and I would see them every day because they were digging a swimming pool by hand in our back garden. This was not a small swimming pool (it was pretty deep at the diving end) and all the earth they dug out was used to build the surrounding ground to a higher level, so nothing was carted away. The same brothers then mixed concrete by hand and plastered the bricks that they had previously laid along the inside of the rather large hole. They did a beautiful job, with crazy paving all around the outside and there was a pool house too, with an enormous pump and a huge number of valves to control the water.

My dad seemed very pleased with the finished job and while he had, of course, been paying them throughout the six months it took to build the pool, he also gave them the Vincent motorcycle as a thank you. I must say at the time I was pretty upset but what a lovely thing to do, giving the fastest and most expensive motorcycle in the world to these two hard-working labourers. I wish I could find out what had happened to that bike…

My Vincent Black Shadow. I only wish that I could find the one that my dad had owned during the 1950s.

> 'Mum was a chain smoker and this is what got her in the end as her lungs just stopped functioning, but she remained glamorous right to the end of her life.'

very sporty. Whereas I was very skinny and probably underweight, he was rather fat and overweight. My mother always led me to believe that he was the clever one but that I was very good at games. Understandably, after losing his father, who he never knew, he was very close to my mother so the family was rather two-sided: me, my nanny Mary, and my father were on one side, and my brother William and my mother were on the other side.

My dad was good friends with Percy Chandler, William George Chandler's younger brother. Our house and Percy's house were, as the crow flies, about half a mile away from each other and I always remember Guy Fawkes' Night being great fun, with my dad and Percy aiming rockets at each other. They'd call each other up and laugh if one of them managed to get it into the other's garden or, better still, on the roof.

From what I remember, the early period of my childhood was pretty nice and special. All my needs were looked after by Mary, I didn't want for anything and I was happy playing games with myself, or football against the wall with the chauffeur, or causing havoc in the garden with Wally the gardener, often throwing stones and breaking his greenhouse windows, with really no one around to tell me off.

My mother was very kind and I never remember her getting cross with me or my friends. I think Mary, my nanny, was left to clear up any mess. Mum was a special person and she really loved all her grandchildren. They would always look forward to visiting her in Kinnerton Street in Belgravia and going shopping with her in Harrods, where she got all her provisions. The doormen always greeted her saying, 'Hello, Mrs Norman,' and had a chat with her.

Mum was a chain smoker and this is what got her in the end as her lungs just stopped functioning, but she remained glamorous right to the end of her life.

The early days – my mum and dad were very much in love.

Chapter two
SCHOOL YEARS

As I grew up, my father was around even less as I'm sure he was gallivanting around enjoying himself and living a playboy lifestyle, and I can see that slowly he was not getting on so well with my mother and there would be lots of arguing at home, on the odd occasion that he did come home. Although he always tried to come home for Sunday lunch (and I really looked forward to his visit) he used to leave quite soon after, which left me pretty devastated because I didn't know when I'd be seeing him again – maybe not for another week or so.

I can't imagine how much damage I must have caused to various bits of gardening equipment since I was always taking lawnmowers to bits, bolting the engines onto wooden planks and making my own soapbox-type carts. These were highly dangerous machines, often with the lawnmower blade still rotating and, of course, with no brakes whatsoever. I used to charge around the garden and down our drive, then across the grass on the verge of the main road and back along the other drive, racing as fast as possible.

I initially enjoyed my early school days because I was very good at sports, and although I had trouble in some of the lessons, particularly English, this might have had something to do with the fact that I was never read a bedtime story and I think the first book that I ever read was James Bond much later in life. I never minded going to school but the most embarrassing part of the day was being dropped off and picked up in the Rolls or Bentley, and I used to insist that the driver, Harry Lovell, didn't wear his chauffeur's hat. I became very friendly with Harry, who was much more than just a driver, and really he became my stand-in father doing all the normal things that fathers usually do, like teaching me how to ride a bike, playing football and, later on, teaching me to drive. He must have done a good job as I passed my test on my 17th birthday. He cycled with me to Southend and back when I was 11 years old, which was a round trip of 120 miles. I was laid up in bed for two day afterwards exhausted.

When I went up to senior school when I was nine, things started to change. The headmaster's son, who used to teach French and who was also in charge of the school rugby and swimming team, took an instant dislike to me. He didn't like the fact that my mum was not frightened to flash the cash and I somehow felt he held this against me.

During his French lessons, and later on in his Latin classes, it seemed to give him great pleasure if I could not answer questions. There were three or four of us who he would definitely lay into, degrading us verbally and, if he got the chance, giving us a couple of whacks with his cane. I must say I got pretty fed up with this and my way of dealing with it was very straightforward – I just stopped turning up to his lessons. The second strange part of this whole exercise was the fact he would still praise me on the rugby pitch, because our team results were very important to him.

As a result I fell more and more behind in French and Latin, but no one at home knew what was going on, or took a particular interest or cared. The truth only came out after I'd been skiving for a whole term because one morning I refused to go to school and locked myself in a downstairs toilet at home with my grandmother. Although the driver and my mother tried to get me to come out and said that they would knock the door down and make me go to school, I still refused to open the door and I took out my pocket-knife and told everyone that I would hurt

Millfield School swimming team 1963-'64. I am in the middle of the back row.

my grandmother if they didn't stop. I actually had no intention of doing it, of course. Instead I jumped out of the window and ran off. This did prompt the arrival of my dad, who asked me very calmly why I didn't want to go to school. I told him the reasons and he said, 'Right. Leave this to me.'

We jumped in his Continental Bentley and drove to the school and he told me to wait inside the car while he went to see the headmaster. Anyway, after quite a short time he came out and said, 'Okay son, come with me. We're going to see the headmaster.' I have to say I was petrified. When we arrived, the headmaster's son was sitting there and the headmaster said to me, 'Norman, you must not worry about getting the right answers in your French and Latin. Just try your hardest, you will not be beaten for getting things wrong.' I later found out that my father had a strong word with the headmaster about his son. Funnily enough, a short time later the French class got all-new dictaphones and desks, and I know who paid for them.

My dad had brought back an early go-kart from America and I starting racing it around the garden, tearing up our front lawn. A friend of my dad's had opened up a track at Tilbury. His name was Big Alf 'Man Mountain' Dean. He was a wrestler and featured in quite a few British movies in the Sixties, always as a bad guy. He was, in fact, one of the kindest men I've ever met. He was also absolutely huge – he couldn't walk through one of the doors in our house unless he went sideways. One time, for a joke, I saw him pick up my father and my father's best friend Bill Larkin at the same time, one in his left hand and one in his right hand.

I got very interested in go-karting and paid several visits to Rye House Stadium in Hertfordshire, and although I was only 12 or 13 I used to take my new go-kart there (a Starfire, which had a 100cc Siata engine). We used to load the kart in the back of a Bedford van with Harry the driver, and I would drive the van to the racetrack. I used to practice like mad, lap after lap, and started doing pretty well in the races.

Go-karting in Nice. My dad later flew my kart out from England so that I could use it in the South of France.

'We used to load the kart in the back of a Bedford van with Harry the driver, and I would drive the van to the racetrack. I used to practice like mad, lap after lap...'

At Rye House and ready to race my Siata-engined Starfire kart. In the November 1962 issue of *Karting*, the author wrote: 'One point of note was the driving of Vic Norman – this boy of 16 years was extremely fast and I have no doubt will develop into a very polished driver...'

There were no junior classes in those days and everyone used to race against each other. I remember some characters, one of them being Roy James, who supposedly was the getaway driver in the Great Train Robbery. Another one was Derrick 'Shunter' Brunt (called 'Shunter' because he was not averse to giving other drivers a nudge), who later raced in the British Saloon Car Championship. In fact, I still occasionally see him because he is very high up in the microlight world and he still calls me 'young Vic'.

I applied for a racing licence with the Royal Automobile Club and had to forge my age, because in those days you needed to be 16 years old to race internationally. I was shortlisted for the British team but sadly couldn't take part in the qualifying races because I had gone back to my senior school, Millfield.

I would never have passed my Common Entrance but it was decided that I might be able to get into Millfield because the headmaster at the time, Jack Meyer, would accept students if you and your parents passed the interview. I think somewhere along the line my dad donated some equipment to the metal-working room. I think it also helped that the headmaster quite fancied my mother.

I ended up really enjoying my time at Millfield. I loved playing rugby, although I wasn't good enough to get into the first team; the second team played most other schools' first teams. I also got into the school swimming team but the real reason for wanting to do this was that we didn't have a school swimming pool so we used a pool in Street, the local town, owned by Clarks (the shoe company), whose children were also at Millfield. If you got into the swimming team you'd be taken to training one evening a week at Bridgwater and you not only missed house prep but you also got fish and chips afterwards, and then a second meal when you got back late to your house because food had been left out for you. I seemed to be always starving at school.

There was no real pressure put on me to work very hard, but some of the subjects I found myself really enjoying – especially maths, physics, and history. Things at school were going along quite well; I had lots of friends, enjoyed my sport, and during my time there the first girls' house opened on the school grounds, which added much interest.

But then one day my world turned upside-down. I was in the middle of a lesson and the headmaster sent a message asking me to go and see him in his study. This was jolly scary because normally the only time you were asked to see the master was if you were in trouble and probably it would end up with you being beaten, which was a common practice at public schools then. I remember knocking on the headmaster's door, having checked that his light system was on green (if it was on red you weren't allowed to interrupt or enter). I gingerly opened the door and the headmaster was there with his secretary, Mrs Sankey, and he asked me to come in

> 'He told me that I had to go home because my father had been ill and I had to support and help my mother. I really had no idea what he was talking about because I knew my dad had been ill but I never thought anything was seriously wrong with him.'

and sit down. He told me that I had to go home because my father had been ill and I had to support and help my mother. I really had no idea what he was talking about because I knew my dad had been ill but I never thought anything was seriously wrong with him. He was such a tower of strength that I could never imagine any illness would affect him.

I was driven by taxi to the local train station and put on the train to London Paddington, where I was told someone would meet me. On the way back to London my mind was racing, just wondering what could have happened. I was met at the station by my half-brother William, who was 17 and had a car. I walked up to him and the first words he said to me were, 'Your father's dead.' I was completely and utterly devastated. I got in the car and didn't say a word, felt very tearful and arrived back at our family home. I walked in the front door and saw that my mother had two of her friends there and it was plainly obvious that they'd been drinking. Without saying a word, I went up to my bedroom and locked myself in.

By now, my nanny Mary had stopped working for my mother because she felt her job was done the day I went to boarding school, and walking in the house it seemed to me that no one actually cared or was that concerned that my father had died. I guess they knew that he had been seriously ill and I subsequently found out that he had Hodgkin's disease, and of course in 1962 there was no known cure. I think it was madness that I wasn't told how ill my father was. I would have loved to have seen him and had a chance to speak to him and then his death would not have been such an enormous shock. It actually took me eight years to live with the fact that he was dead, and before that time I used to dream every week that he was alive and that I would see him again.

The next day I was still locked in my bedroom and no one had really made any attempt to come and talk to me. I was asked through the door if I wanted to go to my father's funeral, which was due to take place that day, but I didn't answer. I remained locked in my room and after several hours I saw lots of cars arriving for the wake. After a while there was a knock on my door and Victor Chandler Senior, the bookmaker and a very good friend of my father's, asked if he could come in and see me. I opened the door and he sat on the edge of the bed and told me how my father had helped him when he was a lot younger and that he was a very good friend of my father's. He told me that any time in my life I needed help or advice that he would be there for me and I only had to ask. I can't tell you how much better it made me feel to have that short and brief discussion with one of my dad's friends, who I knew to be a very kind man.

I stayed locked in my room for the rest of the day and the next morning I went downstairs and said that I was going back to school. I realise now, of course, what a crazy and dysfunctional way I was treated over this whole affair but I don't think I really blame anyone. My mother must've been scared about what would happen financially, about where the money would come from, but by then her relationship with my father had totally broken down. I knew he'd had a girlfriend at this stage and had been 'birding it' for a very long time before he became ill. My brother, I felt, was in no way sad my father had died and I guess that perhaps he felt happier because now I was in the same boat as him, and of course he had a very close bond with our mother.

So I went back to school the next day. My friends and my house master were very kind to me, other than one boy who made some comment about me feeling sorry for myself just because my father died so I whacked him with one punch, nearly broke his nose and laid him out. I was immediately asked to go and see the Head of House because the school didn't take kindly to fighting and I thought that perhaps I'd be beaten for hitting this boy. In fact, after I explained what had happened no action was taken and the boy who had made the comments got a couple of whacks instead.

Millfield is a great school and I found out that the headmaster Jack Meyer had spoken to my mother and told her not to worry if paying the school fees got difficult. In fact, they never did because Leslie, my father's older brother, carried on running the engineering business although, by this time, the jukebox business had died a death. The headmaster, or 'Boss' as we called him, asked my mother to be a governor of the school. I think this arrangement very much suited her and him because most of the school meetings were in London and afterwards they would go out eating and dancing, and of course my mother was very well known in all the top London restaurants and clubs. Boss also knew that if it came to a vote, my mother would always vote on his side on any issues.

Boss was very keen on horse racing, and I guess gambling, and somehow persuaded my mother to buy a racehorse. Luckily, with Victor Chandler close at hand, being a member of the family, everything worked out fine. My mother was instrumental in getting my half-cousin – the current Victor Chandler, the man behind Bet Victor, who is a very good friend – into Millfield School, and I remember on one occasion he was caught in the local town betting shop by one of the masters of the school. This was brought to the attention of Boss, who promptly got Victor and the master into his study and, having questioned Victor about what he was doing in the betting shop, he turned round to the master and said, 'This boy is going to end up running his father's business – of course he needs to put on the occasional bet and obtain knowledge of the horses.'

I don't know if this is true but there was a rumour that Boss had an account with Victor Chandler's father and I think it was a good reciprocal arrangement, with school fees being waved in lieu of gambling bets but, as I say, this is only hearsay.

I don't know why, but after my father died I decided that I should really start studying and try to get a few O-levels. Up until then, it was thought that I might get one or two O-levels but in fact I managed to get six, which for me was a huge achievement and everyone was very, very surprised, including my mother and the school. I decided to stay on to do my A-levels and at the same time I was made a house prefect, which brought enormous perks and life was pretty cushy. I was still enjoying my sport, very involved with house activities and feeling pretty good about myself. Millfield gave me that feeling that I could actually achieve anything.

Chapter three
ANNE

Like a lot of young boys at that time, I was very keen on cars and motor racing. I remember on one occasion with a friend of mine, we missed Saturday morning school and sneaked off to Earl's Court to see the Motor Show, which was fantastic fun and it never occurred to either of us that we might be caught out. I was very used to driving and racing my go-kart, and in fact I owned a Bantam motorcycle that I was always modifying. At 14 years old, I was riding it on the roads around where we lived and I never got stopped.

My 17th birthday was coming up and I was determined to take my driving test on my birthday. Harry Lovell was going to come down in the Mini from Chigwell to Somerset and I had booked a driving test in Street, the local town near the school. I passed with flying colours and, without being big-headed, I don't think I made a single mistake. I'd really swotted up on the Highway Code, which was much simpler in those days, and I also managed to get all the questions the examiner asked me right.

I was absolutely thrilled that I now was legally allowed to drive, and I remember Harry coming down to collect me in the Bentley at the end of term and driving home myself with Harry as my passenger. I definitely didn't hang about on the open roads.

It never occurred to me, as I was still being spoilt financially, that I wouldn't get my own car on my 17th birthday. I really wanted a Lotus Elite, which were small fibreglass cars with a Coventry Climax engine. They looked absolutely fantastic and quite a few of them were being raced by people like Les Leston, who I used to see in the school holidays when I went to Brands Hatch.

My best friend away from school was a guy called Nick Lancaster, who later became the CEO of HR Owen. I first met him when I was five years old, coming out of school to meet my mother after my first day. My mother and Nick's mother, who'd never met before, were chatting to each other and I ran up to say hello at the same time that Nick ran over to his mother, and the main topic of conversation was the fact that both Nick and I had kirby grips in our hair to stop it flopping into our eyes. We became very good friends and, in fact, 64 years later we are still very good friends. There are hundreds of stories about what Nick and I used to get up to.

The brother of another friend of mine, Christopher Craft, was a young well-known saloon car driver who later became one of the leading sports car racers of his time. This was the main reason we used to go to Brands Hatch – to watch Chris race – and the whole thing was really exciting.

When I came home from school after passing my driving test, I wondered how I was going to persuade my mother to buy me that Lotus Elite but, in fact, when I arrived home, there was a brand-new, bright-red Triumph TR4 in the garage. My brother decided that it was a safer car for me to have, and he was probably right. The first thing I did was take the exhaust off and fit a straight-through copper pipe; the noise was just fantastic.

It was during this holiday that I heard a young group called the Rolling Stones were going to be playing at Leyton Baths. This was before they released their first single, which was called *Come On*, but I'd already seen them when we used to go up to London during previous holidays. I was interested in girls and had already had two or three non-serious girlfriends but that night watching the Rolling Stones changed all that.

There were over a thousand people listening to the music but Nick noticed a girl and her friend across the other side of the hall because her younger brother went to his school and he had seen her during one of the sports days. We went over to say hello and I was completely and utterly smitten with the girl, who was called Anne. I was quite shy but managed somehow to ask if she would like a lift back home with her friend. Anne and her friend were very much dressed like mods and it turned out that they assumed I had a scooter and she asked me what type. I told her I had a TR4 and I must say she looked rather vague.

I was totally besotted with Anne. She was beautiful, amazingly kind, and very well-mannered. Her father was a Major in the Grenadier Guards with an amazing war record, which he never spoke about. Her mother was very Scottish and I remember her house being full of younger siblings and golden retrievers, as well as various other animals. We met up virtually every day during the school holidays.

I went back to school and we wrote each other lots of letters that never really said much other than 'I love you' and 'millions of kisses and hugs'. I couldn't wait for the term to end. I knew that I wasn't going to go back to school to finish my A-levels; I told my mother and both her and my brother tried, not for the last time, to get me to change my mind.

Anne applied and was accepted to train as a fashion model at Lucie Clayton in Bond Street and I had to do something so I entered for a Higher National Diploma at the Chelsea College of Aeronautical and Automobile Engineering, which happened to be on Sydney Street, just off the Kings Road. This was not a bad place to be in the 1960s and it taught me basic engineering skills that have stood me in good stead later on in life when working with cars and aeroplanes.

Anne started getting work doing modelling shoots and she was featured in lots of catalogues and magazines, including *Vogue*. She also did some commercials on television, one of them for National Benzole petrol, where she was filmed in an open-top Ferrari in the south of France with some good-looking Swedish guy driving the car. It used to annoy me enormously, seeing Anne with this other person, but every time it came on television she

Anne's modelling career included shots for *Harrods Magazine* and *Vogue*.

> '**Anne and I had been going out now for three years and we decided (although Anne tells me I just told her) that we would get engaged and married. I think, if truth be known, I was scared that someone else would whisk her away...**'

would get around £25, which was a lot of money in those days.

Although Anne and I were Stones fans, we also liked the Beatles. Even my mother's generation liked the Fab Four – unlike the Stones, they were clean-cut and polite boys. My friend at prep school, Micky Martin (who was best known for biting people when he got annoyed), had a job at Finsbury Park Cinema as an assistant manager. He told me that the band were playing and promised let us in through the side door. The place was full of screaming girls. They started playing with a simple sound system so you could not really hear a word, but it was still an amazing experience.

The next day I telephoned Micky to thank him for the tickets and he told me that they had a real problem because the girls had all weed on the cinema's velvet seats and the place stank. They had to get the steam cleaners in.

My father's old engineering business, Balfour (Marine) Engineering, which made component parts for Rolls-Royce and Bristol Aero Engines, was still going, and it was decided that I could and should be employed there. My elder brother also ended up working in the business. It was not a good place to work – it was run by a very strong trade union. The Soviet Union was our biggest potential enemy back then and some of the workers were known troublemakers, so we were told by Special Branch to keep an eye on them. Apparently, some had been trained at the Ford Motor Company. The only good thing was that I was well paid and didn't have to do much.

Anne and I had been going out now for three years and we decided (although Anne tells me I just told her) that we would get engaged and married. I think, if truth be known, I was scared that someone else would whisk her away and I couldn't imagine living without her. She gave me everything I never had when I was growing up: love and attention, true kindness, and she always put herself second. She is without doubt the kindest person I have ever met but that doesn't mean she's not tough and strong –

NORMAN CONQUEST 51

Looking very smart – look at those legs! Right: Major George Hackett and my gorgeous bride arriving at the Guards' Chapel. Anne's Bellville et Cie dress was covered in hand-stitched flowers.

The wedding service was conducted by my uncle, Derek Matton. The altar at the Guards' Chapel survived the Blitz bombing campaign and although the church was flattened, the crypt was left standing and candles still burning.

she can be very determined and she's not frightened to say what she thinks.

Of course, we were going to have a large wedding and it was a golden opportunity for my mother to show off a bit and let her friends and family know she wasn't on her uppers yet. My mother organised virtually the whole wedding and the reception was held in the ballroom at the Dorchester Hotel. The only part she had no say in was the fact that we were going to get married in the Guards' Chapel at Wellington Barracks. George, Anne's father, was an officer in the Grenadiers, so this was the perfect place for his eldest child and daughter to get married.

The Guards' Chapel is a magical place; it suffered a direct hit during the Blitz but the altar remained standing and, I'm told, the candles were still burning even though the rest of the church was flattened. The rebuilt chapel is magnificent and all the original banners that were carried into battle are mounted along the nave. Inside, the building has a very special

Anne and her five bridesmaids at the Dorchester Hotel, shortly before leaving for Wellington Barracks.

atmosphere and you can't help but be moved when you think of all the men that have been killed during those battles.

Our honeymoon was a bit of a disaster. We went to Corfu and our hotel seemed to be opposite the sewage works, or rather the lack of sewage works, so there was a terrible smell the whole time. To make matters worse, it was at a time when you were only allowed to take around £30 abroad and credit cards appeared not to work in Corfu. There was a mad panic because we ran out of money and had to get some sent over in an envelope by post from the UK.

We decided to go to the south of France, which was my old hunting ground because my father used to send us to the Carlton Hotel in Cannes in the summer holidays for a few weeks. We used to walk up the road to E Felix, a restaurant where we had an account for most of our meals, including ice cream cornets during the day. I remember my father being horrified when he had to settle the bill for the ice cream, and it's lucky that at that stage in my life I was still very skinny. Every night, Anne and I used to walk back to the hotel after eating a wonderful pudding called Désir du Roi, or dessert of the king, which consisted of profiteroles filled with vanilla ice cream with hot chocolate sauce poured on the top. When we got back to the hotel, we would collapse on the bed feeling absolutely stuffed, but I have to say it was truly wonderful.

After our honeymoon, life went back to normal. I was working in the engineering business and Anne was becoming more and more successful with her modelling. After moving from my old family home, Manor House, we bought a gamekeeper's cottage near Abridge in Essex. At the time, my mother was going out with a man called Boyd Gibbins, who was a well-known builder in Essex and had obviously done pretty well for himself because he had his own polo team and used to jet around in his helicopter when he wasn't driving his Bentley (which he seemed to be always having minor accidents in).

Anyway, he was a very nice guy. He was given a pair of lion cubs by some Maharajah and I used to go in the compound with Boyd but, as the lions got big, it was very scary and in the end I think they went to Longleat. I got on very well with him. He was a bit like my dad – doing mad things like skiing behind his Bentley around the village after it had snowed. He heard the gamekeeper's cottage was for sale and that the local Colonel who owned the big estate was selling off some of his land and assets. Boyd picked me up in his helicopter and we flew to the cottage, which was very rundown and consisted of a very small building with kennels out the back. We landed nearby and he said, 'This is exactly what you want.' To me, it looked a complete wreck and, after living all my life in Manor House, I didn't really know what to think of it.

Clockwise from right: Anne posing with gun for a photoshoot for Lucie Clayton – one of Britain's top modelling agencies in the 1950s and '60s; enjoying drinks on the terrace at the Carlton Hotel; getting ready to leave the Dorchester Hotel and go on our honeymoon.

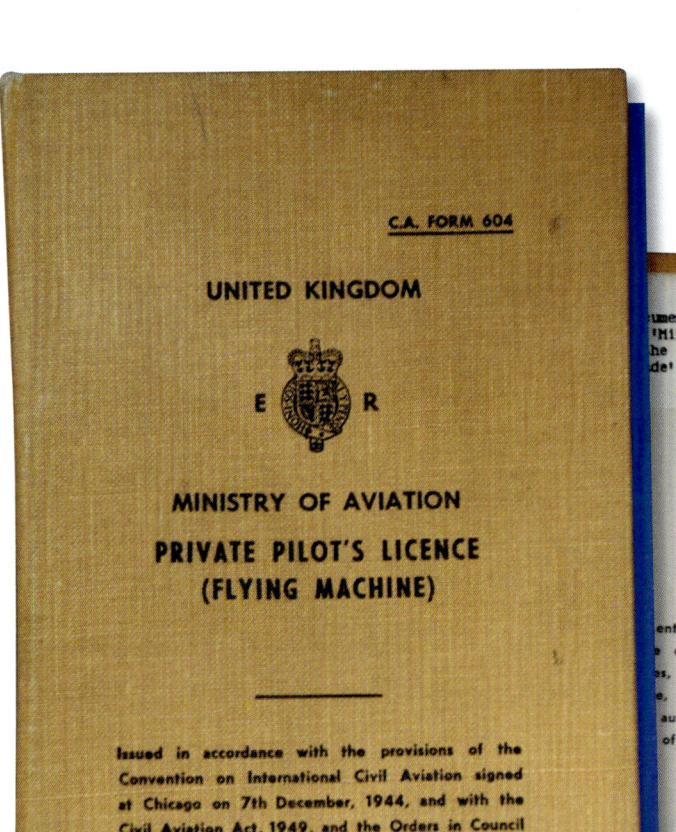

My early pilot's licence – something I achieved when I was just 17 years of age.

We took off, circled round and Boyd saw the big house that the Colonel obviously lived in. We landed in his back garden and Boyd told me to go knock on the door and to say that Major Gibbins was in the helicopter – would it be okay for him to come and have a chat? I'm pretty sure Boyd had never been in the Army and that he surely wasn't a Major. Anyway, I did what I was told and knocked on the door. A housekeeper answered and asked me what I wanted, so I repeated the message and the next thing I knew Boyd and I were in the sitting room with the Colonel. Boyd was discussing the fact that he should sell me the gamekeeper's cottage because I was starting out in life and I had a very nice and attractive wife and the cottage would be just perfect for us. He agreed a price then and there of £7,500. I have to say I was a bit bewildered because I knew nothing about building work but Boyd told me not to worry and said he'd help get planning permission.

It was during this time that I went down to Stapleford, the local flying club. I'd been there many times with my father, and in fact as a very young boy I remember going and having tea with the owner of the airfield, Mr Roger Frogley (the grasstrack speedway racer). I hadn't been to the airfield for a very long time, probably several years, but Mr Frogley and the chief flying instructor Eric Thurston remembered me – or rather, remembered my father.

They were all terribly kind and before I knew it I was having flying lessons. I found the flying very

Top: I learnt to fly in the Alon Aircoupe at Stapleford airfield. Above: a Piper Cherokee Arrow – the first aircraft that I bought new. At the time I had a choice between this and a Ferrari 275 GTB/4. The aeroplane won!

> 'We walked up the road to the local village shop, which was only about 100 yards from where we landed. Neville said hello to the shopkeeper and collected his daily bread, and we trundled back to the aircraft and strapped in and taxied back to the edge of the fence and off we went again.'

easy, I suppose because I was so used to flying with my father and used to taking the controls. I think I went solo in six and a half hours and quite quickly thereafter passed my flying test, so then I was a proud 17-year-old holder of a private pilot's licence but really had no use for it. I remember one of my training lessons in particular, with a wonderful man called Neville Browning, who was a Second World War pilot, local farmer and flying instructor. We took off in one of the club's small aeroplanes, called an Ercoupe, for a general handling test. While I was flying along in the general direction of Ongar, a local village near Stapleford, Neville lent across and closed the throttle and told me in his very quiet, calm voice, 'You have an engine failure and you must prepare to do a force landing.'

I had very little idea of what to do but I knew I had to maintain flying speed and I stuffed the nose of the aircraft down towards the ground to maintain around 60mph of airspeed. Neville pointed out of the cockpit and said to land in a field behind some trees and flying wires. I tried my best to position the aircraft to come in just over the hedge in the field. I thought I was doing quite well and assumed that Neville would open the throttle and that we would actually go around rather than land in the field.

When we were about 20ft above ground level, he gently took the controls and said, 'Follow me through boy.' I could then see, with a certain amount of fear, that we were actually going to land. And we did. We taxied the aeroplane over towards a gate in the field and Neville said to follow him. We walked up the road to the local village shop, which was only about 100 yards from where we landed. Neville said hello to the shopkeeper and collected his daily bread and we trundled back to the aircraft and strapped in and taxied back to the edge of the fence and off we went again.

I subsequently learned a great deal from Neville collecting his daily bread. It made me realise that should you have an engine failure it is often possible, if you (as the pilot) make the right decisions, to land the aeroplane in a field without hurting yourself. Something, in fact, that I had to do on more than one occasion later on in my flying career. Stapleford Airfield I still think of as my base and John Chicken, the current owner, and his departed wife Tania and daughter Pamela were the most straightforward, lovely people.

I carried on working in production control at my father's business and started enjoying parts of my work, particularly visiting our customers at Rolls-Royce Derby and the Bristol Aeroplane Company at Filton. I somehow persuaded the powers-that-be that it would be a good idea if the company bought a small light aircraft so that I could fly around visiting our customers, saving lots of time and carrying on with the tradition that my father started. We therefore bought a Piper Cherokee Arrow with 180hp engine, a retractable undercarriage and a constant-speed propeller.

It was quite a good little aircraft as long as you didn't overload it. Although it was a four-seater (or rather it had four seats), it really was only a two-seater plane if you were going to take any luggage and a decent amount of Avgas fuel. I remember at the time it was the same price as a Ferrari 275 GTB/4, and in fact I'd arranged a demonstration drive with Mike Salmon, the well-known racing driver who worked for Colonel Ronnie Hoare at Maranello Concessionaires in Egham. Still being a rather spoilt brat, I was torn between choosing the Ferrari or the aeroplane, but my passion for flying made me choose the aeroplane.

Work was going along swimmingly even though it was a constant fight with the trade unions, and I just couldn't understand why everyone in management was so frightened to say what they really thought and be a lot stronger with them. There were various walkouts and one-day strikes, and every time the company seemed to give in. Without doubt, the managers were very downhearted and depressed because they couldn't control the workforce who, I might say, at the time were the highest paid for what was undoubtedly the very skilled jobs that they were doing with the machine tools.

Overnight this suddenly all changed. I remember the day well. I was down visiting the Bristol Aeroplane Company delivering some parts that they urgently needed and a big meeting was called, which I was allowed to attend, and the factory were told that a receiver had been appointed. This all happened following the collapse of Rolls-Royce.

No one really knew what was going to happen. I went back to the works in Ilford and it took a long time to think it through and find answers to all of our questions. Should we carry on working on the parts in the factory? Would we be paid, and what was going to happen to the £130,000 the company was owed? For our company to break even we had to invoice around £65,000 a month and we had two months of outstanding invoices with an enormous amount of work in progress and not yet invoiced on the shop floor.

Barclays, our bank, panicked and also appointed a separate receiver to run our business, dispose of the assets, pay our preferential creditors and the outstanding bank loan, and make a contribution to the non-preferential creditors. Anything left over after their large commission went to the shareholders, who were principally my mother, myself, and my brother.

The next day the receiver arrived and came up to the boardroom and gave everyone the sack. I was immediately re-employed by the receiver's manager, Mr Flynn, on a greatly reduced salary. My job was to be his runner, driving around and generally asking and answering all the hundreds of questions he had. Initially it was obvious that he was only there to dispose of the assets as quickly as possible but, in fact, all this changed because the receiver for Rolls-Royce desperately needed the parts that our factory was manufacturing. An agreement was made between the two receiver-managers and our workforce pretty well carried on working as before.

There was, however, one big change. The unions backed right off because they could no longer threaten to walk out and go on strike because the receiver would have just closed the business, so common sense at long last prevailed. The company carried on trading like this for over a year and became more profitable during that period of time than it was before because many unnecessary overheads were gotten rid of. At the end of this period of trading, a lot of money was generated to pay off all outstanding debts to the creditors, including the company's bankers. The receiver no longer had a job to do and the company was handed back clear of debt to the shareholders.

It didn't take very long for the unions, or rather the troublemakers within the union, to start making impossible demands and everyone quite frankly had had enough so the business was gently run down. Everyone was paid proper redundancy money, the property was sold and a distribution was made to the shareholders (my mother, my brother, and myself). This left me and my brother with around £200,000 each and we decided together that we would purchase an arable farm in Wiltshire and farm the land ourselves. This was never going make us rich but it was a nice way of life, particularly after all the aggravation of trying to run my father's old engineering business.

I enjoyed working on the farm and driving the

combine harvester and getting in the harvest – we employed two good men who we'd inherited with the farm and who taught me everything that needed to be done during the farming year. My brother, however, became very bored. His family's gambling business at Walthamstow Stadium was involved in legal wrangles over shareholding and control. There ended up being a court case between various members of the Chandler family – one side of the family was trying to get control and the other side of the family was resisting them. It all became very complicated and legal and ended up in the High Court. During the judge's summing-up, he said that he'd never heard so much lying in court and that he quite frankly did not believe anything that anyone had said, and that he would therefore follow the wishes of the founding Chandler, William George Chandler Senior, and it was his wish that the company remained within the family.

The result of all this was that some shares that had been obtained by the Coral Group were up for grabs but could only be purchased by family members. My brother wanted to cash-in his money from the farm and free himself to go ahead and purchase some of the shares and get himself a position on the board of Walthamstow Stadium. I'm not sure why, but I agreed to go along with this and we ended up selling the farm and he ended up working at the stadium, although how much work he actually did is open to debate.

It was a terrible shock to Anne, who had made our young family a lovely home there. I also put some of my funds from the sale towards buying shares and at the same time was paid a small salary as a director. I had to turn up at monthly board meetings, which actually was a waste of time because, after trying a few times to make suggestions to build the business up and diversify without any success, I pretty well just gave up. I got on well with most of the board but everything was decided by a committee of eight directors so no decisions were ever quick. That said, it suited me well and allowed me to get on with my own business while providing me with a sound basic income, which helped with the school fees. Anne and I ended up moving to Gloucestershire without me really knowing how I was going to earn a living.

Prizegiving at Walthamstow Stadium. I persuaded F1 driver Jacques Laffite to hand over the prize – he clearly fancied a day out after qualifying at the British Grand Prix!

Chapter four
A NEW DIRECTION

Around about the same time as all this was going on, I met a man who became a big influence on my future life. His name was Alain de Cadenet. We were both quite young at the time (in our early 20s) and the person who introduced me to Alain was Chris Craft, the racing driver. Chris had met Alain at a European race circuit; I'm not sure what car Chris was meant to drive but I believe Alain had a very pretty little Dino Ferrari race car. Chris told me that Alain was working on his car in the paddock at some race track, his head was down in the cockpit, and his oily well-worn Gucci shoes sticking out from the door. They got chatting about racing cars and I'm sure they got on very well since they shared the same passion.

It was some time later, probably towards the end of 1971, that Alain had gone upmarket and bought a Formula One Brabham BT33. I think he got it from Bernie Ecclestone, who had just bought the Brabham team and later became Mr Big as far as Grand Prix racing goes. I'm not sure exactly how it came about but Alain asked Chris to drive the car at the Canadian Grand Prix and the United States Grand Prix, and although they didn't finish either race they went on to establish a long-standing entrant-and-driver relationship.

There was no doubt about it, Chris was a very quick and good driver, and Alain had a very sound basic understanding of the mechanics of a racing car. At some point during this period, Alain met Gordon Murray, who was working for Bernie at Brabham. Murray, of course, was to become one of the most successful Grand Prix car designers of all time, winning championships with his designs for Brabham and then McLaren. He later went on to design the McLaren F1 road car, which is still recognised as the most definitive road car ever built and, with some modifications implemented by Gordon, the GTR version went on to win the Le Mans 24 Hours.

Alain had made up his mind that he wanted to have his own car designed for him, and for Chris to drive it with a view to trying to win the Le Mans race with a completely British team. Gordon agreed to design the car, making a completely new, aluminium, small, lightweight tub and using some of the suspension components from Alain's Brabham BT33. Gordon was working full-time during the day at Brabham for Bernie, and during the evenings he was designing Alain's new car.

Alain and his team arrived at Le Mans a few days before the race. The car was hardly finished and everyone was working on the thousand-and-one little jobs that needed doing. The car was now known as the Duckhams Special because the oil company had given Alain free oil for the race and also, I think, some sponsorship. My job during the race was to be part of the signalling pit crew, which was positioned just after the tight and slow hairpin at the end of the Mulsanne straight. The problem was, we had no equipment to be able to do the job.

The signalling pits consisted of open-fronted concrete bunkers – the open side looked out onto the track just after the very slow corner and each team had a separate section to set up their equipment. When we entered our pit there was absolutely nothing there, but looking next door to our right-hand side, one of the Porsche factory-backed teams had already got their equipment in place. This consisted of electronic display boards, computers, radios to talk to the main pit area, catering equipment and motorhomes set up for their crew to take turns sleeping during the 24-hour race.

We were a bit taken aback with this, but our crew consisted of people who were used to getting on with the job and we were all very good friends. To mention one in particular, Barry Cox was a butcher's boy and worked in one of his father's butcher's shops at the weekends from the age of 13. He had his own shop, and I think the main reason he was in the team was that he had promised to bring a load of sausages, pork chops and steaks with him down to

'My job during the race was to be part of the signalling pit crew, which was positioned just after the tight and slow hairpin at the end of the Mulsanne straight. The problem was, we had no equipment to be able to do the job.'

Alain de Cadenet looking dapper; this was a British stamps promotional picture.

Le Mans, 1975. My friend Nick refuels the de Cadenet Lola while I look on from the passenger side. Alain attempts to get a drinks sponsor to go with the Tic-Tac mints – no bad breath that year!

Far left: 'de Cad' has been a long-term adviser when it comes to buying classic vehicles. Left: Barry Cox, better known for his role as one of the Mini drivers in *The Italian Job*, was also part-owner of the Hyde Park Hard Rock Café and presented me with a card so that I could jump the queue!

Le Mans in the boot of his BMW. This was all very well, but he broke the springs on his rear suspension and the rear end of his car was nearly dragging on the floor when he arrived.

Barry later became the part-owner of the Hard Rock Café on Hyde Park Corner. However, his main claim to fame was being one of the Mini drivers in the original *Italian Job* film with Michael Caine – but of course Barry was the star. Barry gave me a Hard Rock credit card called the Hard Cheese Club and there was always a big queue outside Hard Rock with people waiting to get in. If you flashed this card you went straight in, and it was 'Hard Cheese' for the others waiting – all very East End Essex.

Another one of my best friends, Nick Lancaster, was there too. He was a terrible joker and always getting all of us into trouble. As mentioned earlier, he become a well-known car dealer and part-owner of Lancaster Garages and, later on, HR Owen's Rolls-Royce and Bentley dealerships, as well as Ferrari and others, but it all slightly ended in tears. I am pleased to say he is very happy and doing well now and is based in Monaco with his wife Jane, who we are very fond of.

With no signalling equipment, we had to come up with a solution and, of course, we did. By chance, there was a public toilet just behind the signalling area and we all popped in to have a pee – but one of us noticed a wooden crutch propped up outside one of the cubicles. I guess there was no room for

> 'Alain is the most knowledgeable person I know regarding old motors and I always listen to his advice before purchasing yet another one.'

it to go in with its injured owner. We nicked it and after much debate came up with the idea of nailing a square of wood on the end, painting it black, and with a bit of chalk we used it for the whole 24-hour race, taking it in turns to lean out with it whenever Alain or Chris came by. There was an old-fashioned telephone in our pit which, if you turned the handle, would ring up the main pits, who then instructed us to put various signals out, like 'PIT FOR FUEL', or the lap time.

We somehow survived the whole race with no food, no kit, and no passes, but we were laughing and joking the whole time and the Porsche crew could not believe what was going on next to their Germanic, efficiently run set-up – on top of which, we were ahead of their car.

Early on Sunday morning, around six o'clock, the grandstand opposite the tight hairpin corner had only a few die-hard fans in it watching the race. We were worried about Chris getting tired and also we were getting bored, so Nick had a cunning plan to liven things up. He stood on the top of the barrier next to the track dressed in a long trench coat and, as Chris came past and looked to see if there were any messages from us, Nick dropped his coat and stood stark naked with an erection holding the message board out. We creased up laughing, the few people in the grandstand started to clap, and even the Porsche crew were laughing.

Alain's Duckhams car, designed by Gordon Murray, was one of the fastest cars down the long straight, timed at 212mph. During the race, the car had worked its way up to fourth place and was just about to overtake an Alfa to snatch third when a downpour of rain soaked Tertre Rouge corner. Chris spun and hit the barrier. The car made it back to the pits and the team of mechanics worked to replace the broken parts because we wanted to finish the race and do the last lap to qualify as a finisher. The Chief Marshal said that the car wasn't allowed to go out again because he couldn't be sure that it was safe. Alain took the Chief Marshal behind the pits, pulled out 500 francs and explained in fluent French that we wanted to do that last lap. Deal done, we finished in 12th place – what a great adventure.

The party after the race was pretty special, too, and again involved Nick running around in the nude, food fights, setting off the fire extinguishers and us eventually doing a runner from the police.

The next day, after the race, I was sitting down talking to Alain and he suggested that I should not bother going to work and that I should just buy a couple of old cars, have fun doing a bit of racing, and sell them for a profit at the end of each year. This is exactly what I ended up doing. Alain is such a dear friend, and Anne and I enjoy our times together with him and Allison, his wife, and my godson Aiden. I introduced Alain to flying and found him a really nice Boeing-Stearman B75 with 220hp, which he used a great deal when he had his château in France.

We both go out riding our motorcycles in the hills near his home in California and also back in the UK sometimes on the Pioneer Run for pre-1915 motorcycles. Alain is the most knowledgeable person I know regarding old motors and I always listen to his advice before purchasing yet another one. I went to Le Mans every year for 15 years and I had various jobs, all involving a limited skill level, but what fun and great results.

We would often race our old Grand Prix cars at various Vintage Sports-Car Club meetings in the 1970s and '80s, and we were founder members of the Historic Grand Prix Cars Association. We talk and plan adventures nearly every week and long may it continue. He would also telephone me every week when I was diagnosed with cancer and supported me all the way through my chemotherapy treatment. *Mon ami mate*.

Chapter five
MY CARS

Berkeley and Messerschmitt

When I was 16, I went out and bought a Berkeley three-wheeler, which I soon blew up and replaced with a three-wheeler Messerschmitt with a glass-like plastic roof. It would go up on two wheels if you overdid it cornering, but I got pretty used to giving the steering a twist the opposite way and putting it back on all three wheels.

However, one day I had a big argument with my brother and went off in a storm with Nick in the back, and I overdid it on the drive and rolled it upside-down with the motor revving its nuts off. Nick managed to crawl out from the back through the broken roof, but I was stuck in the front and smelling petrol. I was worried it would catch fire but in the end only my pride was hurt.

Triumph TR4

This was my first proper car – bright red, brand new, and I soon fitted a straight-through copper exhaust pipe. When I was dating Anne, we would go up to London a few nights a week but always on a Saturday night. The standard procedure was to have a meal at the Hungry Horse on the Ifield Road in Chelsea or later on at Nikita's, which was just opposite. We would also go to the *Playboy* Club, where for five pounds each you got a steak sandwich and we would put another fiver on red or black and then leave; we never really gambled. We went there for the food and to look at the Bunny Girls – or rather I did.

We would then go via the Hyde Park Corner underpass to hear the car's exhaust, or to the Ad Lib club and later on to Sibylla's or Tramp. At around three in the morning we'd leave, and I'd take Anne home, stopping on the way in the East End for a salt-beef sandwich. I had to be very quiet pulling into Anne's house on Teasdale Road because I got told off by Major Hackett's next-door neighbour for making a lot of noise. Not difficult with that copper exhaust! I would coast to Anne's house, have a kiss and cuddle outside, and then push the car down the road until I was all clear, start it up and leave, making as little noise as possible.

I had my first road accident in that car on Silver Street. The traffic had stopped and a pretty girl was walking down the pavement, so I was revving the car up and she was smiling, but then the car in front moved off and, still looking at the girl, I dropped the clutch, there was much wheelspin and I slammed into the Austin in front, knocking the boot catch off. The girl was still laughing when I got out to apologise to the man, who was going away with his family on holiday. Both cars were drivable and I felt like a complete idiot, which I was.

In a few days I was going to drive down to the south of France and meet Anne, who was already there, having travelled with my mother by air. My mother used to rent a small house next to the Carlton Hotel and how lucky we were to be spoilt like this – drinks on the Carlton Terrace, dinner at E Felix and a walk along the seafront before bedtime.

I got the front of the car bashed out but not properly painted and I had a fantastic race with a Continental Bentley all the way down south. The driver was an older man and his wife was charming, and we had a good chat when we both pulled in for fuel. The race continued for a total of about 200 miles on and off.

Marcos

I loved the shape of the new Marcos. Mine had the Volvo engine and it went very well, except I had two issues: the doors would fill up with water when it rained and one wheel kept coming loose. Luckily the wheel never fell off because I used to feel the car whopping around and would stop and hammer it tight. I soon discovered that it had the wrong-thread hub on one rear wheel and instead of it tightening itself, it would slowly come undone.

Above: AC Ace Bristol – just one of many cars I have owned and enjoyed over the years.
Right: 16 years old and I was legally allowed to drive a three-wheeler, two-stroke Berkeley. Friend Nick is in the passenger seat, holding aloft a bandaged thumb – he tells me that I'd shut his hand in the door!

AC Cobra 289

There was a programme on the television called *Honey West* and the opening sequence included a white Cobra filmed passing under a bridge – it looked just fantastic. We also used to see a ruby-red Cobra always parked outside the Ad Lib that was owned by Lord Ruby Russel.

Anne and I went to the 1965 Earl's Court Motor Show when we were 18 and 19 years old, and I had very long hair, but of course Anne always looked stunning whatever she was wearing (sometimes clothes that she had run up herself). The Commissionaire at the stand gate didn't want to let us in, but a man who I later knew to be Adrian Judd was the only salesman to wave to us and he was absolutely charming, as indeed he was for the whole time that I owned the car.

I went to the factory the next week, which was at Thames Ditton, and was shown around. I was rather surprised to see that the three-wheelers were being made next to the Cobras. AC was just updating the Cobra from the Mark II leaf-spring car to the Mark III coil-spring new model. Adrian Judd let me drive the factory demonstrator and I was offered the second or third car, which at that stage was only a bare chassis.

Several months later, my white Cobra was ready for collection. It cost £1,760, with Dunlop chrome wire wheels and a working detachable hardtop. It was a wonderful car and I never should have parted with it. Anne used to drive it to the local shops.

Radford Mini Cooper 1275 S

This was a fun car and it looked really great in silver with a black top – the inside was all black and fitted out in leather and thick lambswool carpets. I had a Downton conversion and Minilite wheels with spacers to make the wheels stick out more, which was a mistake because during hard cornering the tyre rubbed against the wheelarches.

I remember making a trip down to Monaco to watch the Grand Prix when it was still partly snowing and raining in the mountains, and I was driving pretty fast on what was a very twisty road with low visibility. I saw these headlights in my rear-view mirror getting closer and closer and we were on the long, downhill section of the road dropping down to the coast. The next thing I knew, a small Renault van was right up in my jacks trying to overtake. I tried to leave him behind but could not shake him off so I pulled over and watched him disappear into the mist. He must have been a local who really knew the road.

One evening, or rather morning, on our way home from Ad Lib we stopped at the lights by the entrance to Regent's Park. We pulled up and next to us was another Mini with Peter Sellers and Britt Ekland in it. It was just too tempting so we raced all around

> 'We pulled up and next to us was another Mini with Peter Sellers and Britt Ekland in it. It was just too tempting so we raced all around the Park… we both waved to each other and with a huge laugh made our way home at a more leisurely pace.'

the Park and then stopped again at the next set of lights leading to the Seven Sisters Road. We both waved to each other and with a laugh made our way home at a more leisurely pace.

In the same car, Anne, Nick and I were going to Brands Hatch to watch our friend Chris Craft race in the Saloon Car event. There was always a great dice, with drivers like Sir John Whitmore, Doc Merfield, John and Mike Young in their Red Rooster Ford Anglias and the Broadspeed cars (plus the works), and the Ford Lotus Cortinas driven by Clark and co – it was all very competitive racing.

It was raining and I got involved in a dice (I can't remember what the other car was). I left my braking very late going into a roundabout and I overtook the car I was chasing but then the brakes locked up and I went straight on over the roundabout until I hit a metal signpost. The car stopped very suddenly and Anne's knee hit the dashboard, and Nick in the back hit his head on the roof and made a large, head-shaped dent. The front was caved in, the radiator was broken, there was steam pouring out and that was the end of the Mini. It was rebuilt and is still around today in Ireland, which I know because the owner somehow managed to find my email!

Superspeed V6 Escort

Mike and John Young's Superspeed racing team was converting new Ford Escorts from their father's garage next door by putting in V6 engines, lowering the suspension, fitting a limited-slip diff, and putting in better seats to hold you in place, so in the end they were the perfect Q-car. That car could really go and it handled so well and, being rear-wheel drive, it could oversteer in a controlled way with power.

I honestly think that it was the quickest car I ever drove from A-to-B on country roads. I turned up one day at Stapleford Airfield, where the West Essex Car Club was holding a sprint around the perimeter track. I paid my entry fee, did two runs, and got the fastest time of the day.

Ford GT40

Shell was selling three roadgoing cars, which I think it had used in an advert, for around £3,500 each and I just missed getting one. However, a short time after, another roadgoing car was up for grabs. It was owned by an American TV host and he used to drive to his show in the car, which is pretty cool. It was white with two blue strips and looked fantastic.

I used it for a while and so did Anne but it was not a great car to take down to the shops and park, partly because it had Firestone racing tyres and was not good on the road. Anne used to take our younger daughter Nina in her carrycot, somehow perched on the gap behind the seats, and would see her cot jumping around in the rear-view mirror.

I was asked by Shell if I could take the car to Brands Hatch. There were about 10 cars there in total. Noel Edmonds was in a new mid-engined Ferrari, which had been lent to him by Elton John, who I was told had paid a huge amount of cash over and above the list price to get one of the first cars – why not?

I gave Noel a circuit or two in the GT40, which he loved, and later on he bought his own car. Anyway, we all then went to the local pub for lunch and returned to Brands for a few more laps in the afternoon. I went out with Noel in the Ferrari and we went past the pits and were just about to turn in for Paddock Bend and dive downhill when another car appeared and flashed past us going in the opposite direction! It really was a near thing. Apparently, after Noel and I had left the pub, all the others agreed it would be more fun in the afternoon session to go around the track anti-clockwise!

Eventually I decided to sell the GT40 because I was getting more and more into Ferraris. A guy arrived to see the car who was a dealer called Monkey Brown (and I now know why). I was asking £11,000 for it and Monkey offered me £7,500 and a very large gentleman's (or, rather, not a gentleman's) diamond ring. I told him that I had no interest whatsoever in the ring and he said we could just go down the high street and stop at a jewellers to get it valued. Stupidly, I went along with it.

We arrived at the first jeweller and showed him the ring. Monkey asked what he would give trade-price for the ring and he said £3,000. We went back to my office at my dad's engineering works in Ilford and Monkey somehow got me to agree to take £7,500 in cash and the ring, and he drove off in the car – but I kept the logbook because it had my registration number in it, which I needed to get transferred to one of my other cars.

Well, you guessed it right. I went back to the shop with the ring and told the shopkeeper that the ring was his for £3,000 as agreed, but he said that he didn't want the ring anymore. What a fool! Monkey had been to the jeweller and set the whole scam up.

A week later I got a phone call from Hexagon Cars asking me for the logbook. I told them what

My GT40 had previously belonged to US television host Vic Damone before becoming Anne's shopping car.

had happened and said that I was not prepared to hand over the paperwork, and that afternoon a driver arrived with the balance of the cash. It was a lesson well learnt.

Dino 246

I always longed for a Ferrari but they were just too much money. Then the 206 Dino came out, followed by the 246, and the price was about half the cost of a 12-cylinder car. The UK importer, Colonel Ronnie Hoare, had the clever idea of adding the Ferrari name to the back of the car so you could pretend that you had a real Ferrari.

It looked fantastic – mid-engined with a V6, and very lively performance and great handling. I arranged to collect the car with Anne from the Ferrari factory in Italy and a driver was sent to collect us from the airport and take us to the works. I was very excited because my dad used to buy cars direct from the factory. We were met in the waiting area by the sales director and when I mentioned that my father was Sam Norman he proceeded to tell me that he used to have huge arguments with my dad because the cars were always late. I think he enjoyed the banter and he went rushing off and bought back a big red book and said that Mr Ferrari wanted me to have it as a gift for old times' sake.

Paperwork presented to me when I collected the Dino 246 GT. I think I was actually supposed to hand it to customs!

At long last my red Dino turned up in the courtyard – it just looked fantastic. We drove very carefully to Paris and as a treat I booked us in for the night at the George V, a wonderful hotel where my mother and father used to stay. I asked the doorman to put my new car down in the hotel garage. We had a lovely evening, I paid the large bill happily and the Dino was waiting outside on the pavement, so we jumped in and to my horror I noticed that the ashtray had a cigarette butt in it. I jumped out and caused a huge row, which went nowhere, and drove off in a bad mood.

It was a great car which I never went to the engineering works in because the trade unions would have caused such a fuss. I kept the Dino for quite a long time but although it was very beautiful I never considered it to be a proper Ferrari – they have to have 12 cylinders.

Bentley Corniche convertible

In 1971, I met Victor Barclay, whose father, Jack Barclay, had been a very good friend of my father's. I think they used to get up to some naughty stuff (girls, enjoying the good life) since Jack's showroom and my dad's office were both in Berkeley Square.

My dad's registration number was KUU 1 and he had this on all his cars over the years. I believe Jack Barclay gave my dad this number, which had been on an old car, because the number nearly matched the registration on one of the aeroplanes my dad had just after the war. When my dad died, my mother kept the number on retention and gave it to me on my 17th birthday. I have always had the number on my current car ever since.

So I met Jack's son, Victor, who was the Managing Director of Barclays and he told me to go and see him the following week at the showroom. I couldn't really understand why, but when I turned up he was very kind and pleased to see me and talked about what great friends our fathers were, which was very nice. He told me that he had a cancelled order on a light blue metallic drophead Bentley Corniche and that I should buy it, and that if I kept it for a few weeks he would be able to buy it back off me for a profit. I was slightly concerned, but raised some cash and got a lift up to London to collect the car.

It did look fantastic, and just as I was about to drive it away from the showroom we all heard a large explosion and soon after police and fire-engine sirens. It was the first time an IRA bomb had been set off in London. It was all a bit of a shock but after a few hours I plucked up the courage to drive the car very carefully back home.

Anne's sister, Jane, was going to be dancing for the Royal Ballet in Dortmund, Germany, the following week and we decided to take the Bentley across the Channel on the car ferry. I did feel rather embarrassed, being only 24 years old with my gorgeous 23-year-old wife next to me. We booked into the best hotel in Dortmund and I did not want to leave the car outside in the street so the doorman arranged to have it parked downstairs in the hotel car park. That evening we went to the ballet, which was very nice, to see Jane dancing and went out for a lovely meal after the show.

The next morning, I went to settle and check-out and asked for the car to be brought up. I noticed after a while that a lot of talking was taking place in German and discovered that the driver collecting the car had started it with the automatic choke still on, so the engine was running fast – he had put the car into reverse with the driver's door left open and smashed the door against a pillar.

Well, I was so upset I very nearly started World War Three, and also now worried whether Barclays would still be interested in buying the car off me. I rang Victor Barclay, who was very nice and told me not to worry. I drove the car back to the UK and took it straight round to the showroom and they got the door repaired. I claimed off the hotel insurance and still managed to make a very good profit on the car. Thank you, Victor.

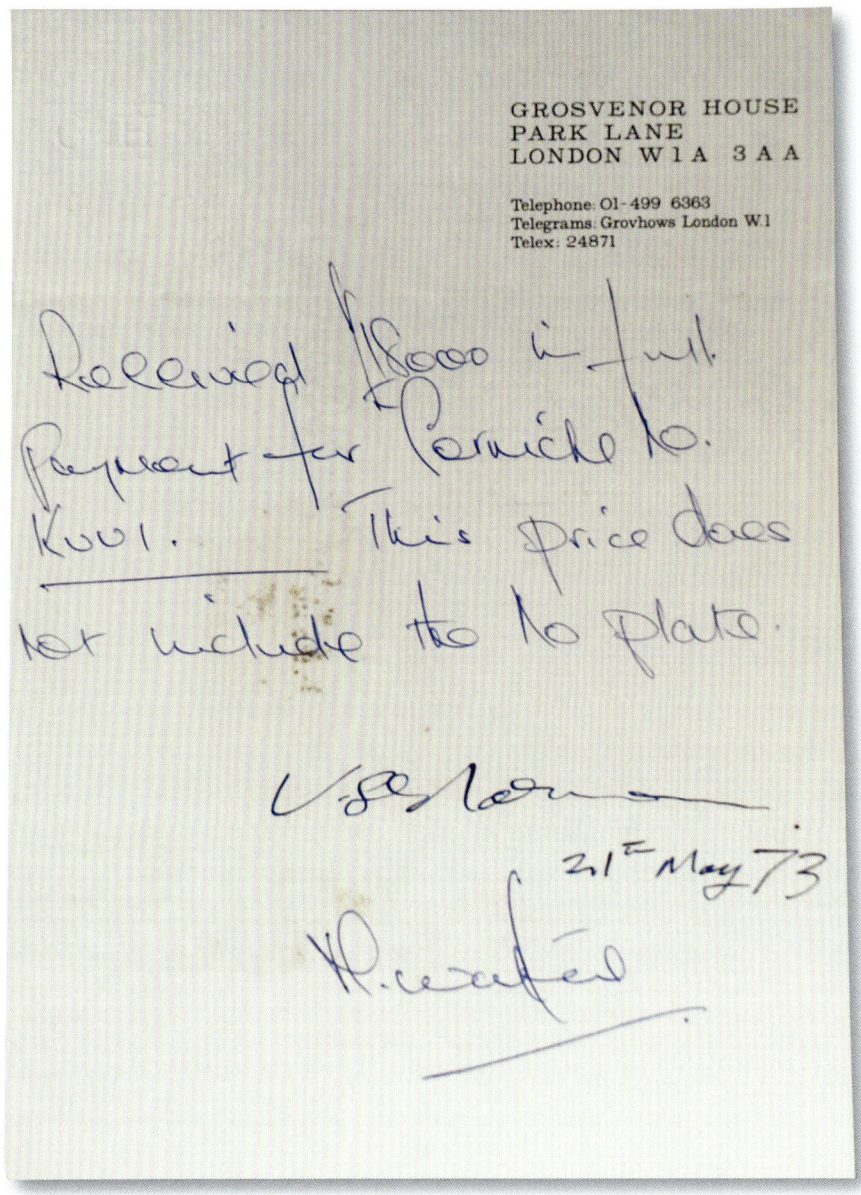

The receipt for selling the Bentley Corniche convertible – I even made a profit, despite the damage to the driver's door.

1973 Porsche 911 2.7 Touring

My friend Alain de Cadenet had told me about the new 911 Porsche. Everyone wanted one but they were pretty hard to get hold of. I managed to find out that Frank Sytner, the racing driver, had a new car up north from a cancelled order. He delivered it himself but en route it got a cracked front windscreen caused by a stone thrown up from a lorry. He promised to replace the screen as soon as he could but it took some time because the glass on these Touring and Lightweight cars was extra-thin to save weight and it had to be sent over from the Porsche factory in Germany.

I really loved that car and I used it every day. It was my first experience of owning a Porsche and it was bulletproof, so very fast, and great to drive, except in the wet – if you went into a corner too fast it would understeer. I remember on one trip back from the Highlands in Scotland – where I had been salmon fishing with my uncle Henry Ewer, who owned Grey Green coaches – I left at midnight and got back to Wiltshire in seven and a half hours. It was the fastest I had ever driven on the road.

I then always ran a 911 as my everyday road car and I used to upgrade to a new model every few years. My current car is a 997S, which has done 130,000 miles and I think is the last of the 911 cars that I would want. From then on, they all just got bigger, wider, and for me lost the appeal.

I currently have a 356C Porsche, which I really love. Mine has a slightly uprated engine that puts out around 110hp and goes really well, as well as stopping nicely with its disc brakes. It is a 1964 car, right-hand drive, and as an old car it could be used every day. I have taken it on various rallies, including sending it to South Africa and breaking down in Botswana around dusk in the middle of the desert, where the only thing in sight was a family of hyenas slowly walking towards us. The back-up rescue truck finally arrived and we were towed for 35 miles across the sand at night on the dirt road with a very short tow rope. When we eventually arrived at the overnight stop, both the car and us were covered inside and out in sand, but it was an adventure.

I also have a 1971 Porsche 911S, right-hand drive, 2.2-litre car with the open-gate five-speed gearbox and that wonderful revving engine. For a 50-year-old car, it ticks every box. Such a joy to their lucky owners – everyone should have one, but they have become bloody expensive.

Above: I bought my first Porsche 911 in the 1970s, and still own a 1971 911S.
Below: Anne and I have had many adventures in the 356C, including breaking down on a rally in Namibia.

Fast driving on a loose surface in a classic Porsche – possibly the perfect combination.

Ferrari 550 Maranello

I have always had a love of 12-cylinder Ferraris. I suppose this all started when I had that first ride in my dad's 1956 Ferrari 410. Having been out of the car business for several years, I noticed around 15 years ago that the 550 was coming on the market for less than £50,000 and so I found a 1999 car with less than 10,000 miles in one of my favourite colours, Tour de France Blue.

I bought it and really love it. It's got the classic open-gate manual change. I have driven it a few times with Anne down to the south of France and I always think how lucky I am when driving it. A real value for money, proper Ferrari. I don't like these eight-cylinder cars with paddle shifts. If you can find one, do buy it before the value creeps up and people realise how special they are.

Alpine A110

My friend Gordon Murray, of McLaren F1 fame, was the designer of numerous winning Grand Prix cars, including the Brabham BT46B 'fan car', which won first time out before it was withdrawn from racing. Gordon phoned me after he got back home from the Geneva Motor Show and he was very excited about a new Alpine A110, which was being shown to the public for the first time. He told me that he had ordered one to be his everyday road car and that the first edition of right-hand-drive cars was limited to around 125 cars, and also that the whole first production run of both left- and right-hand-drive cars had sold out on the first public day of the show.

I asked Gordon if he could get me a car and the next day, after he had spoken to his boss friend at Renault, I somehow managed to get the first right-hand-drive car delivered to the UK. It is such a fantastic lightweight car, built like a racing car – all-aluminium monocoque construction, a small turbocharged engine giving 249hp, but so light that it goes like a rocket.

Ferrari 250 GT Short Wheelbase

While I was farming with my brother at Cowage Farm in Hilmarton, Wiltshire, I still had some cash left over from the wind-up of Balfour (Marine) Engineering so I decided to buy a 1959 Ferrari SWB ex-North American Racing Team car, which was also the 1959 Paris Motor Show car on the Ferrari stand. I bought it from a Mr David Piper, an ex-racing driver who had lost one of his legs while filming *Le Mans* with Steve McQueen. He was proper wheeler-dealer who kept most of his old racing cars, including a GTO, LM, P4 Ferrari and also a 917 Porsche, as well as a huge selection of spare parts from his old racing days, just down the road from his house in his ex-racing workshop, which was an old church building.

The Ferrari was a runner but very smoky and it needed some bodywork repairs. I had read in the Ferrari Owners' Club rag that David Clarke, who had a very successful box-making business in Mountsorrel near Donington Park Circuit, was himself a long-time owner of exotic Ferrari and had set up a restoration business. I went up to visit, and the work being carried out there, both mechanical and bodyshop-wise, was fantastic. I left my car with them and said I wanted it like new and I knew what this meant because they were just finishing a GTO Ferrari rebuild for JCB's Anthony Bamford, later to become a good friend.

Anne and I went all over Europe in that Ferrari and we got on well with the members of the French Owners' Club. They would arrange races at great little circuits like Nogaro and Pierre Bardinon's private test track, and the racing was very competitive. I would race it with the VSCC, at the Aston Martin Owners' Club events at Silverstone and Brands, and also enter it for concours events run by the UK Ferrari Owners' Club.

Ferrari GTO

I was on the lookout for a GTO Ferrari having spent some time with Jess Pourret, who later wrote the first of many books dedicated to GTOs – giving chassis details, race history, owners. When this book was released, the price of GTOs doubled. Luckily, I got mine before the hype. My mother lived in Kinnerton Street, and before I met Alain de Cadenet he rented the garage at the top of her road and used to charge about in one of the several GTOs he owned at various times. They did look good.

I heard that a car might be for sale, owned by Pete Newens, who owned the famous Newens cake shop. I turned up at his house behind the shop and after a cup of tea and one of the delicious Maids of Honour cakes, he took me out to see the GTO.

Racing my Ferrari 250 GT Short Wheelbase Competizione.
Left: a brace of Alpine A110s at Heveningham Hall, where I was chief judge at an aeroplane concours.

My Ferrari GTO (chassis 3757 GT) competed at Le Mans in 1962 in the hands of Léon Dernier and Jean Blaton.

The GTO, polished and ready to bring our son Sam back from his christening, having arrived in our Maserati 300S.

Well, it looked great, not too bulled up and with nice straight panels. He was asking more than I really wanted to pay and his reason for selling was because he wanted a very good Rolls-Royce Silver Ghost. I remember him telling me, 'You know Vic, one of these days this will be worth a million pounds.' I thought he was completely off his rocker.

I was trying to knock the price down but then the doorbell rang and he looked outside and said to me, 'It's Brian Classic, a car dealer from up north.' I stuck my hand out and said, 'OK, I'll have it.' Peter went to his front door and I heard Brian say, 'I understand you have a GTO for sale.' Peter told him that he was sorry but he had just sold it to me.

Later that week, I went up to collect the car with Anne and on the way back to Wiltshire she fell asleep in what was a very noisy cockpit. I did like the GTO (who wouldn't?) but to me my Ferrari SWB, which I still owned, was a much nicer car. I never raced the GTO because I would always choose the SWB.

My son's christening was coming up and Anne had asked family and close friends along to our local church, with drinks and food afterwards. I drove our son Sam, named after his grandad, to the church in my 300S Maserati racing car and back from the church in my GTO. Not bad means of transport.

One of my cars had to go to pay a tax bill and the axe fell on the GTO – it went to a car dealer and his friend who were only ever going to move it on for a profit. I never bought a car or anything else with a view of making a turn. I was only motivated to purchase because I wanted to use and sometimes race my cars and bikes and I had the passion. It's funny, because nowadays it seems so important that chassis numbers and engine numbers match up, but I never checked any of that. I just wanted the car.

> 'Pete Newens was asking more than I really wanted to pay for the GTO. I remember him telling me, "You know Vic, one of these days this will be worth a million pounds." I thought he was completely off his rocker.'

I have kept a lot of paperwork for our vehicles, including these bits of correspondence relating to the Ferrari GTO.

Maserati 300S

I always loved Maserati racing cars and, of course, Maserati had a much longer history making and racing cars back in the 1920s and 1930s, which carried on right through to the 1970s. The 300S was a beautiful, simple race car with that tough, easy-to-maintain, straight-six engine. This was not a car to be used on the road. It needed careful warming-up with soft plugs and a toe start; it had a dry clutch and you had to select first gear and move off before the plates overheated. Today, people put a modern clutch system in the cars so that you can use them on the road.

It was a lovely car to drive and I won my only historic race in it in 1980 at Thruxton. On the fast sections of the circuit around the back, the car would really fly and it was a delight to race.

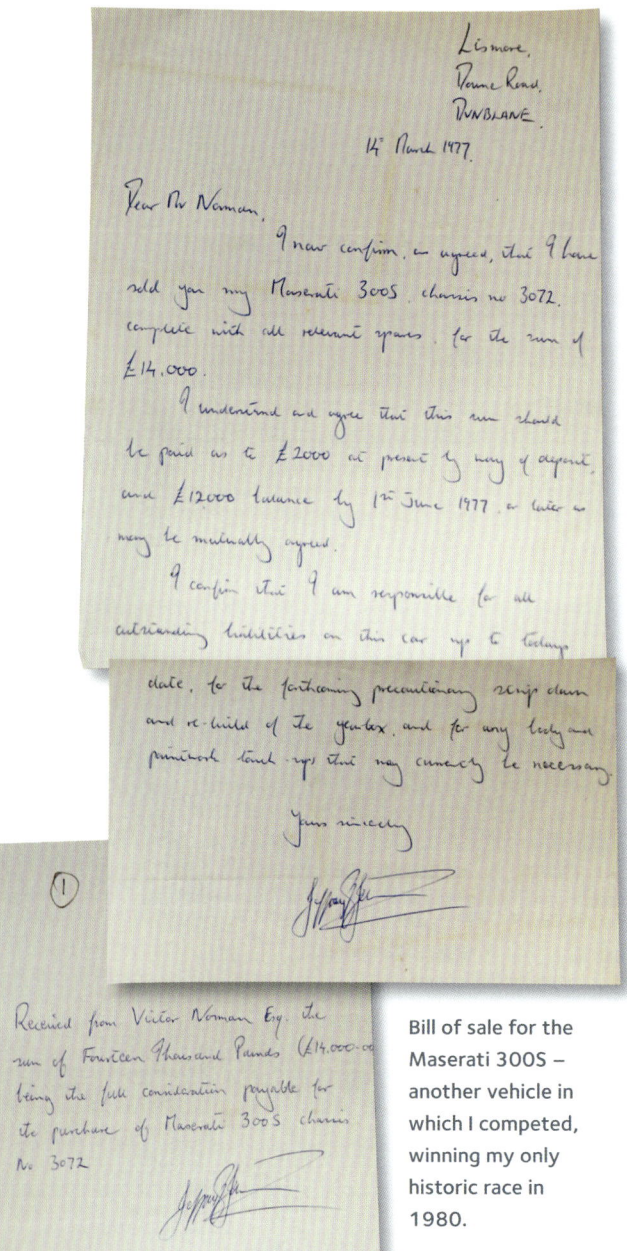

Bill of sale for the Maserati 300S – another vehicle in which I competed, winning my only historic race in 1980.

Jaguar D-type

My D-type was an ex-Ecurie Ecosse car (registration MWS 302), which had won at Spa in 1956 with Ninian Sanderson driving and was well campaigned in period. It had been raced and modified in the 1960s and 1970s, but it still needed a rebuild when I bought it. I took it down to Guy Black at Lynx Engineering and they rebuilt the car with a long nose, which looked great but it was not how it should have been done. It would have been much nicer to return it to its original short-nose spec, but back then no one was too fussed.

I raced the car on the continent at Zandvoort and Le Mans Historic in France in 1978. An amusing thing happened at Le Mans – the organisers insisted on knowing all the drivers' blood groups so I was escorted to the medical centre and was very worried because I had a real fear of needles.

A pretty French nurse came in and took me to a cubicle, and I thought that she had asked me to take my clothes off and lie on the bed so that's what I did. When she came back in, I was stark naked and she let out a scream and motioned for me to put my trousers back on. She then came towards me with a needle so she could sample some of my blood. I looked away and she said she was finished so I turned around – and fainted. No more pretending that I was a cool racing driver!

Anne and I used to drive the car everywhere we went. I remember that I had a section of wood that I would place by the rear wheels when driving onto the ferry to stop the exhaust pipe grinding out. It was a nice road car but not so good on the twisty short circuits.

I was racing the D-type one weekend at Silverstone and we had become friendly with Neil and Freda Corner and Patrick Lindsay. Neil and Patrick had their Maserati 250F 1957 Grand Prix cars both parked next to Neil's transporter. I asked Neil if I could sit in his car because I always wanted a 250F single-seater Grand Prix car, which to me is the best-looking car of all time and from the best period of Grand Prix racing.

While waiting for my race, I was in Neil's motorhome having a nice cup of tea and Neil asked me if I wanted a 250F. Well, of course I did, but they were always a bit more money than I could find. Neil said that Patrick really liked my D-type so we could swap if I wanted. The next thing I knew was that I was next to Patrick and on an old piece of torn-off paper we agreed to swap cars with no money changing hands.

Neil agreed to take the Maserati back to Yorkshire in his transporter and Patrick drove off in the D-type. I had to phone Anne, who was at home with the children, to get her to come and collect me. She said, 'Oh dear, have you crashed the D?' When I told her about the swap I'm not sure how pleased she was, but she soon changed her mind because we had the best time ever racing the Maser.

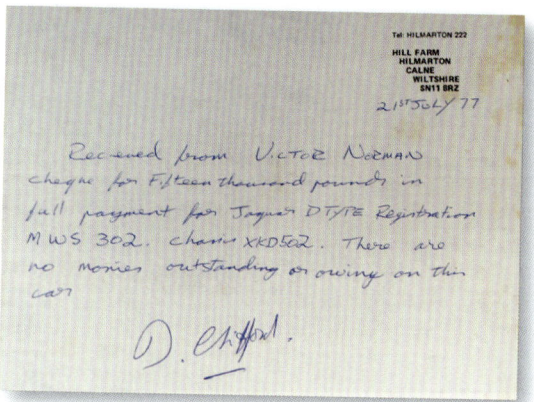

Another bill of sale – this time for the Jaguar D-type.
Right: Anne calming me down before an outing at Le Mans Historic in 1978. After the race was over, we drove it back to our hotel and stopped in the woods for a picnic!

In 1978, we drove the D-type to Le Mans for the four-lap historic race, which was a real experience and home turf for D-type Jaguars. After the race, which Stirling Moss won, we were all very happy and a French TV crew turned up and must have found out that Walter Hill had sent his car all the way over from Texas. They started interviewing him asking what was it like and was it worthwhile, and other pretty stupid questions. The last question was, 'Walter, what do you think about your race?'

Walter said, 'It was great to bring my D-type all the way back to Le Mans and drive over 160mph down the Mulsanne straight. It was just the best and I have to tell you that no black man has ever done that!' That was the end of the interview, and he had no idea that he had said anything offensive...

At Le Mans in 1978 with the Maserati 300S and Jaguar D-type (left). I drove the Jaguar in the Grand Prix Historique de l'ACO, whilst my good friend Clive Richardson took the 300S to a class win.

BRITISH SPEEDMAN IN ITALY

Stirling Moss, British racing driver who is in Monza, Italy, to test the modified version of the B.R.M., seen with Miss Sally Weston in his 2,500 c.c. Jaguar.

In 2004, I bought this Jaguar XK 120 fixed-head coupé – the first owner of which had been none other than Stirling Moss. Not only did Stirling enter rallies with it, he used it for travelling around the continent as his career began to take off. He even towed a matching two-tone caravan with it, until the caravan broke loose and destroyed itself en route to the Swiss Grand Prix!

NORMAN CONQUEST 85

Maserati 250F

Juan Manuel Fangio won the World Championship for the fifth time in 1957. His mount for that season was shared between one of the three Maserati 250F lightweight cars (chassis numbers 2527, 2528 and 2529). Without going into detail, his best race of all time was at the Nürburgring when he was driving 2529. After a fuel stop he caught up with Peter Collins and Mike Hawthorn, lowering the lap record on every lap to overtake them both and take the chequered flag.

I had always wanted a single-seater to race in historic events, having seen them race in period with my dad and, much later on, seeing the likes of Charlie Lucas and Neil Corner and, of course, Willie Green drifting around Woodcote Corner with the tail hanging out in a wonderful four-wheel drift. Well, my own chance finally came when I was racing my Jaguar D-type at Silverstone. Without any doubt, my 250F, 2527, gave me more fun – attending wonderful events and being with my wife Anne, who always joined in and supported me. Of course, the racing was the icing on the cake.

I did all the VSCC races and other invitation-only events that were organised by Baron Emmanuel 'Toulo' de Graffenried and sponsored by Marlboro. These were support events at Formula One races in France at Circuit Paul Ricard, Monza, Monaco and the Nürburgring. We used to get start money given to us in a Marlboro envelope, together with a thank-you note when we arrived. Not only this but we were put up in lovely hotels where the F1 guys stayed, we had seats for the Grand Prix and a black-tie dinner in the evening – no better way to go historic racing.

I ended up selling 2527 to have cash that would enable me to buy what was at the time The Best Aerobatic Aircraft in the World.

BRM P25

Christie's was selling a 1959 Grand Prix-winning P25 BRM that was still owned by Rubery Owen. Chassis number 258 had won the Dutch Grand Prix with Jo Bonnier, and the factory had kept the car rather than break it up to convert into a rear-engined model. It was very special, with magnesium lightweight body panels, and everything on it was so beautifully made.

After having some work carried out on the car at Crosthwaite & Gardiner, I entered it for the historic race at Monaco. I had never driven the car before and in the first practice session, having only completed three laps, the gearbox packed in but I was still the fourth fastest without really trying. It had fantastic power low down compared to my Maserati, and going up the hill into Casino Square it was flying.

I was getting more and more into building up and running my flying team. It was my main source of income and I really loved the flying. My good

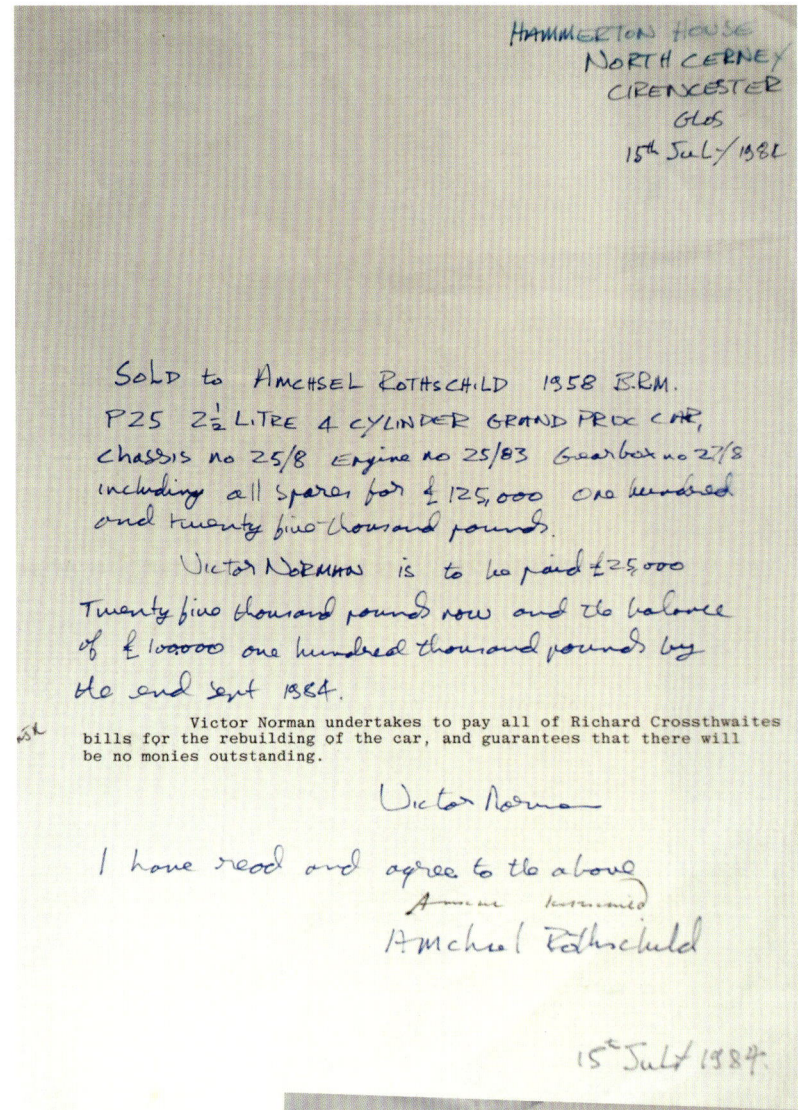

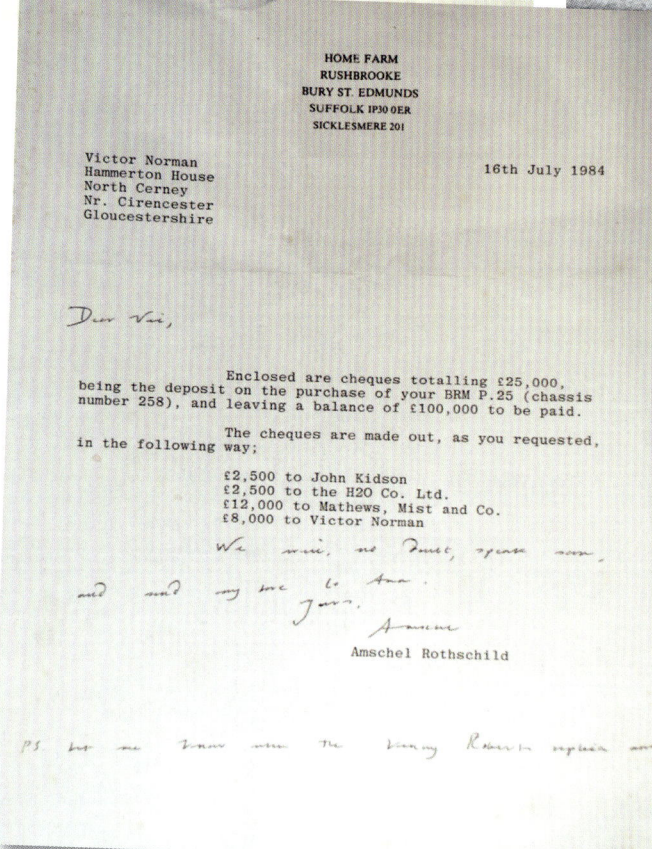

I sold my BRM P25 to my great friend Amschel Rothschild in 1984, but I first had the pleasure of driving it at Monaco (far right) where it was impressively quick.

friend Amschel Rothschild, who was also a very good and keen motor racer, later became interested in flying as well, and bought a Stampe biplane like mine, painted in his family colour of dark blue. Anita Guinness, his wife, had a navy blue windsock made for his farm strip, which was not the easiest thing to see, but fun. Amschel really wanted the BRM, being very British himself, and so I sold him the car. It could not have gone to a more special and great man, and friend.

Amschel used to harvest apples on his farm and sell the bottles to Sainsbury's. He told me that it was not great business because he lost about a shilling on every bottle. Anne and Anita spent hours together at Silverstone, normally sitting in a car to get out of the wind, while Ami and I mucked about with our cars – lovely memories.

Amschel took his own life, which was so sad. I really miss him and often think about our chats on those wet days at Silverstone, and also sitting in a de Havilland twin-engined Mosquito fighter in Scotland during the Christie's sale of Sir Willy Roberts' Strathallan Collection, thinking we were fighter pilots from 633 Squadron.

After I sold the BRM, I still missed racing and the chance came up to purchase the ex-Bob Gerard Cooper-Bristol Formula Two car. I raced it for a while but it was not like having a proper Grand Prix car and my flying soon took over all my time.

NEWS FROM THE RUBERY OWEN GROUP

For immediate release.

The Rubery Owen Group are pleased to announce that they will be maintaining an interest as the entrant of the only original B.R.M. P25 which is to be raced in selected historic events this year by Victor Norman. The car was purchased by Norman at the B.R.M. sale organised by Christie's South Kensington at last October's Motorfair. Christie's are particuarly pleased to have been involved in formulating this arrangement, as one of the car's earliest appearances is expected to be the Monaco Historic Grand Prix on May 23rd, which will be exclusively sponsored by them .

For further information, photographs etc. please contact :
Robert Brooks
Tel: (01) 581 2231 or 581 3491
Telex 922061

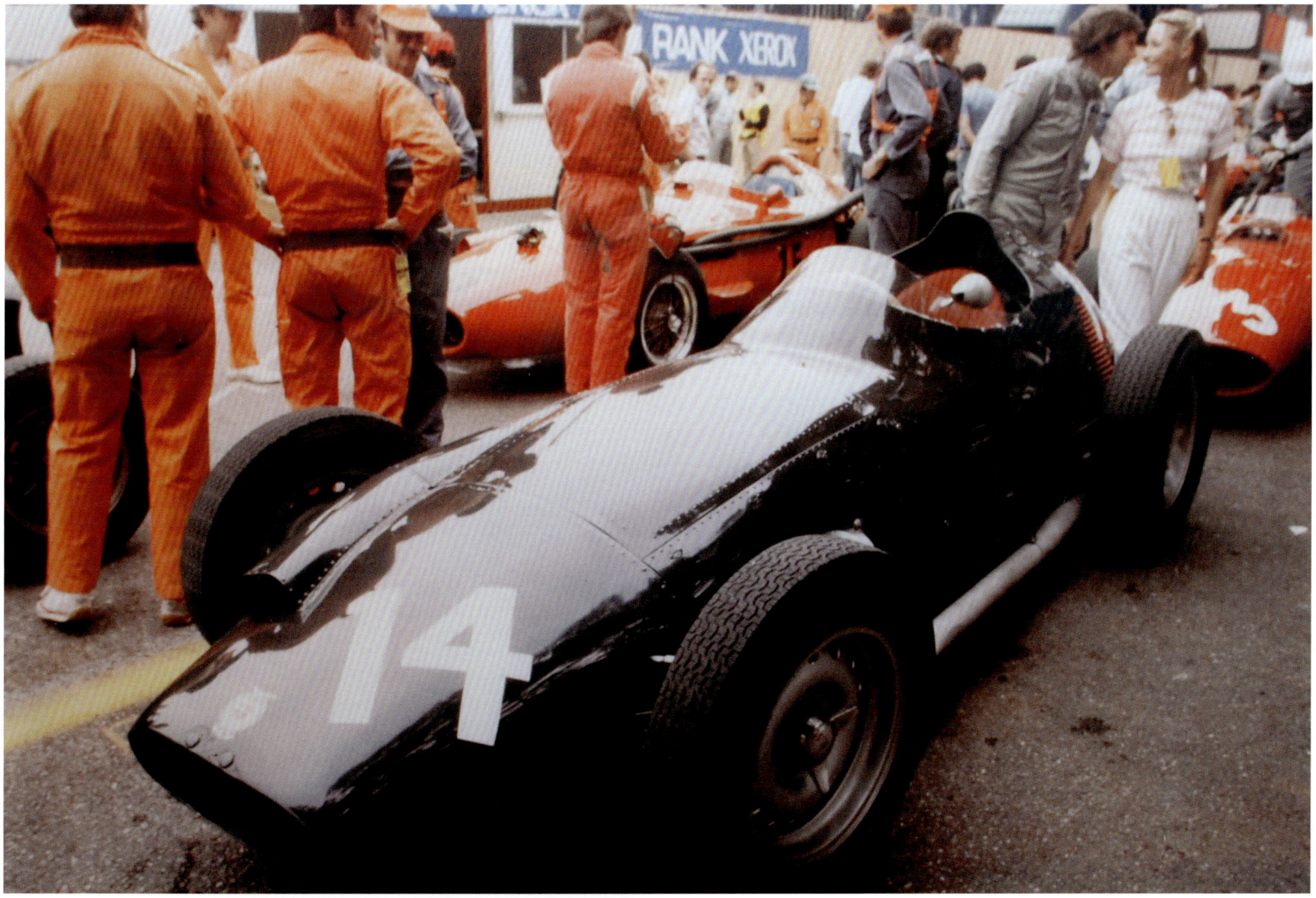

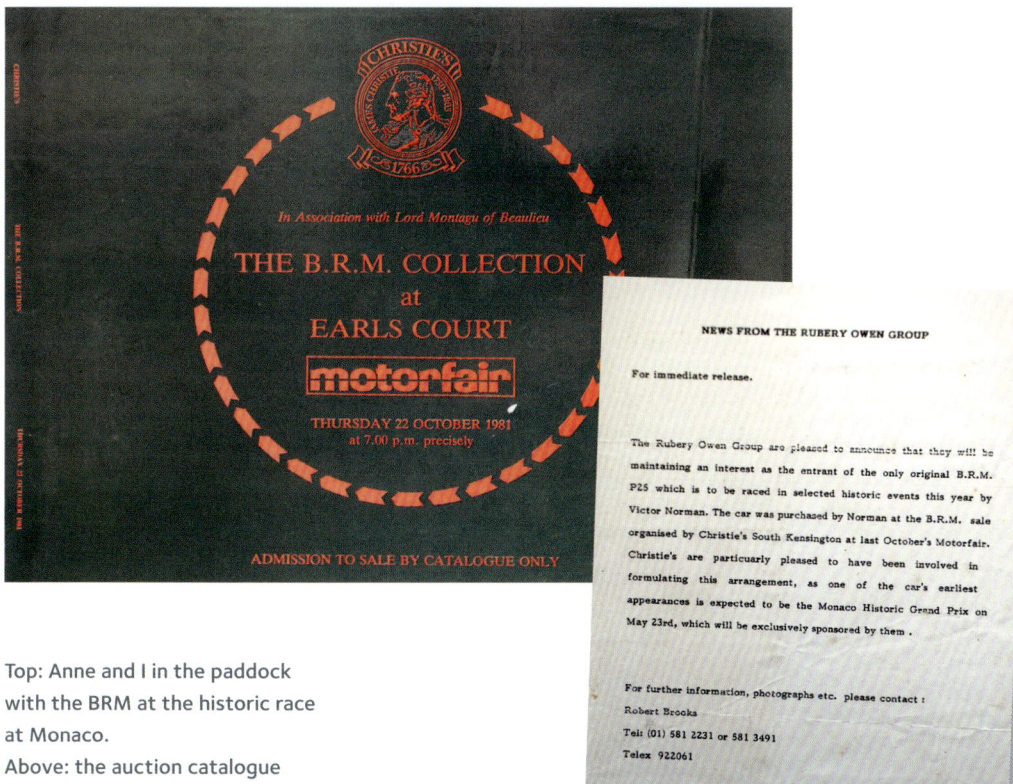

Top: Anne and I in the paddock with the BRM at the historic race at Monaco.
Above: the auction catalogue from 1981, when I purchased the car.

Anne's cars

I once bought Anne a black Mini Cooper 1275 S. She had learnt to drive in Manor House's run-around standard Mini and was used to rushing about in London doing her photoshoots. She was, and is, a very good driver.

The next car she had was a Lotus Elan Plus 2 in bright yellow. It came to a sad end when someone jumped the lights in Oxford Street and rammed into her passenger side, which totally destroyed the car. Luckily Anne was completely unhurt but the car ended up in thousands of plastic bits scattered across the road. I guess that this helped displace the energy of the impact and saved Anne from harm, thank goodness.

Anne needed a replacement and a bright orange Morgan Plus 8, which had just come out, was her next car. I bought it from Rob Walker's garage in Warminster and it was great fun, but had very heavy steering and used to jump all over the road. She also had a fun white Volkswagen Golf convertible and then a series of boring but practical road cars...

The ex-Bob Gerard Cooper-Bristol and my first Zlin-50, photographed at Kemble airfield.

Lockdown, no time to spare

It's rather boring not being able to feel the joys of speed, and what shall I do to get my fix if and when flying and motoring get back to normal? Well, I have got the answer! For several years I have been looking at the Vintage Hot Rod Association's activities and the racing on the sands at Pendine in Wales, thinking what good fun it all looked.

Before the COVID lockdown, a friend, Peter Stevens, the well-known British car designer, was telling me about how much he liked competing in his hot-rod and what great fun it all was, with no posers and a great bunch of people. He suggested that I could put on a wingwalking display and maybe even land on the beach while all this was going on.

I kept thinking about this and started looking for a suitable hot-rod with a flathead V8 engine. I have taken the plunge and purchased a 1928 Model A Ford Roadster and am now working out what I need to do to get more power because I would really like to join the exclusive club and get the 100mph t-shirt. I think that I have even convinced my good mate Nick Mason to follow suit in between his drumming, and for us to have a team. DOUBLE VINTAGE.

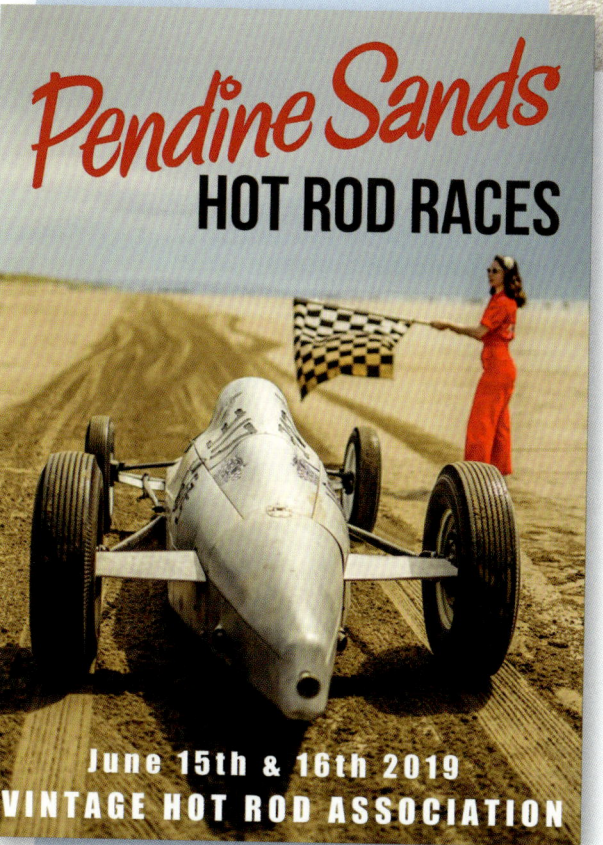

One of my latest buys has been this 1928 Ford Model A Roadster, the aim being to run at the famous Pendine Sands and hopefully join the exclusive 100mph club. Above: the Model A as I bought it, following a listing on eBay.

Clockwise from left: Alfa Giulietta Sprint Veloce is the perfect transport for Gordon Murray's 'Old Alfa' trips out with the Murrays, de Cadenets, and Anne and myself – the Alfa is parked in front of my first Stearman, which has never ceased to work since I bought it in 1986; enjoying my Jaguar XK 120 on a rally; winning my class at Thruxton at the wheel of the Maserati 300S.

Chapter six
ROSSO RACING

I had just moved my family out of Cowage Farm in Hilmarton, Wiltshire. It was all a bit of a rush and came about because my brother got the chance to buy back into his family's business, Walthamstow Stadium, and unlike me he had not gone out and bought old cars but, as my mother used to remind me, invested in stocks and shares.

I moved with Anne and our three children to a nice house in North Cerney, Hammerton House, with a stable block that soon became my workshop and garage for a few motors. I'd met Bob Houghton up at Graypaul Motors and he wanted to leave, and we also had a small spare cottage that he moved into so my old racing car business, Rosso Racing, was in action from day one.

The work just grew and grew and we ended up with three more engineers, all doing historic car race preparation, and rebuilds on road cars, with Bob being a great engine man working on all sorts of engines, not just Ferraris. I was racing my Ferrari 250 GT SWB all over the UK and Europe, and also later on my Maserati 250F and D-type Jaguar, promoting the business.

We were asked to race-prepare Ferraris for Le Mans and at the same time more and more work was flocking into the business. Rosso Racing was getting a high-profile reputation in the Ferrari world and work was being done for owners from many different countries.

I was approached by Colonel Ronnie Hoare, who was 'Mr Ferrari' in the UK and the distributor for all right-hand-drive cars. Ronnie was a proper gentleman and he had a real love for Ferrari racing cars. I think he took a shine to me and Rosso because we were a very small set-up (running and preparing cars to go racing) but we were also

Myself and Clive Richardson chatting to Denis Jenkinson as he tries the P3 Alfa for size at Hammerton House.

'We had a grand opening and I asked along all my racing chums, and we had some wonderful older competition Ferraris, including GTOs, SWB and racing Daytona.'

becoming a bit of an embarrassment because we were getting much more media coverage than the current crop of Ferrari dealers selling new cars. Their only interest was making money, which was all rather boring. It was never about making money for me. Yes, I had to make enough of it to provide for my family but having a fun, challenging time was more important.

I was asked if I would like to become the Ferrari dealer for Gloucestershire, Wiltshire and Avon, but I had to find a garage because we were still working from my back garden. I found a small garage in Cirencester, our home town, that was closing up and was on the market. The premises were not grand or big enough for Renault, but I felt would be perfect for Ferrari since it had a large workshop area and a small showroom big enough for two cars. We had a grand opening and I asked along all my racing chums, and we had some wonderful older competition Ferraris, including GTOs, SWB, racing Daytona, 1960 front-engined Grand Prix cars, Boxer BB LM, 250 LMs, as well as various road cars.

The business carried on as before. Eighty percent of our work was from historic and current racing cars but we were now on the 'Ferrari map' and getting much more service work. Although it was difficult at times, we were also selling a few new cars but we always had to discount because all the other larger dealers were almost giving cars away to move them on. All in all, it was not a great time to be selling new Ferraris.

We had some really nice customers and many became good friends, although there were a few who weren't our type. One very interesting restoration was a Ferrari 250 LM that had been totally modified in period with a shortened chassis. It had been

Top: I raced this Ferrari LMB with my good friend Chris Craft and its then-owner Steve O'Rourke – manager of Pink Floyd – in the 1980 6 Hours of Silverstone. We finished second in class and seventh overall.

Above: restoring a Ferrari 250 LM proved to be a challenging experience but resulted in becoming good friends with Eric Stewart of 10cc.

turned into a lightweight hillclimb car with a Porsche-like body. It arrived to us as a basket case. The first job was to get the tubular chassis put back to original so, being a Ferrari dealer, we took it down to Modena. Anne and I towed it on a trailer all the way there. After about six months, Ferrari came back to us saying that it had been modified too much and they no longer had the toolings or time to rebuild a new frame.

Eric Stewart (the owner of the car and lead singer of the band 10cc) and I were getting pretty fed up and we had another customer with an LM, so I suggested that if we rebuilt his car free of charge, would he mind if we copied his frame? He was delighted and we made a fully comprehensive jig locating on every separate tube of the chassis, which worked a treat, and the car turned out really nice and Eric was thrilled.

The word got out through the grapevine that we could make new Ferrari frames and a well-known dealer and racer asked if we could make a frame for him. I think we probably made two new frames and then, sometime later, we sold him the jig and I think he made several more. Funnily enough, one of the cars with our frame was sent back to the factory for certification and several tens of thousand pounds later it was certified as being an original car. Well, I suppose it was if you count continued history, but you can't take history away from the old frame we junked, which was the frame that did all the period racing.

Someone has now rebuilt another car and there are now two cars purporting to have the same number. The values of these old cars have gone through the roof and buyers now need to get authenticity before investing their millions. In my day, all we wanted to do was race an old historic car, we never cared about numbers. How times have changed.

Eric and his wife Gloria became our closest friends. We would go away on holidays and spend a lot of time together. Eric is one of the most gifted people that I know and he sings like an angel. He thought of the name for Rosso Racing and would sing and play at all our parties. He even wrote a song about Anne and I – *Norman Conquests II*. We of course went to all of his gigs and became close friends with Rick Fenn, the lead guitar player, who now lives in Australia in a fantastic small town called Byron Bay, and we managed to see him when my flying team was displaying at The Avalon Airshow, Melbourne. Not only does Rick tour all over with 10cc, he also has a great band where he lives and we managed to go to see him play at the local pub.

Through racing the old cars, I also met Nick Mason – I think at Silverstone. He was racing one of his old Aston Martins and I was racing my 1959 Short Wheelbase Ferrari 250. I had no idea that he was in Pink Floyd and we obviously shared a common interest in old cars.

Rosso Racing worked on a car for Nick and we got the job because my mechanic and partner Bob Houghton had met Nick before coming to Rosso Racing. Nick was also racing his Connaught Type A in some of the same races that I was driving my Maserati 250F.

We rebuilt a Ferrari 512 S for Nick – a car that had been in a fire during Steve McQueen's filming of *Le Mans*. Later on, when I bought a Ferrari 250 GTO and ended up selling it to a car dealer and his friend,

'Through racing the old cars, I also met Nick Mason – I think at Silverstone. He was racing one of his old Aston Martins and I was racing my 1959 Short Wheelbase Ferrari 250.'

Through my friendship with Nick Mason and then with other members of the band, Anne and I were lucky enough to see Pink Floyd on numerous occasions in Europe and the USA, and were treated to VIP passes.

100 NORMAN CONQUEST

On a break in Barbados with Nick Mason, Steve O'Rourke, Eric Stewart and our respective families. With *Jaws* having just hit the big screen, we decided to make our own version: *The Rubber Duck*. The children were petrified to jump into the swimming pool in case it ate them!

Above: tea in Nick Mason's flash hotel in San Sebastian, Spain. We had just completed an air display at the opening of a casino in Biarritz and Nick kindly invited us to the Pink Floyd concert that evening. Over the years, Nick has become a great friend and we share a passion for both cars and flying.

Nick bought it from them not long after. He still has it and it takes pride of place in his collection.

Nick and I are great friends and Nick paid for my flight tickets for my family – all five of us – the very first time we went to Barbados at Christmas in 1978. I think we did some work on his cars in return. Anne and I have an ongoing relationship with Nick and Annette as well as with Lindy, his first wife. Our families are very close. Anne and I were honoured to be asked by Nick and Annette to be godparents for both their sons, Guy and Cary, and Nick's two daughters, Chloe and Holly, are best friends with Zoe, Nina and Sam.

We went to so many of the Pink Floyd concerts and we always got VIP passes but with three extra stars, which were like gold dust and there was a real one-upmanship when you went back-stage. I also helped Nick overcome his fear of flying and he has since become a qualified flying instructor on helicopters. He just loves flying and so does his wife Annette.

Rosso also prepared and looked after Robert Horne's Ferrari 512, which Derek Bell drove at RAF Fairford to get the British Land Speed Record. Derek and his wife Misti have subsequently become good friends and we took them wingwalking when we were in Switzerland working for Breitling, but more of that later.

Alan Jones turned up at Rosso the week before the British Grand Prix at Silverstone and it was great to see him and show him around. He ended up sending us two Ferraris for restoration – a 330 GTC and a 365 Daytona. He wanted both cars to be like new and we put a lot of effort into doing a really good job. He made regular payments and was very pleased when the first car was finished.

The second car was going along really well but then the payments for the last two months stopped coming. He said he would settle up when the car was ready for collection, by which time he owed us a lot of money. We were offered, from memory, about half what we were owed but we never had any reserves. I just took the money because I knew a legal action would be a complete waste of time for us, other than the lawyers getting rich.

Ferraris were getting very difficult to sell at this time. Interest rates were in the high teens and I was getting disillusioned with the business and, if truth be told, I was only ever interested in the race cars. I had a bit of luck because another Ferrari set-up called Modena Engineering, owned by several well-off Ferrari owners and run by a good chap called Michael Scott, wanted to become official dealers but they were never going to get given a dealership being so near to the importers (they were based near Egham, just a few miles away from Colonel Hoare's showrooms). I was flying much more and most of my attention was on learning how to fly aerobatics. I was really hooked.

Michael Scott approached me and asked if I would sell him our dealership. In truth, it was worth very little. The freehold property was owned by Walthamstow Stadium and I was now a director and shareholder. Michael and I went up to see Colonel Hoare and he agreed that Modena Engineering could buy my dealership. I got a banker's draft there and then and was very pleased to walk away from the car business.

The story didn't end there. A few days later, I heard that Michael and one of his partners had bought Rosso for themselves and that they were trying to move the business on to Modena for a large profit. There's nothing wrong with that, other than one of the partners in Modena was a good friend of the Colonel's and so the dealership offer was withdrawn. James Hunt's brother David came down to run the business and I tried to help them as much as possible but it carried on for a year or two and then packed up. Michael Scott started the 96 Club, which is still going strong.

George Daniels' Millennium watch

The late Dr George Daniels is recognised as the greatest watchmaker of the 20th century. He invented the coaxial escapement, which is arguably the greatest British contribution to watchmaking.

I first met George in the early 1980s through Ronald 'Steady' Barker, who was a dear friend of mine and a much-liked motoring journalist. Steady was an old-car buff and a vintage car driver. I took him wingwalking on his 70th, 80th and 90th birthdays, as well as doing many other exciting things with him. George was also a real enthusiast and he ended up with a wonderful collection of cars including the Birkin 'Blower' 4½ Litre single-seater Bentley.

George, Steady, Anne and I used to meet up at one of the local pubs and sometimes George would come for supper at our house. He did have a good eye for anything exquisite, which, of course, included Anne and they used to chat about things other than motors or aeroplanes so I would feel rather left out.

I used to ask George when he was going to make a wristwatch as a joke because he would make just one or two highly complicated pocket watches every year. They provided him with more than enough funds to support his motor racing. In the mid-1990s, he told me that he was going to make a limited run of wristwatches, all to be fitted with his coaxial escapement. They would, of course, all be handmade and limited editions of fewer than 50 pieces.

He showed me the first one he produced and it was simply stunning with a gold case, a sterling silver dial, gold hands, a sapphire front and back, and a brown alligator strap. He told me that he would like me to have one of his watches, but after he told me the price, I said that I could not afford to buy one. We met several times that year and, on each occasion, he would always tell me that he would like to make a watch for me.

I told George that I simply could not wear a gold watch because it would be much too flash for me so, after some thought, he said that he could make me a one-off in white gold. I then told him that I didn't like gold hands and would much prefer blued steel hands. He said that I was being awkward but that he could do it if I insisted. Finally, I said I would only want a plain black leather strap. I also reminded him that I could not afford one of his watches. He just told me not to worry about the money because I could have a special price if I supplied him with some spare parts for one of his cars.

I gave in and, because I knew he used to engrave each watch with the owner's initials, I asked him if he could leave mine plain. I have wonderful letters from George where he tells me that I was the most difficult customer he had ever had.

Anne and I went up to collect my watch from his home in Herefordshire and it looked amazing. To me, it looked so much nicer than the normal gold version. I was thrilled with it and he had engraved 'AEROBA' on the case. It's a special thing and he went on to produce a further six of the 47 watches he made in white gold, but none of the others were exactly like mine. Thank you, George.

Chapter seven

TAKING TO THE AIR

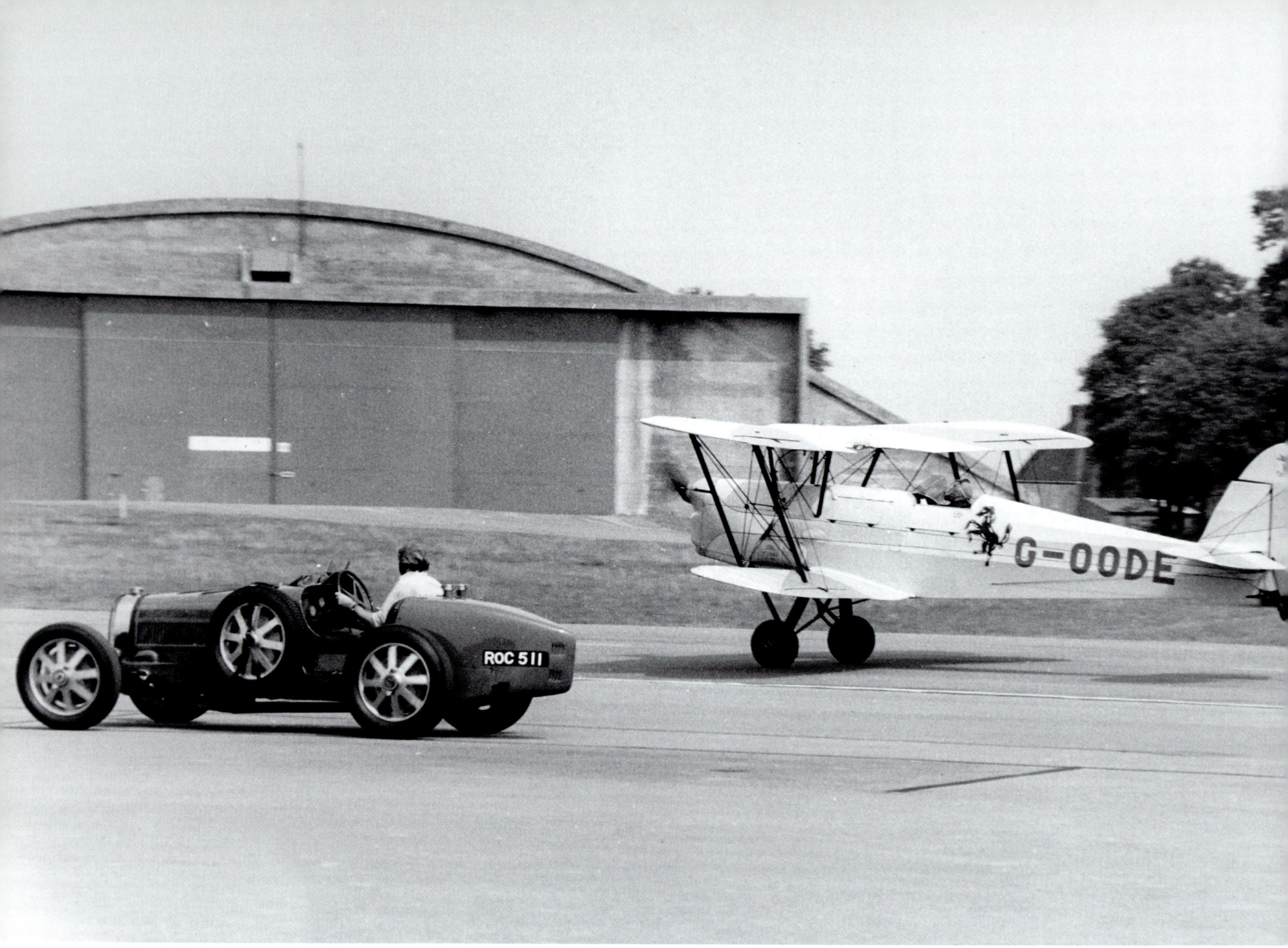

Neighbour and close friend Geoffrey St John racing his Bugatti against my Stampe biplane at RAF Kemble. The whole thing was filmed by HTV West and the Bugatti narrowly beat the Stampe over a quarter-mile standing start.

010181 329375

APPLICATION FOR CZECHOSLOVAK VISA

Registration No. of vehicle | State identification sign
Factory mark of vehicle | Colour of vehicle

Surname: NORMAN
First name: VICTOR
Day, month, year of birth: 18 2 47
Male ~~Female~~
Place of birth - State: HOSPITAL LONDON
Place of birth - Town: LONDON
Address of applicant State
Place of residence: HAMMERTON HSE
Street: NORTH CERNEY, CIRENCESTER
Citizenship: BRITISH
Profession: PILOT, DIRECTOR
Name of employer: SELF EMPLOYED
Employer's address: HAMMERTON HSE NORTH CERNEY, GLOS
Place of stay in ČSSR - District: OTROKOVICE
Name of visited person - institution - hotel in ČSSR: FACTORY MORAVAN
Purpose of journey to ČSSR: VISIT FACTORY MORAVAN TO DISCUSS TECH DETAILS. Z50L
Length of stay in ČSSR: 3 DAYS
Accompanying children under 15: —
Series No. of passport: N 131353B
Stamp of border control - ARRIVAL
Signature

Upon arrival in the Czechoslovak Socialist Republic you are obliged to register with the Czechoslovak police authorities within 48 hours.

Please type or print in Roman letters all the parts of the application. In case of illegibility the application will not be considered.

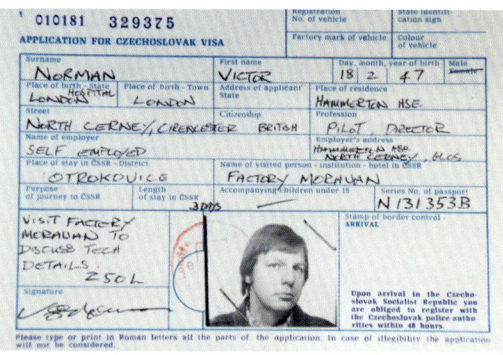

In 1978, when I was very much still into cars and racing, and running my Ferrari business, Anne and I were invited for lunch by Patrick Lindsay at his house near Hungerford, which had its own small landing strip. Patrick had his Stampe aircraft parked in the field and he took both me and then Anne up for a flight. I'd never been in an open-cockpit biplane before and I fell in love with the whole thing there and then, and Anne was also smitten.

Fate is a strange thing because, by chance, we went to a friend's drinks party and met this real character, Richard Goode, who was Captain of the British Aerobatic Team and, surprise surprise, he had his Stampe for sale. I agreed to buy it on the spot for £7,500, which was very little money compared to the cost of old cars.

My pilot's licence had expired and I had to do a refresher course with an instructor, and then I couldn't wait to fly my Stampe. Well, there was a Vintage Sports-Car Club event coming up that weekend and I was going to race my Maserati, so I asked a friend of mine who was in the RAF flying transport aircraft if he would like to come along because Anne was driving to Silverstone and bringing the children and a big lunch.

I was so excited but I also discovered that flying a vintage biplane and landing in a crosswind was not for the faint-hearted and that you needed to learn the skills over a period of time with a good biplane instructor. Well, I thought, how hard can it be?

The answer, I found out, was very hard as I ground-looped on landing, smashed the wing, broke the propeller and damaged the undercarriage – luckily with no harm to Peter or myself, and just my pride in tatters. Peter was shell-shocked; although he'd flown for 20,000 hours, it was the first crash he had ever been in.

I still raced the car but felt pretty rotten. As always, Anne was there to calm me down and tell me not to worry and that the aircraft can be rebuilt. And rebuilt it duly was, and I then went about getting some proper instruction.

Richard Goode was going around airshows, displaying his other aircraft, which included a high-performance Pitts Special. He suggested that he would try to get the show organiser to book the

Stampe for him to display and that I could position the aeroplane for him and he would then split the fee with me. It was a great way for me to learn about display flying and it was something that I really enjoyed doing. Well, it did lead on to greater things and a total change in my life.

The flying bug had really taken hold of me and all I wanted to do was fly. I sold my Maserati 250F Grand Prix car for £120,000, which was a huge amount in 1982, and Richard became my mentor, pushing me to practise doing aerobatics and different manoeuvres, not just sticking to the easy ones. He would say you shouldn't waste time doing loops and rolls when you go up flying – you had to practice the harder stuff. It wasn't about enjoyment, it was about getting better.

Richard had heard that the Spanish aerobatic team had ordered a batch of five new Z-50 aerobatic aircraft from the Zlin factory in the Czech Republic. To me, these were the ultimate competition machines and no one in the West had one, so I knew it would be a big attraction for the UK and European airshow organisers.

The Zlin factory would only manufacture batches of five aeroplanes at a time and the cost was $120,000 each. However, the dealer who had done the deal for the Spanish team had in fact charged them for all five aeroplanes and only delivered four, which meant that he had a spare new aeroplane that was standing him in for zero money.

The word got out and my friend Richard Goode told me that one could be purchased for $50,000 in cash. Richard did the deal for me and he jumped on an airliner with a black suitcase full of cash that I'd drawn out of my bank following the sale of my Grand Prix Maserati. It all went according to plan and I had what was the best aerobatic aircraft in the

The race was deemed to be cover material by the publishers of *Classic and Sportscar* – it probably helped that the car won!

Left: the Stampe in preferred light blue colour scheme and a friendly handshake between 'rivals' before the Bugatti vs biplane dash.

Above: Ryan PT-22 – the original owners of the aircraft enjoying the fresh air in an exercise that is a far cry from its original role as a military training machine!
Right: I prefer to fly the PT-22 with a few more clothes on...

AeroSuperBatics Ltd

AeroSuperBatics was the first Stearman aircraft wingwalking company in the UK. It started wingwalking in 1987 and in 2019, before the coronavirus pandemic, we flew more than 1,000 members of the public with about 70 percent of the flights raising money for charities.

I have often been asked how I came up with that name for my aviation company. Well, I discovered that a small book was published every year that listed all known outdoor events that would be taking place in the forthcoming year. This included fêtes, carnivals, concerts and, of course, airshows. When I started displaying my aeroplane at shows, the book gave me a list of all the events that might want, and be prepared to pay for, an aerobatic appearance. My main competitors all advertised in the book, too – in fact, there were about five of us who were all chasing the same bookings. AeroSuperBatics was alphabetically one of the first on the list of airshow performers, which, for some reason, I thought was a good thing. Whether it really made any difference, I shall never know.

AeroSuperBatics
EXCELLENCE IN WINGWALKING

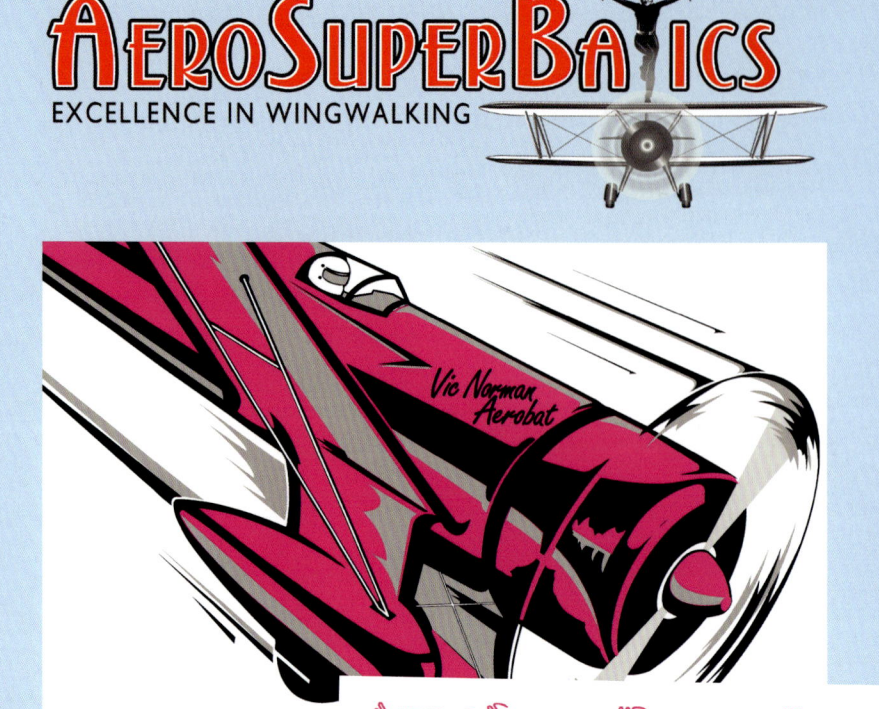

Right: current and the first incarnations of the AeroSuperBatics logo. Below: me with the Zlin.

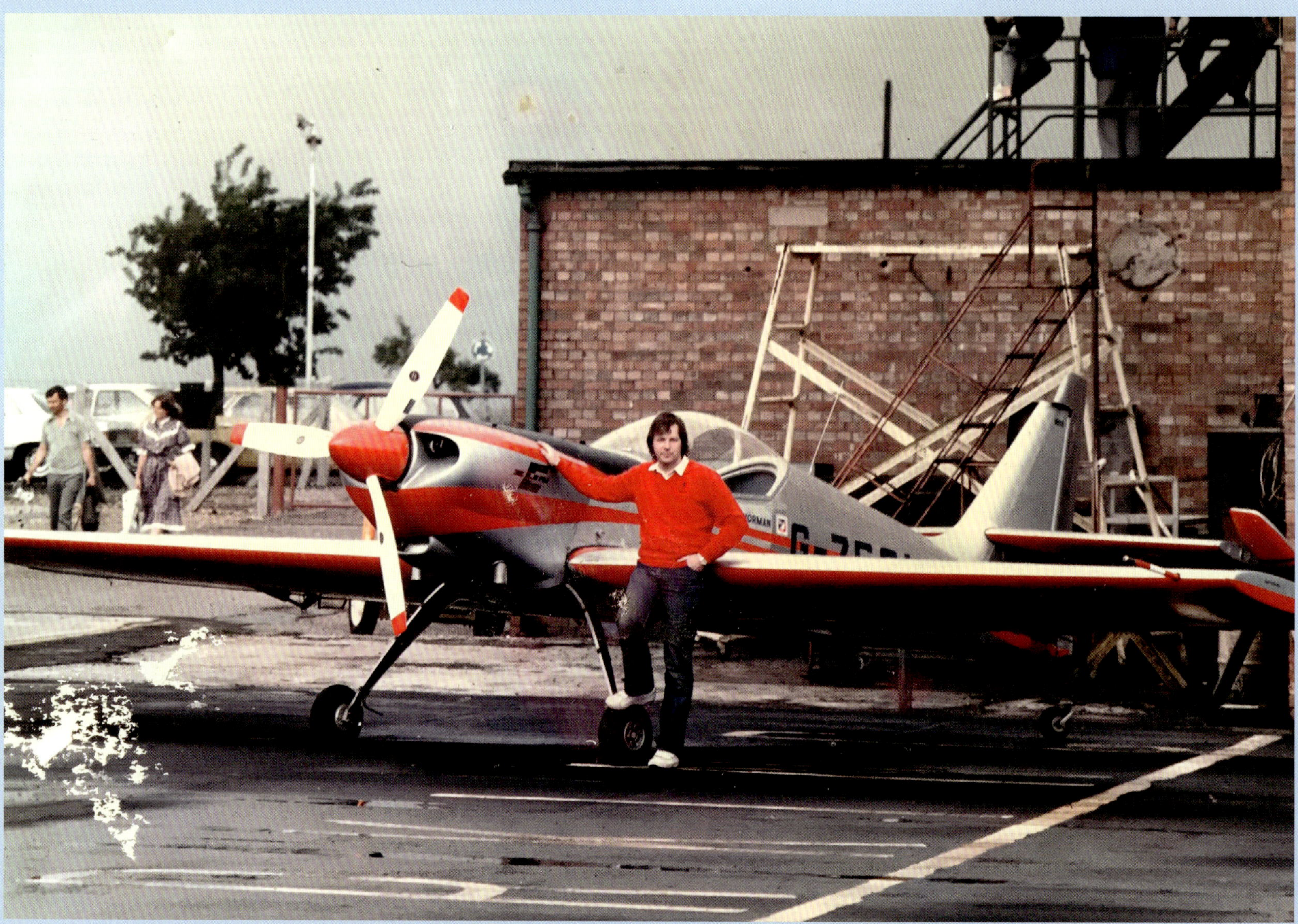

Eric Stewart of 10cc and myself taking to the skies in the Stampe.

world, but with no idea how to fly it.

I bought the Neil Williams book *Aerobatics*, which was the bible on how to teach yourself basic and advanced manoeuvres. I read it over and over again. The first chapter dealt with the importance of checking your aeroplane, and the most important note of all advised against practising anything unless you had a great deal of height to enable you to recover from unusual attitudes should one mess up and fall out of manoeuvres. Or, worse still, get into a spin and not know how to recover, which would be a matter of life and death if you got it wrong.

My training, which went on for a year, started with me flying every day when the weather was good. I would read a chapter and the next day I'd practise whatever I'd read about the evening before. I also had weekly chats with Richard, when he would question me in detail about what I had done. He told me not to waste my time – practise the manoeuvre until I could do it and move on to the next chapter.

I did have another problem, which was the fact that, very quickly, whenever I flew I would start feeling sick and would have to land and pack up for the day. The feeling would last the whole of the next day and into the evening, and it was only after a night's sleep that I felt alright again, but this was something that I really wanted to do so I just pressed on regardless. A funny thing happened after about six months. I went up for a practice flight, did a full 20 minutes of aerobatic flying, landed and suddenly realised that I wasn't feeling ill. In fact, I never felt sick ever again in an aeroplane, but I still get very ill in the back of a car or, worse still, on a cross-channel ferry. I am told it is all to do with balance and ears and bodily fluids, but flying for me is only ever a joy.

I was now able to fly the aeroplane reasonably well and had worked up a simple display routine. Airshow organisers wanted to book the Zlin for their shows because it was new to the West. I had to find a sponsor because I needed to get some income to cover Anne and my family's life. Just down the road in Cirencester, the Colt Car Company was doing very well importing Mitsubishi Motors and they had a love of flying, with their own corporate jet and helicopters, and they liked the high life and they felt (or rather I convinced them) that I could help provide some razzmatazz by appearing at air displays, motor-race meetings and the like, to add value to all their outdoor events.

I had sold them the idea but it still all depended on the directors coming to see me display at South Cerney Airfield, which was next to their headquarters. It went very well and it helped that Richard Goode, the British Aerobatic Team's Captain and my good friend, flew the aeroplane for the display and we did

'My training, which went on for a year, started with me flying every day when the weather was good. I would read a chapter and the next day I'd practise whatever I'd read about.'

Above: a scantily dressed model poses with the Stampe on a shoot for the racy Pilots' Pals calendar series that ran from 1981-2000.

My second Zlin Z-50 in polished aluminium and before SEAT sponsorship. The registration 'G-MATE' was referring to a new condom manufacturer, aimed at a younger audience. The Civil Aviation Authority didn't notice and instead thought that it was named 'MATE' after a friend. The coloured lettering was also a 'no-go'!

Inverted and running in for a low-level pass down the runway at RAF Kemble.

Just some of the promotional photographs and material produced as part of my sponsorship deal with Mitsubishi Motors. These were often distributed to the national and local press.

a quick change behind the hangar – Richard jumped out and I strapped in to taxi up to the directors and get the handshake and a signed contract. I know this was a bit naughty but I had to get some income to keep my family afloat and Richard was a much better pilot at that time than me.

Funnily enough, the next weekend I had to do a display down at Fowey, where Colt were holding their summer party. The display went really well and I went back to join them for the evening. The CEO, Michael Orr, came up to me and said my display was much better than at the South Cerney event. In truth, it wasn't but it was lower and more hairy-looking flying low (but safely) along the river. I became very busy with around 120 shows every season, which lasted for eight years and it worked out well for them and me.

One of the highlights was when HTV Television wanted to make a TV programme about me being at that time one of only five aerobatic pilots in the UK earning their living from flying air displays. The programme followed me around at various events and also featured my family of three young children and, of course, Anne, who was running her own fitness and dance studio called STUDIO 23 in Cirencester. To my embarrassment, they filmed me working out.

Left: ready to give 16-year-old Michael Figures his prize, after dad Roger won a flight in a charity tombola at the Colt Car Company's Christmas ball.

In 1985, HTV chose me as the subject for a documentary. *Aeroplanes Bite Fools* was aired in April of that year and showcased the life of an aerobatics pilot.

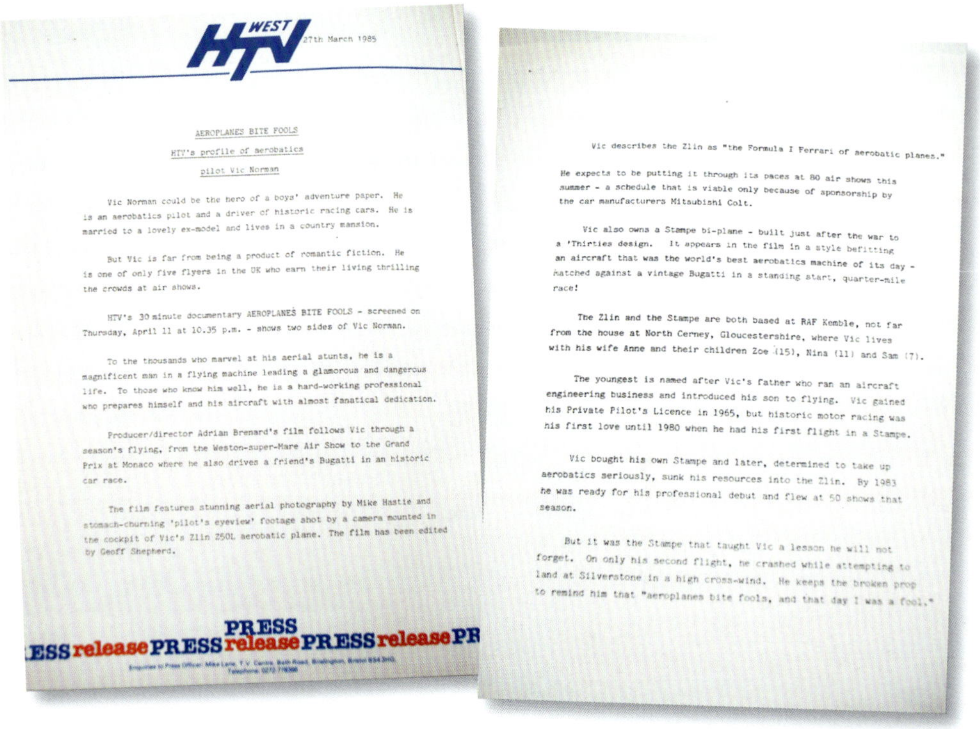

HTV WEST 27th March 1985

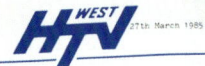

AEROPLANES BITE FOOLS

HTV's profile of aerobatics

pilot Vic Norman

Vic Norman could be the hero of a boys' adventure paper. He is an aerobatics pilot and a driver of historic racing cars. He is married to a lovely ex-model and lives in a country mansion.

But Vic is far from being a product of romantic fiction. He is one of only five flyers in the UK who earn their living thrilling the crowds at air shows.

HTV's 30 minute documentary AEROPLANES BITE FOOLS - screened on Thursday, April 11 at 10.35 p.m. - shows two sides of Vic Norman.

To the thousands who marvel at his aerial stunts, he is a magnificent man in a flying machine leading a glamorous and dangerous life. To those who know him well, he is a hard-working professional who prepares himself and his aircraft with almost fanatical dedication.

Producer/director Adrian Brenard's film follows Vic through a season's flying, from the Weston-super-Mare Air Show to the Grand Prix at Monaco where he also drives a friend's Bugatti in an historic car race.

The film features stunning aerial photography by Mike Hastie and stomach-churning 'pilot's eyeview' footage shot by a camera mounted in the cockpit of Vic's Zlin Z50L aerobatic plane. The film has been edited by Geoff Shepherd.

ESS release PRESS PRESS release PRESS release PR

Vic describes the Zlin as "the Formula I Ferrari of aerobatic planes."

He expects to be putting it through its paces at 80 air shows this summer - a schedule that is viable only because of sponsorship by the car manufacturers Mitsubishi Colt.

Vic also owns a Stampe bi-plane - built just after the war to a 'Thirties design. It appears in the film in a style befitting an aircraft that was the world's best aerobatics machine of its day - matched against a vintage Bugatti in a standing start, quarter-mile race!

The Zlin and the Stampe are both based at RAF Kemble, not far from the house at North Cerney, Gloucestershire, where Vic lives with his wife Anne and their children Zoe (15), Nina (11) and Sam (7).

The youngest is named after Vic's father who ran an aircraft engineering business and introduced his son to flying. Vic gained his Private Pilot's Licence in 1965, but historic motor racing was his first love until 1980 when he had his first flight in a Stampe.

Vic bought his own Stampe and later, determined to take up aerobatics seriously, sunk his resources into the Zlin. By 1983 he was ready for his professional debut and flew at 50 shows that season.

But it was the Stampe that taught Vic a lesson he will not forget. On only his second flight, he crashed while attempting to land at Silverstone in a high cross-wind. He keeps the broken prop to remind him that "aeroplanes bite fools, and that day I was a fool."

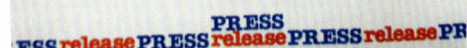

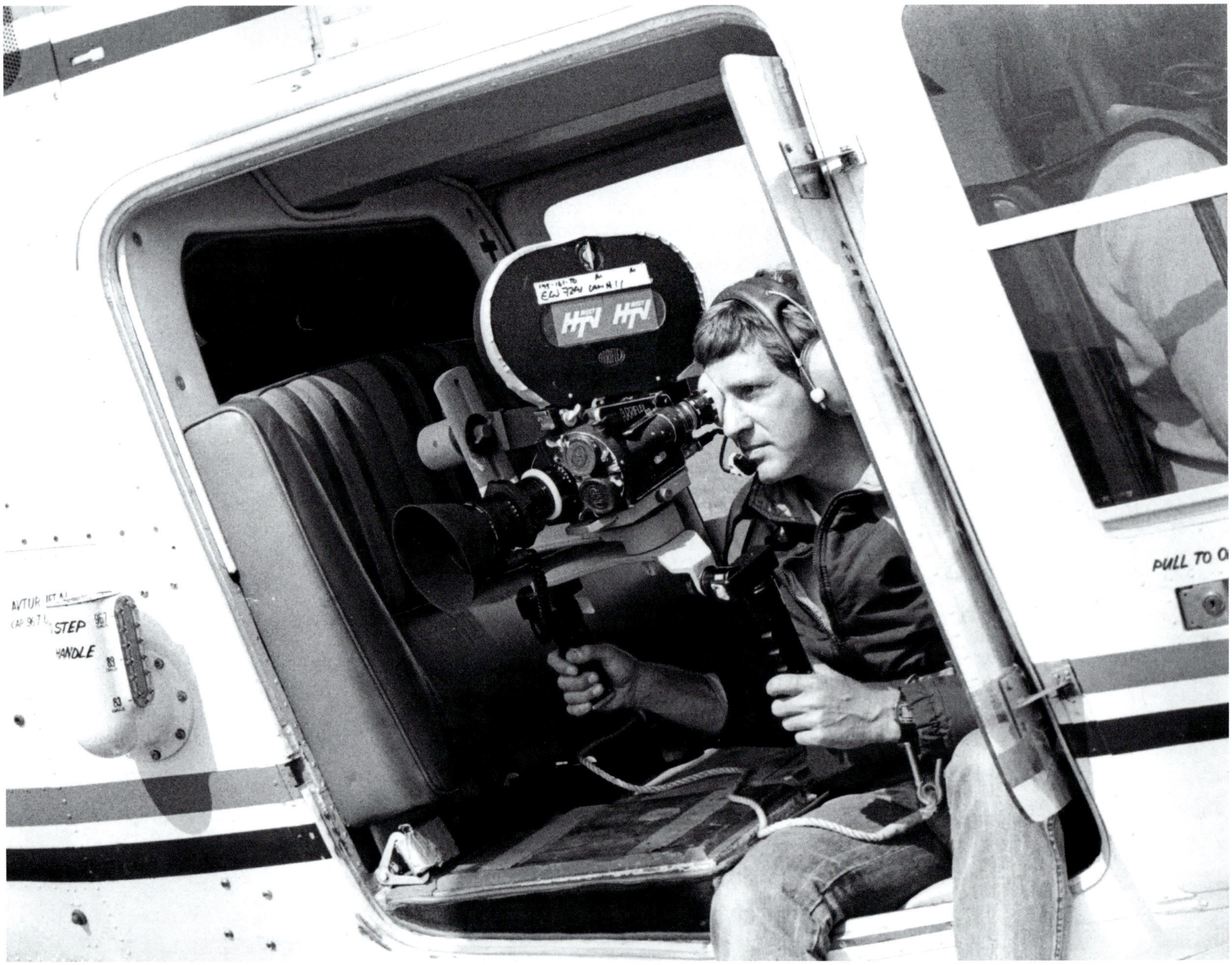

I was booked to give an aerobatic display on the morning of the Grand Prix at Monaco on the Sunday, and on the day before Eric Stewart was going to let me race his Type 35 Bugatti Grand Prix car in the historic race.

The event started for me when I left the UK to make my way down to the south of France. I had left early on the Monday morning and the flight across the Channel was fine. I stopped to refuel at Le Touquet, my dad's old hunting ground, and on checking the weather I saw it was very low cloud and foggy, so I decided to stay at Le Touquet for the night and do a weather check the next morning. If you have time to spare, go by air.

The next morning, Le Touquet was fine and my next refuel stop, near Lyon, was also clear of cloud. I had no instruments in my aerobatics aircraft and so I navigated by dead reckoning and map reading. This was before the arrival of GPS and sat-nav, which eventually made the whole job much easier.

Before setting off, there was another four-seater private aircraft heading south and they had a full set of instruments and could fly in cloud, so I asked if I could follow them because I still suspected some areas of broken cloud before it all opened up and cleared. In retrospect, this was a big mistake – I should have just done my own thing. We both took off and everything was going well but the cloud started to build up and we were flying in and out of small areas of cloud.

The cloud was getting thicker and I should have just turned back but I kept in close formation with the other aeroplane. I kept asking for the other pilot to climb. We were up to about 7,000ft by now and in solid cloud, with me just keeping my wings level with the other aeroplane. He then told me he could not climb anymore and I looked down at my instruments for a split second and when I looked back the aeroplane had gone. I was now in cloud and didn't know if I was the right way up so I just opened up my throttle and I saw a slight pin prick of light above me, which I aimed for. The next moment I shot out of the clouds into bright sunshine on top of the clouds.

I was so relieved but I knew I had to work out what to do. I decided to turn around and head back towards where I came from because I knew sooner or later the cloud cover would break up and that I could see the ground and find out my position and land at the nearest airfield. I checked my height and realised that I was in controlled airspace so I decided to make a 'pan-pan' call declaring that I was uncertain of my present position. I called up Paris' radar and they got me to do some turns and headings and asked for my height. I told them that I was at 10,000ft and they told me to descend because I was in controlled airspace. I told them that I could not descend because I had no instruments and they got very agitated and gave me a heading to steer for the nearest airfield that was clear of cloud.

I settled down to flying the aeroplane. After about 20 minutes, the cloud had cleared and I told them that I could now descend as requested. By checking

Receiving my cup for an aerobatic competition from the station commander at RAF Finningley.

122 NORMAN CONQUEST

Left: Eric Stewart and his Bugatti Type 35 at Monaco – my good friend John Hewitt serving as his mechanic.

my map I worked out my position, which was about ten miles from Beauvais-Tillé airfield, where I was passed onto the local airfield air traffic system and cleared to land. After landing, I asked to go to the fuel pumps, which was refused. I was directed to park in front of the control tower and a very official-looking policeman escorted me to a room in the building where I was told to wait.

I knew that I was in trouble. I was put under open arrest and told not to leave the terminal building. About two hours later, a senior official from Paris came to take a statement from me and I decided the best policy was to own up and just tell the truth. I explained exactly what I had done and then the official went off and told me to wait. Half an hour later, he came back and told me how stupid I had been but I was free to go.

I got myself a quick cheese sandwich and refuelled my aeroplane, having checked the weather, which was now all clear, and I took off on my way south to Mâcon, which was my next refuelling stop. The rest of the trip to Nice airport was straightforward and I landed between jumbo jets and got permission to park next to the airport fire station. I made friends with them and told them that I would be back the next day to get the aeroplane ready for my display just around the coast at Monaco.

I met Anne and the film crew at our hotel and at last I could relax for a while, although I was still on edge. The next morning I had to visit the airspace controller who oversaw Monaco and I was told that I had to display over the water and that I would be arrested if I flew over the Principality.

I then went with the HTV cameraman and my mechanic and friend John Hewitt to mount a huge 35mm camera behind my head and seat, and also two small Zap cameras (this was before anyone had GoPros!) on the wingtips. Then I fuelled up and got ready for Sunday.

The next day, Saturday, was the race and the Bugatti had a few problems in practice. I was hopeful that it would be better in the actual race itself, but unfortunately it broke down. While it lasted it was great fun, we had a good evening, but the next morning I woke up and I guess the bad weather had caught me up. It was pouring with rain in Monaco.

I got to Nice airport with the visibility still very bad and low cloud, and was told that the helicopters had stopped flying taking VIPs from the airport to Monte Carlo. I just had to do the display, the film crew were waiting and the pressure was on. I took off in drizzle and decided to just follow the coast along to the harbour. It started clearing a bit and I managed to climb to 1,500ft, which was the minimum height that I needed to do the display. It went very well and I could not wait to get out of the aeroplane and back to the hotel. The film crew were pleased and I slept really well that night and woke up to even more rain. I just could not face getting in my aeroplane and fighting my way back to the UK, so I arranged for my friend Brendan O'Brien to fly the aeroplane back home and I went with Anne on British Airways.

The programme must have been pretty good because it won an award and the director flew Concorde to New York to collect the gong. I, of course, was never told about it until much later. I did, however, do some presenting later on in the programme about the 1986 World Aerobatic Championships and I got paid union rates.

> 'The next morning, I had to visit the airspace controller who oversaw Monaco and I was told that I had to display over the water and that I would be arrested if I flew over the Principality.'

Filming with a new type of camera fitted with a fish-eye lens. This had to be operated from the cockpit — something which is much easier now that we have bluetooth connections.

Chapter eight
WINGWALKING AND BEYOND

I was sponsored by Mitsubishi Motors and was doing about 100 air displays each season, sometimes three or four different events each day. I had competed in a few aerobatic competitions but I always found them rather boring and was not prepared to train enough, so I was never that good and I much preferred airshow flying. I guess it was the show-off in me – plus I also got paid and I needed the cash to support my lifestyle.

The British Aerobatic Association needed to find a sponsor to underwrite the 1986 World Aerobatic Championships and they were getting desperate. I heard about this from Richard Goode and I was asked if I had any ideas. They needed £120,000 to cover all the costs, which included accommodation, food, and transport for all the teams.

My motoring friend Ronald 'Steady' Barker arranged for me to attend a meeting with Volkswagen and I managed to sell them the idea that they should be the main sponsors for £120,000. We now had to find a venue and an organisation that could handle the logistics needed to bring teams from all over the world, including teams of pilots and engineers from behind the Iron Curtain – from the Soviet Union, East Germany, Czechoslovakia, Poland, etc. There was also the arrival of competitors' aeroplanes to organise, plus accommodation, catering, transport, and keeping an eye on the activities of the KGB spies who we knew would turn up.

The Royal International Air Tattoo took the job on and with their close connection to the Royal Air Force and Special Branch the security measures would be covered. I knew the Colonel in charge of RAF South Cerney Airfield, just down the road

His Royal Highness Prince Michael, looking forward to our flight in Lindsay Walton's Stearman G-THEA at the World Aerobatic Championships. As a result of the rather special passenger, I was afforded a 'purple airway' – restricted airspace where no-one else is permitted to enter when a member of the Royal Family is being flown.

One of a number of publicity shots taken for our sponsors at the time, Mitsubishi Cars.

'We could do only very limited flying at the weekends so as not to upset his afternoon tea. He did not like aeroplane noise, but the funny thing was he was actually the Minister for Aviation.'

from where I lived in Cirencester, and he agreed to let the event use the airfield, having got clearance from his headquarters. South Cerney was an all-over grass airfield and a perfect venue for the tricky acrobatic aircraft to operate from because they were able to land and take off into wind.

Accommodation was organised at the Cirencester Agricultural College since the event was during the college's holiday. The Air Force organised all the transport for the teams and it gave our security people a chance to talk about aeroplanes with the Iron Curtain teams, which was deemed to be a good idea and opportunity. The Czechoslovakian team were put up with me at our house and I managed to get them the loan of a Mitsubishi Shogun, and we all flew the Zlin-50 aircraft.

The event was plagued with bad English weather and it was either too windy or wet for much of the time for the teams to fly and everyone was getting very tense. The situation was not helped by a certain Lord Fanshawe, who lived near the airfield and was, apparently, a personal friend of Lady Thatcher. Unofficially, the flying had to stop around 5pm each day and we could do only very limited flying at the weekends so as not to upset his afternoon tea. He did not like aeroplane noise, but the funny thing was he was actually the Minister for Aviation.

With all the bad weather, the event was turning out to be a disaster with no official results, so the Colonel decided to put his job on the line and allow flying to take place whenever the weather would permit it, including late into the evenings and at weekends. It was the right decision because we had the world's press in attendance and would have been a laughing stock.

The Sunday after the event, which in fact carried on until lunchtime, we were to have a small airshow and the public could come in numbers to watch. Volkswagen had invited HRH Prince Michael to attend and be the guest of honour and the directors were very excited. I was chosen to take him flying for five minutes in a vintage 1940s Boeing-Stearman aircraft and was instructed to be by the aeroplane parked in front of the VIP area 30 minutes before his arrival. I was told that I was not allowed to do any acrobatics because the thought of him getting out of

NORMAN CONQUEST 129

the aeroplane and either feeling or being sick was a strict no-no.

The next thing that happened was an ambulance turned up and parked nearby. I asked what it was there for and was told it was a medical team in case Prince Michael had an accident; they had Royal blood on board. I commented that was good, but who would look after me if we crashed? I had the St John Ambulance team and I am sure that I would have been looked after very well.

HRH was escorted to our biplane and I gave him a short briefing and strapped him into the front seat. We took off and of course I had a purple airway so the airspace was all mine. I was circling over the airfield and after a while he said, 'Aren't we going to do some aerobatics?'

I said, 'Well, yes sir, if you would like to.'

We did a few loops and stall turns and rolls, and HRH really enjoyed it. When we landed, the boss of Volkswagen was ready to meet him and of course nothing was ever said. Everyone was happy.

That evening after the flying, I invited everyone back to my house for a barbecue that Anne had, as always, laid on beautifully. Everyone got very drunk and the Colonel and one of the KGB men from Russia ended up jumping into the swimming pool with all their clothes on and became good friends for the evening. They even ended up telling each other that in the morning they would both have to write up reports on each other to their authorities.

Prince Michael would often fly over to my airfield, Rendcomb in Gloucestershire, with my close friend Micky Suffolk and he was always pleased to take a box of Crunchies back with him when we were being sponsored by them.

Yugo cars approached me when I was flying my Zlin-50 with Mitsubishi sponsorship. I knew Yugo's sales director and he asked me if I had any good ideas for an aeroplane act to go around the airshows and dovetail sponsorship with their dealers. They'd also be attending the shows displaying the cars, which, at the time, no one had ever heard of.

Luckily, I had recently been to California and we had attended an airshow in Salinas with our friends; it was nice to be watching rather than flying for a change. There was a Stearman wingwalking act and it really impressed me. It's a big biplane, fully aerobatic, with a wonderful-sounding engine and lots of smoke. We only had Tiger Moth wingwalking in the UK and although they're lovely aeroplanes, they are underpowered when you have someone strapped to the top wing, and aerobatics are definitely out of the question.

I got the go-ahead and signed a contract and had to buy an aeroplane, get the Civil Aviation Authority to approve both the aeroplane and its wingwalker rig, and find a pilot and a brave person to stand on the wing.

My new 450hp Stearman N54922 in Yugo Cars colours. I still have this aircraft and it has never stopped earning money.

One of my idols at the time was Ray Hanna. Ray was the most famous leader of The Royal Air Force Aerobatic Team, otherwise known as the Red Arrows. He'd left the Air Force and operated a Boeing 707 for two businessmen who were based in Switzerland. I believe that they headhunted Ray because they wanted the best of the best, and they obviously got it.

I would bump into Ray and his son Mark at airshows. They also had their own company called The Old Flying Machine Co, and Ray would fly his famous Spitfire MH434, which he now shared with Sir Adrian Swire, owner of Cathay Pacific. Mark, also an ex-Air Force fighter pilot, eventually took over the running of the business with his sister Sarah. They slowly ended up with a fantastic collection of World War Two fighters and their formation flying was very exacting and close.

Ray had a large-engined Stearman built up from an ex-crop-dusting aeroplane by his friend Gordon Plaskett, who later, with his wife Barbara, became very good friends of ours. We would spend time with them in California and they would come over to stay with us in the UK and we would venture over to France. Gordon ran a crop-dusting business in King City, California and he had a large collection of old surplus Stearman crop-dusters. He had spent over 12,000 hours crop-dusting and to see him fly under the trees in and out of fields was mind-blowing – it needed such precise judgement.

I asked Ray if he would sell me his red Stearman and he suggested that I meet him at Duxford to talk about it. He said that he would want a lot of money for the aeroplane and told me to fly him around the block and do a couple of circuits and some aerobatics. I was pretty nervous having to fly Mr Perfection, but it went pretty well and I didn't make too much of a mess of it.

After we landed, we went into his office and he said again that the price would be very high. He quoted a price and I quickly stuck my hand out and said that I would take it. This rather took him by surprise but I had an arrangement that whatever I paid for the aeroplane would be added to the sponsorship fee.

That night, Ray phoned me and said that he had spoken to Gordon, his friend in California, and that he was just finishing off a bright yellow aeroplane and that it was just like his but much cheaper. Ray really did not want to part with his biplane, and I can understand why.

Anne and I popped over to King City, met Gordon and Barbara, and agreed to buy the yellow aeroplane. It was good that it was yellow, since that was Yugo's colour. I now had to get an approved wingwalking rig made and I discovered that there was only one man in America who had a fully approved set-up. His name was Art Scholl, and the airfield he was based at was later named after him. He was one of the best and well-known aerobatic pilots in America and he had a Super Chipmunk on both the East Coast and West Coast, and would jet between the two doing shows.

We went to see him and met his wife Judy. I explained that I wanted to have a wingwalking act in the UK and asked if he would manufacture a rig for me with all the approved paperwork. He explained that he never had done this for anyone because he was worried about liability issues in the US should an accident happen, but he said that he would think about it.

Art was filming the movie *Top Gun*, doing all the spinning sequences in his Pitts Special biplane, when sadly he spun into the sea and died, and his body was never found. It was thought that a camera mounting had come loose and jammed his controls. In the end, the film was dedicated to Art.

I wrote a letter to his wife Judy saying how sorry I was to hear about Art and got a very nice letter back. At the end of the letter, she said that Art had liked Anne and I, and that he was going to help me with manufacturing a rig. She explained that she still had the engineering business at the airfield and that she would build a rig for me. Without the rig and the paperwork, I don't think that I would have ever gotten the act off the ground and so I will always be thankful to Art and Judy for helping me out.

As a 'by the way', Art had a little dog called Aileron, and he would fly with this dog. When he was taxiing in, Aileron would jump out onto a wing wagging its tail to the crowd – wonderful.

Yugo were great sponsors and we had a lot of fun with them. I signed up Bob Thomson, a well-known display pilot who used to be part of the Rothmans Aerobatic Team, and later he worked for Marshall of Cambridge flying their modified jet fighter and testing ejection seats. Bob was a very safe pair of hands.

We now had to select a wingwalker and, although it was not very PC, it had to be a girl with a bubbly personality because she would be talking to the media at all of the shows. We put an advert in *Pilot* magazine and got lots of enquiries. I decided not to employ a mother – the reason being that, if worst came to worst, we did not kill a mum. We also wanted someone who was small and lightweight, simply because flying with a wingwalker on top of your aeroplane was like having a big barn door on top of you acting as an air-brake and slowing you down all the time.

We received hundreds of applications and shortlisted the number down to three, all of whom I'd spoken to and who had good previous backgrounds skydiving, and bubbly personalities. We arranged a selection day at Kemble airfield, and myself and a director from Yugo Cars attended. All three could have done the job but what turned it for one girl was she had turned up about 15 minutes

A Yugo Cars press shot with Helen Tempest in her brand-new suit, which had been specially designed to fit in with the motoring sponsor – note the secondary harness around her waist for safety.

'We also wanted someone who was small and lightweight, simply because flying with a wingwalker on top of your aeroplane was like having a big barn door on top of you acting as an air-brake...'

late (which was not a good start) and, dressed in a very short white dress, explained that she had left really early to make sure that she would arrive on time but she had got a puncture. She had started to change the wheel but she didn't want to get her white dress dirty and make a bad impression, so she took the dress off and started changing the wheel in her undies! Well, it apparently didn't take very long before a couple of young lads pulled over and changed the wheel for her...

Her name was Lesley Gale and she did a fantastic job for Yugo Cars. She was very bright, quick to learn and the media obtained for Yugo in all types of publications was fantastic. We could not have asked for anyone better.

Sometime in the team's second season, Yugo Cars got a phone call from the local police station and they were asked if their aerobatic wingwalking team employed a girl called Lesley Morris. I said no, but that I did employ a Lesley Gale. They felt sure that it was the same person and they told me that the girl was being pursued for carrying out a lewd act in Scotland in a pub with a snake. I asked Lesley and she told me it was not her but, of course, it came out that it was her and the media man at Yugo told me that she had to go. Regrettably I fired her, not for doing the act but for lying to me.

We remain good friends and she went on to be one of the country's leading skydivers and in fact ended up running the British Parachute Association. She is a very bright girl and she did a great job for AeroSuperBatics and Yugo Cars.

I was now without a family run-about and I heard that the RAF were selling off their Queen's Flight Dove aircraft, which were based at RAF Northolt. Myself and a friendly mechanic went to inspect all eight aircraft, and the foreman in the hangar was very helpful and went through all the technical paperwork with us.

At the end of the day, there were two that we felt were better than the others. I had to submit a sealed bid for both aircraft but I mentioned that I only wanted one of them. A few weeks later, I became the proud owner of a fantastic aeroplane that was in first-class condition and it had cost me £5,800.

I kept it at RAF Kemble and the engineers there knew these aircrafts inside-out because they used to do all the service work when the RAF owned them. If anything needed fixing, I would pay the guys to work after hours and at weekends, which worked out really well. I also got permission to leave the aeroplane in the Air Force's livery, and to me it brought back special memories of when I used to fly with my father in his Dove.

The family went on a few good trips in the aeroplane and we had one amusing rule that whoever used the bucket-type toilet first on any trip had to empty it when we arrived at our destination.

All the children would be sitting there with their legs crossed and after a while I would make sure that one of the grown-ups used it. Then there was always a rush for everyone else to try and fill it up.

One of the trips in the Dove was to go to Italy for the Mille Miglia retrospective. My motoring friend 'Steady' Barker had been sent an invitation from Countess Maggi, whose husband had been a co-founder of the event. The Mille Miglia was a race on public roads from Brescia to Rome and back to Brescia, totalling 1,000 miles. In 1955, Stirling Moss with Denis Jenkinson won the race in a Mercedes-Benz 300SLR, averaging nearly 100mph for the entire route.

Anne, Steady and Ian Fraser were invited to stay with the Countess and what better way to travel than by our 1960s de Havilland aircraft? We stopped at Lyon for refuelling and lunch, and then set off across the Alps directly to a military airfield that was only a few miles from the chateau.

When we arrived, the Ford Motor Co's private aircraft was parked on the apron and we went through to customs where Walter Hayes and his guests, including HRH Prince Michael, were being held up because HRH's private security officer had a gun and the Italian customs were not keen to let him keep it. We said hello and goodbye, and were collected by the Countess and ushered back to her chateau, which had that wonderful, slightly rundown look about it. That evening, we were taken by the Countess to a local restaurant and had fresh pasta with meat and fish, and much laughter and fun was had by all.

The Countess drove us back but when we got to the gatehouse the gates were closed. The car horn was activated and moments later an elderly man came running out in his nightshirt and opened the gates, bowing and saluting *La Contessa*.

After breakfast the next day, we were taken outside to see the terrace where the pre-event drinks would take place. It overlooked a lovely valley and I jokingly suggested that I could do a fly-by in the Dove at the start of the party. The Countess really liked the idea and said that she would of course come in the aeroplane cockpit with me.

I was now getting a bit concerned with the legalities of such a flight and whether the military airbase would let me do it. As it turned out, I needn't have worried because we arrived at the airbase and the Countess was very well known. She spoke to them in Italian so I've no idea what she said, but we were escorted to the aeroplane and were soon on our way to her home with the Countess waving like mad from her co-pilot's seat. All highly illegal but I got away with it.

When Kemble Airfield closed, I put the Dove into a Christie's auction at Duxford and got back £15,000, which was a good profit. It was then converted into a VIP aeroplane with new paint, a proper loo, and leather seats. VP962 became G-OPLC.

> 'I've no idea what she said, but we were escorted to the aeroplane and were soon on our way to her home with the Countess waving like mad from her co-pilot's seat. All highly illegal but I got away with it.'

Helen Tempest

Helen's father Barry was an outstanding biplane pilot, instructor and display pilot, and also became the man in charge of air displays for the Civil Aviation Authority (a classic case of a poacher becoming the gamekeeper). Helen turned up to see me and she told me that she wanted to become the wingwalker for Yugo Cars' second season. She got the job and she became my right-hand girl; she had even more drive than me, and a real passion for aviation having been dragged around the whole of the UK with her dad to various airfields since she was a baby.

Helen and I developed our wingwalking act over the years, test-flying and dreaming up mad ideas, and she very much was partly responsible in helping me to turn AeroSuperBatics into what it has become. She was the perfect team member and I must thank her for all her hard work and friendship.

Anne helped Helen with her wedding arrangements and her and Steve's wedding reception was held at Rendcomb. They have a lovely daughter who is a great dancer, and it's only a matter of time until she becomes a team wingwalker too.

Before we were brave enough to touch hands, we set a world record for passing the shortest pole between aircraft. Below left: at the Royal International Air Tattoo, Fairford, with His Royal Highness King Hussein of Jordan and Falklands War veteran Simon Weston, who we had just taken for a flight on the wing.

Clockwise from main: filming for TV programme *Help Squad*; in flight over South Cerney lakes; left to right – Simon Ward, Matthew Hill, myself and wingwalker Sara Cubitt after setting the pole-pass world record.

138 NORMAN CONQUEST

you might lose your chance. Well, the next day he phoned me and said that Cadbury would like to go ahead and could I send them a contract? This was a really big break for my company. Being partnered by Cadbury was as good as it gets.

Cadbury had a media company in London called Hill & Knowlton that we had to work with. Their managing director was a very high-powered lady who used to power-dress, a bit like the women in *Dallas*. We were looked after by one girl whose other account was American Express and one other international company, and we got really into trying to get media coverage for them and came up with new ideas all the time. The great thing about our team, unlike any other display act, was that we could strap anyone onto the wing, a journalist or a celebrity, and get great coverage.

We would split the UK up into TV regions and make sure we came up with ideas for each region. This really came into its own when we needed to select a new team wingwalker. We would put our contact details in all the regional newspapers and TV stations, along with an advertisement for a new team member, and they would all run an article about us and follow the story through to the final selection day at our airfield. We got so many applicants that we had to be very selective. Our requirements were as follows:
- No taller than 5ft 6in.
- Light, ideally under 8 stone.
- No mothers. We didn't want anyone to have an accident, but especially not a mum.
- Dance training was essential, and ballet was the best for graceful movement.
- Very flexible with working hours. We often got back late after a weekend flying.
- Bright, bubbly, fun and good at talking to the media.
- No show-offs. They had to mix in with the rest of the team and do all the not-so-glamorous jobs, like cleaning the aeroplanes, the office, loos, and just about every other job you could think of.

We would go through their CVs very carefully. We dismissed anyone who said they had no fear because we were always fearful. Our jobs were dangerous, we flew low at airshows, and had to fly around the country and across to Europe in bad weather, always below cloud, keeping contact with the ground, map-reading and following a compass heading.

The final selection was a bit of a fix because we had already spoken at length to all 13 finalists (one each from the 13 TV regions) and had already

Top: flying my good friend Simon Ward out on the wing – another silly idea!
Above: Philip Castle's clever paintwork. It was all airbrushed by hand to show a part-open Crunchie bar with a bite taken from it.

Perfecting the low-level 'skirt snatch'. When it was hot in the summer, we often used to all just fly around in our underwear!

Myself and Helen up in Scotland on a press flight. The Stearman was painted in Save the Children colours – Cadbury's chosen charity at the time.

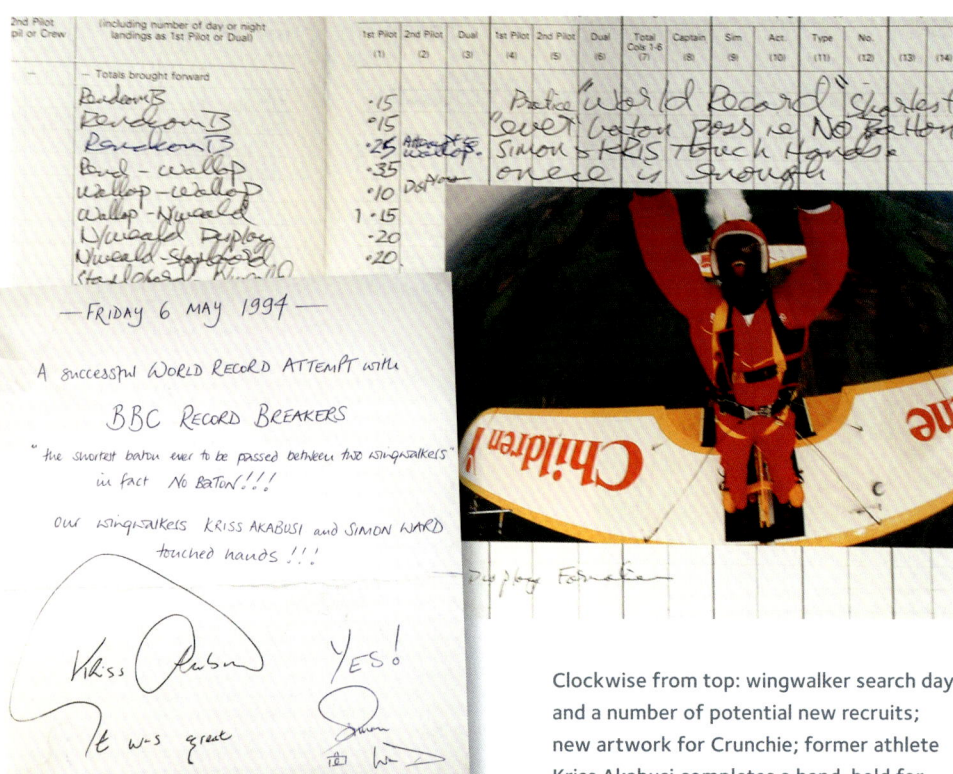

Clockwise from top: wingwalker search day and a number of potential new recruits; new artwork for Crunchie; former athlete Kriss Akabusi completes a hand-hold for the BBC's *Record Breakers*.

> 'Our media coverage was independently valued and was worth three to four million pounds each year, while we were getting around £550,000 so, as far as Cadbury was concerned, AeroSuperBatics was good value for money.'

asked the favourite four or five to come and visit the airfield. After this I would have a pretty good idea which ones would stand out, but sometimes we were proved wrong and someone who we had not picked out really shone. It was all about personality.

The media coverage that first year really blew Cadbury away and we could do no wrong. The girl at the media company told us that we were so easy to look after that she spent nearly all of her time on American Express and the other company.

Well, that gave me an idea. I had heard how much Cadbury were paying Hill & Knowlton, which was about a quarter of what they were giving us as sponsors. I spoke to our boss at Cadbury and proposed that we take over the media in-house at AeroSuperBatics for the same fee as the London agency, but, for that fee, I could employ someone full-time. The deal was done and I employed a very together young lady and in that second season, with us running the media, we trebled the coverage both on TV and in print. Truthfully, it was not that difficult. The media could not get enough of the team and it made us all feel like we were stars.

Cadbury taught us so much. The whole company was very motivated and key positions were changed every two or three years so we always had to be on our toes to impress our new bosses and, of course, they had their own ideas too. Our media coverage was independently valued and was worth three to four million pounds each year, while we were getting around £550,000 so, as far as Cadbury was concerned, AeroSuperBatics was good value for money.

They did spoil us at the end of each season and gave the whole team a great evening out in London. On one occasion, we were all taken to the south of France for a few days living the high life, which was made even more memorable by one of Cadbury guys throwing up in his five-star hotel in Cannes.

I'd been to the Zlin factory at Moravan a few times and before the Berlin Wall came down I was always met at the International Airport by both a representative of Zlin and someone from the KGB, then driven at high speed in a black limo to the factory. I also flew my second Zlin-50 back to the UK from the factory, and when I was ready to leave I discovered that I needed to give 48 hours' notice for an international flight. I really didn't want to wait that long and was much relieved when the local air

My engineering team celebrating another Crunchie scheme rebrand. Chief engineer Tony (back right) is the glue that holds the team together and keeps us off the ground.

Linda Lusardi

We received a phone call from the organisers of North Weald Airshow in Essex asking if we could come to their press day because the glamour model Linda Lusardi wanted to wingwalk to raise awareness and money for her friend's son, who had cancer. They also said that the *Daily Mirror* was going to cover the story with a full-page photo in the paper. This was great news for Cadbury, and I suggested that we could meet the day before the press day so she could have a practice flight with no press present.

I arrived at the airfield and met Linda, who had brought along her boyfriend and her mum and dad. Linda was easy to talk to and she was switched on, and took in all the details and the briefing that I gave her. Her flight round the block went well and she enjoyed it a lot. We arranged to meet the next day for the press call.

I telephoned the Cadbury Crunchie brand manager with the good news that we would be on the front page of the *Mirror* with Linda. I told him that we would be doing a fly-by for the press and that she was planning to lift her skirt up as we flew past and show a glimpse of her knickers. I was told that I must not allow that to happen because Cadbury was a Quaker-owned business and it would not go down well with the shareholders.

The next day, I met Linda and told her that she was not allowed to flash her knickers and would have to fly in a leotard. She burst out laughing and told me that I was the only man who had ever told her that.

Anne and I met her for supper one evening at Walthamstow Stadium and she brought along the footballer Paul Gascoigne (or Gazza), who was great fun but he did get very drunk and throw up in the gentleman's toilets.

Sketches produced with French photographer Alain Ernoult, planning the first 'hand hold' link-up. We achieved our aim and managed to get some stunning photographs at the same time.

NORMAN CONQUEST 147

This display team photograph was featured on huge posters that were created for an airshow in Cannes and displayed all along the promenade of La Croisette.

traffic controller said that if I was prepared to not fly above 250ft I could leave straight away. I questioned this because I had to fly across various towns on route and he assured me that I was clear to go. It was an amazing flight.

We got an invite to fly to a military airfield near Prague because they were organising a big public airshow and a wingwalking display, which was a real first. Matthew Hill and I were displaying at Biggin Hill Airshow the weekend before and we decided to leave together and head east. We were fine making our way across Germany and had to route via a specific entry point. Before leaving, we managed to get some military maps via our friends the Red Arrows and, of course, it was before the amazing aid of the GPS so the whole way was by dead reckoning. We had to land every two hours for fuel so we could not afford to get lost.

The final leg of the journey was interesting and we finally turned up over a large grass field and saw, on the west side, a bank of rocket launchers all pointing west. In the middle of the field, a very old open tractor was cutting a strip across the field that was just wide enough for us to land. We circled overhead, did a low pass in order to let the tractor driver get out of our way, and we landed in the middle of the field and switched off.

We were totally puzzled but in a very short time some excited people came running over and a man, who we later discovered was our interpreter, welcomed us and said it was fine to leave the aeroplanes where they were and that later on, when the whole field was cut, we could move them towards a large hangar.

We had our first meal of many, all consisting of white sausage and onions, which we wolfed down. Talking to the organisers, we discovered that the local flying club mostly flew gliding aeroplanes and that they organised the whole event in the hope that it would raise enough money to buy the club a new aeroplane from Zlin.

There was a new building being put up that consisted of blockwork walls, a roof and not much else. I thought that I had misunderstood them when they told me this was going to be the airshow office, VIP eating area and toilets (which at that moment in time meant a hole in the floor). Well, at 5pm a great many workers turned up – carpenters, plasterers, plumbers, electricians and painters. In fact, all the trades, working at an amazing rate, with everyone working even after it had gotten dark, still going under sets of builders' lights every single night until the evening before the Saturday airshow when the public arrived.

But the job was finished, and all they needed for the final touch were some flowers for the flower beds they had built, so a team went to the town square and borrowed some plants! I discovered that the workers were all pilots and they got flying time for hours they spent building the new clubhouse, a bit like British Airways Air Miles.

Anne and our wingwalkers arrived the day after, courtesy of British Airways, and the media men were all over the girls. They were whisked off to the local TV centre and chatted to live. Matthew and I were asked to fly over the local town, which they called a media flight. There was a river that ran alongside the town and we asked if we should fly along there and also at what height. Oh no, they said, fly right over the town centre and go as low as you can. We questioned this but we were assured that we would not get into trouble. This had an instant result because about an hour after we landed mobs of people started turning up at the airfield.

We had a great few days – everyone was so kind and pleased that we were there. The organisers were very pleased with the turn-out and they did make enough cash in the end to buy the club a new aeroplane. Our displays went really well and we were allowed to fly as close to the crowd line as we wanted so we chose to operate at 25 metres from the crowd line. It was very exciting.

That night there was a big party with even more types of sausages and we filled our aeroplanes up with Avgas, which had arrived on the morning of the show. The next day we said our goodbyes and set off, but Matthew's engine quickly started running very rough and we turned around and headed back to the airfield. Upon examination we found the fuel was contaminated with a black substance. We drained all the fuel from the aeroplane, cleaned the fuel filters and, having both checked my aeroplane and the fuel bowser, which seemed clean, we filled up Matthew's Stearman again and set off for the UK a second time. We believed that the first time we filled up Matthew's aeroplane, the delivery hose must have had some contamination inside it, which was transferred to the aircraft.

We came through some terrible weather and got lost but Matthew managed to find an airfield for us to take shelter in. There is nothing better than landing after a scary flight.

We were with Cadbury for almost eight years when a new managing director from Australia took over the top job. We were keen to get our sponsorship agreement renewed because we had an 18-month contract but the new boss, who had so many more important things on his agenda, was delaying talking to us, so when we were approached by St Ivel, another company that wanted our wingwalking team, we said yes.

The Antonov An-2 is a large, single-engined biplane and proved to be quite a spectacle during our time with Utterly Butterly.

Renowned artist Philip Castle designed a complete rebrand when we moved over to sponsorship by Utterly Butterly. His original poster was turned into the colour scheme for the aircraft, flying suits and team patches.

St Ivel were really pleased with the media coverage and the excitement our wingwalking team were generating for the Cadbury Crunchie brand. They were launching a new butter-like spread, Utterly Butterly, and they came and asked me if I had any ideas on how to push the brand forward. After much consideration, I suggested that we operate the world's largest biplane for them, using a Russian-designed Antonov An-2 aircraft, which, once painted up, made a huge advertising billboard.

The Antonov An-2 is a mass-produced, Soviet, single-engine biplane designed in 1946. It has remarkable durability and high lifting power so it can take off and land from very small fields. It really is a flying truck.

My good friend Laszlo Toth, who was the team leader of the world-famous Malev team in Hungary, flew three Zlin-50s in close formation at all the airshows – the same type of aircraft that I flew for Mitsubishi. I arranged a quick trip over to Hungary to meet Laszlo and I was taken to a small airfield where retired An-2 aircraft lined the taxiways, all looking rather sad. We selected the best of the bunch and I agreed a purchase price for a restored aircraft painted in bright yellow, with a smart new interior and eight oxblood-red seats. The price was £15,000,

all in. I now had to put together a parachute team and, with the help of my friend Simon Ward, who knew all that one ever needed to know about parachuting, we managed to get a team together. We were all set to go.

The aeroplane was ready to collect, and Laszlo and I were going to fly it from Hungary to the UK. I first had to obtain a Hungarian pilot's licence and have a check ride with a flight examiner. I somehow managed to pass the test and we set off to the UK via Austria. It was a hairy flight because we picked up a load of airframe icing and had to keep descending to try to get into warmer air. We were having difficulties maintaining height but we did make it to Austria eventually, rather tired and very pleased to be on *terra firma*. The rest of the trip back to the UK was uneventful, other than the huge quantity of fuel we used.

I decided that I would employ a Hungarian aircraft engineer whose job it would be to look after the aeroplane, prepare it for every flight and walk along the top wing to refuel it, which was no easy task in a strong wind. Zoltan soon settled into life at Rendcomb and he really enjoyed being in the West and going to all the airshows – he was very skilled

A good-looking crew! Andy Offer (top right) went from being 'Red One' with the Red Arrows to 'Yellow Five' with the Utterly Butterly team.

Helen in the javelin out along the wing. The pilot has to maintain positive g-force all around the roll in order to keep her in place!

Fireworks and other fun

We were always coming up with new ideas to keep the sponsors happy, and we tried to inject something new and exciting into the display every year. Either a new flying-suit design, paint scheme on the aircraft, a new display routine, or any other crazy ideas we could think of.

One year, I had the fun idea of adding fireworks to the display. Nowadays, many teams have some form of pyrotechnics or lights on their aircraft, but back then it was very new. We had a system where the fireworks were fitted into metal containers and attached to the aircraft near the tail-wheel. The roman candle fireworks produced a colourful display trailing behind the aircraft. We were always careful not to fly too low and set fire to the farmer's field, but it did happen on at least one occasion! When the large roman candles went off you felt a really big kick from the rear of the aeroplane.

On one occasion, after our display but still during flight, I saw that it looked like one of our team pilot's aeroplanes was on fire and the firework outer casing was burning. I told Mike, the pilot, on the radio to follow me in for a quick emergency landing at a small private airfield. I landed first, taxied to the cafe building and quickly filled up a bucket with water from the outside tap. Mike taxied in behind me and I rushed over and put the flames out before it could set light to the aeroplane. After that event, I don't think we ever did it again.

Other ideas included giving the wingwalkers long ribbon streamers to hold, having the formation tied together with bunting, putting bright lights on the top wing, using coloured smoke, and putting flags onto the struts between the wings.

Utterly Butterly wingwalkers in co-ordinated outfits. Below: setting a world record with Nick Mason as we cook the world's largest crumpet in 2000. At 9ft wide, it was suggested that it could feed 5,000 people!

Clockwise from top: myself and Mark Hanna – 'Mr Charisma', as I used to call him. He was dating 'Tinks' (one of our wingwalkers) and sadly died shortly after this while flying a Messerschmitt 109; Norman Lees in Alain de Cadenet's Spitfire. He died while training another pilot in a two-seater version; Hanna and 'Tinks'.

Soapbox racing

Our good friends Gordon and Stella Murray had a lovely holiday home in the Dordogne that was perched on top of a hill with wonderful views all around. Anne and I used to visit that area every year during the summer for a few days' break from my flying. We would fly ourselves down to Bergerac and stay in a lovely hotel in Trémolat.

Gordon would take a few weeks off from his busy Grand Prix and McLaren racing season, and his manufacturing and designing of the McLaren F1 supercar. Boys being boys, it didn't take long to start making very simple wooden carts, firstly with foot steering and bits of string, and a brake consisting of a lever rubbing on a tyre or wheel.

The competitive friends and the younger generation started planning for the following year's event with more sophisticated designs of carts, all similar to the early days of Formula racing. The event consisted of one and then finally five separate courses and an old course, the deadly Long Drive. The original wooden starting ramp developed into a purpose-built concrete and stone ramp for three carts with a starting release system.

The races were run on a points system: three points for winning your heat, two for second place and one point for third. The winners would end up racing the other winners, and the final points decided the starting position for the last and most dangerous race of the day, the Long Drive.

There were crashes every year and mainly minor injuries, but sometimes more serious crashes meant a visit to the local A&E in Bergerac, including myself with a badly broken collarbone.

Every year there was a theme and, during the morning scrutineering, the teams had to dress up. This became totally outrageous and enormous fun. There would be around 20–25 carts and the fastest 10 were very serious about trying to win. I am pleased to be able to report that I did win outright for three years on the trot. The racing was very close and drifting down the Long Drive, which was lined with trees, bushes and the odd brick wall, was pretty frightening. Thank you, Gordon and Stella, for 25 years of amazing fun.

We have participated in a number of soapbox races and below are Gordon Murray's sketches of one of our creations – the 'Invisible Dog'.

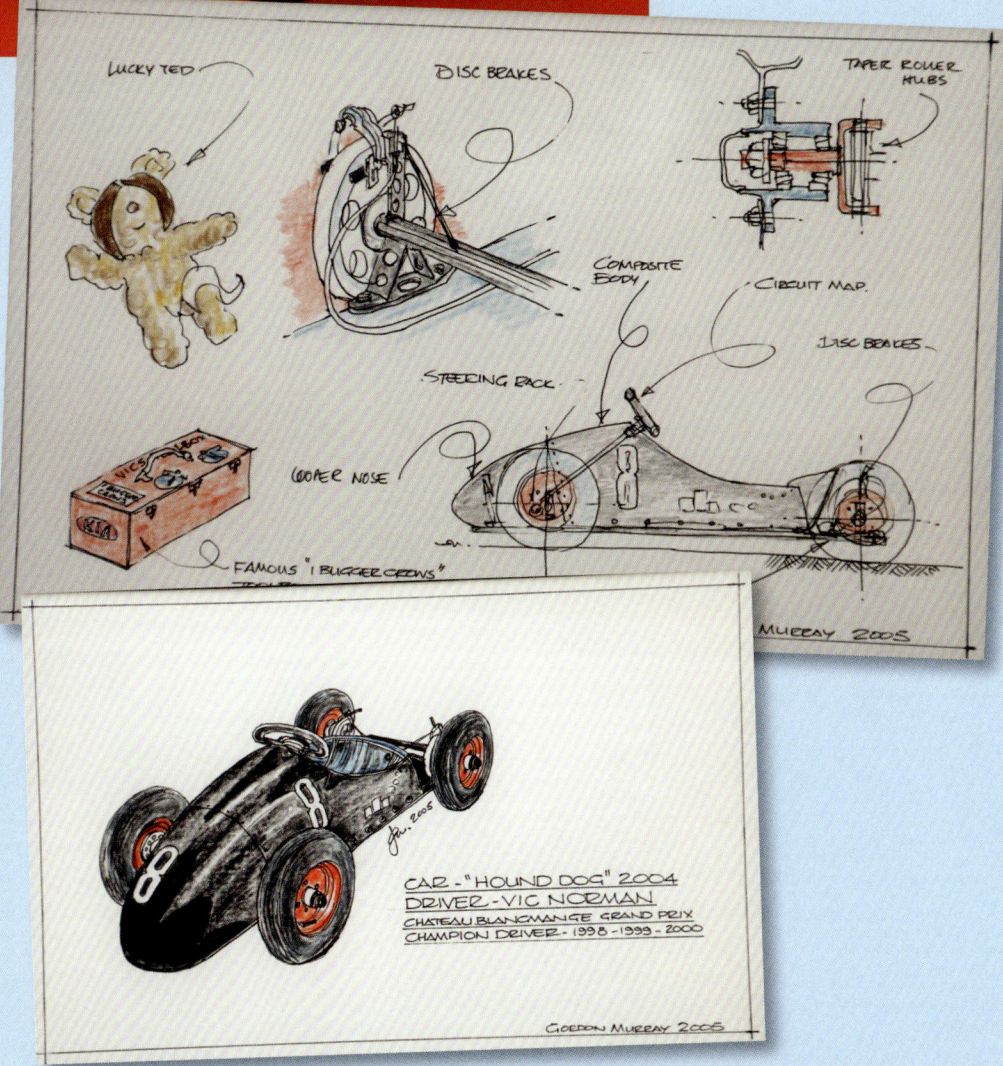

NORMAN CONQUEST 157

> 'Without any warning and when all pressures and temperatures were fine, there was a slight smell and the next thing we knew the engine blew up.'

and could turn his hand to anything. We had a good couple of years operating the team and I had earned well from the sponsorship. When it finished, I still had the aeroplane and we would do the odd air display both in the UK and in Europe.

The An-2 was on one occasion booked to do a show at La Roche-sur-Yon. Anne and I flew down south to do the show. In fact, Anne now had her pilot's licence and she liked flying the Antonov, and was very good at holding a heading and navigating from her map. We did the display and the next day carried on down to Bergerac because our good friends the Murrays have a lovely house up on the top of a hill and Gordon has a soapbox race every year with five separate tracks, which is very competitive. Needless to say, we had a great few days and I came away with the odd trophy.

We loaded up my soapbox and, after checking the Antonov, left for our return flight home, which was about four hours away at 100mph. We had just passed Angers and our next reporting point was Laval when, without any warning and when all pressures and temperatures were fine, there was a slight smell and the next thing we knew the engine blew up. The engine cowling flew off and flames and oil covered the front windscreen and we had no power.

Anne reacted very quickly and spotted a field almost directly below us. We could not see out of the front windscreen due to the oil, but by sideslipping I could see out of the side windows. The big An-2 does not glide well and we were going downhill quickly but I knew I had to keep the speed up to avoid stalling. Luckily, the flames had now stopped. Within seconds I was over a bunch of trees and there was a short 150-metre field that was long enough to flair and carry out a landing.

Anne and I just looked at each other. We knew how lucky we had been to land in one piece unhurt. We made our way to the back of the aeroplane, opened the door and jumped out. What a sight – the whole aeroplane was covered in black engine oil, the cowling was missing, and we discovered that one of the large cylinders had fallen off and taken the cowling with it.

We just stared and thanked our lucky stars to be back on the ground. A farmer arrived and very kindly took us back to his house, where we were made a cup of tea, and before too long the local policeman arrived. He was very excited because the aeroplane was registered in Hungary and was actually rather upset that we were from the UK. He inspected our paperwork and I had to wait for a telephone call from the French air traffic control. I explained what had happened and we then got driven to Laval airfield and I arranged for a lift back to the UK.

My aircraft insurance had always been looked after by Mark Church, who has since become a very good friend. Mark is a proper East End boy made good, and he has been headhunted and moved from one large aviation insurance company to the next and my insurance always followed him. I told him that even if we managed to fit a new engine, the field was not big enough to fly the aeroplane out, so he arranged a lunch meeting with the underwriter and he managed to convince him that I should be paid out the full amount that the aircraft was insured for and that I should keep the aeroplane too.

He told me he started discussing it with the underwriter when they'd just finished eating lunch in a very expensive restaurant and he said, 'Look, either you're going to pay for lunch or I am, so this is what happened: Vic and his wife were flying along on their way back from France and a large bird flew up the exhaust pipe causing the engine to explode!' The guy looked at Mark in utter amazement and they both started laughing. Mark reminded him who would pick up the lunch bill, which included some quality vintage wine, so all was agreed and I got my cheque for £15,000 and the aeroplane.

I had two lucky breaks, because the aeroplane had about 700 litres of Avgas fuel in the tanks and I managed to sell it to the local flying club for one euro a litre, and the mechanic from the club also wanted to purchase the aeroplane, which I agreed to for another €2,000. I had already sent a van over to rescue my soapbox and also the rather smart eight passenger seats, which are still being used in our officers' mess at the airfield. All in all, a rather good result! Thank you Mark, and someone above was looking after me and Anne.

The added attraction at our Utterly Butterly airshows was that we were also operating a sampling unit where people could try the product. This consisted of four people and an Airstream display unit, which was essentially a large dome. It gave us a strong presence at the shows and became a meeting point for lost children, aircrew, and visitors.

We also had to sample the Utterly Butterly replacement for butter ourselves, of course. We had a mid-week delivery at our airfield of loaves of white sliced bread, and we took a lot of them to the shows and spread the butter on them and offered them to the public for people to try. Most people really liked the taste and we gave away thousands of samples at all the shows. We were sent far too much bread, though, so we used to leave some out at our airfield gate for anyone to help themselves to. We became very popular in the village.

We were very lucky again with our sponsors, who were great fun to be with, and the media coverage we obtained surpassed everyone's expectations. We had a very happy eight years with St Ivel.

Shape yoghurt and the Broussard

While things were going well with the Utterly Butterly contract, we were asked if we could put together a team to promote St Ivel Shape yoghurt as well. This was because St Ivel were really pleased with the media coverage and excitement our wingwalking team was generating for the brand, so they wanted to know if I had any ideas on how to push Shape yoghurt forward.

After much consideration, I suggested that we operate an all-female parachute team using an MH1521 Broussard aircraft. The Broussard was repainted in the brand's psychedelic colours, with a matching Kia Sedona people carrier as the base for a ground sampling team to promote the yoghurt at airshows, giving away 50,000 tubs a day!

It all went pretty well for a couple of years, other than the fact that it was very difficult to get the team to help with basic chores. My wingwalking team, including me, used to love keeping the aircraft really clean, but the parachute lot had no interest at all. They just wanted to jump out of the aeroplane and then chill out and do nothing. I have to say that in the end I got fed up with trying to get them motivated and I just gave up.

On the back of the Utterly Butterly sponsorship, we established a parachute team to promote Shape yoghurt. Presenter Davina McCall was just one who jumped from the Broussard.

NORMAN CONQUEST

Chapter ten
CHINESE ADVENTURE

While Utterly Butterly were still sponsoring the team, we received an email via Helen (our chief wingwalker) and my PA from someone in China. The gist of it was that they had seen a videogame featuring our display and they wanted us to come to China. Helen asked me what I thought and I said it's just not possible.

Luckily, Helen ignored me and worked out the cost for the shipping of two aeroplanes, with spares, each in their own 40ft container, plus flight costs for the team. She came back to me with figures and I still thought it was madness. But Helen pushed me and we sat down and worked out the engineering fees and all the other costs we could think of, and came up with a rather large figure. She asked if she could go ahead and find out more details and then send them the quote.

I was worried we might never get the aeroplanes back from China and was still convinced it would never happen, so I said it was fine so long as she doubled the quote. Within 24 hours the Chinese lot came back to us and agreed to our quote. I was now getting worried we might actually be committing to going, so then said we needed 50 percent of our fee up-front with the order and a further 25 percent before the crates left the UK. They asked for our bank details and the next morning we had the money in our account.

This was the start of such an exciting adventure. The team consisted of Rachel (our media girl), Anne, myself and two other pilots, three wingwalkers, and two engineers to assemble the aircraft in case one of us got ill. Rachel went out a week before the rest of the team to do Chinese media for the show, which was going to be at a new international airport in Zhuhai.

We arrived in Hong Kong and were met by a young girl called Coco, who spoke to us in very good English and led the way to the shipping terminal with us hurrying behind pulling loads of suitcases full of tools and spares. We could not understand any of the signs, what was going on or indeed where we were, and everyone was staring at us – particularly at Tania, a very pretty blonde, because they were not used to seeing blonde hair.

We made it to the hotel, which had put out a large sign to welcome us, and we were greeted by every member of staff. Coco was a godsend and stayed with us 24/7. The meals, though, were something else and took a bit of getting used to. Tony, our chief engineer, was not that keen on coming to China. He had never been separated from his wife, other than the night that she gave birth to their daughter, and although he'd been an aircraft engineer since he was 16 and worked for the Royal Air Force, he'd also never flown. We wangled ourselves into Virgin's VIP lounge and Tony, white with fear, was being consoled by the girls. He had packed baked beans in the aircraft containers and planned to live on eggs and beans for the full three weeks.

The day after we arrived we were taken to Zhuhai airport. Our hotel was on a small one-lane track but about six miles from the airport the road became a six-lane motorway with grass verges being cut by hundreds of Chinese men using only hand tools. The airport itself was huge, with one or two aircraft parked but no movement until the Russians arrived with their pair of aerobatic Sukhoi Su-27s, a full back-up transport aircraft and lots of personnel. We assembled our aircraft in a large, empty hangar. The next day we were asked to attend a briefing and it was just us, the Russians, and the Chinese aerobatic display team and parachute team, who all turned up in four big An-2 single-engine aircraft.

There were more than 10 high-powered generals from the Chinese military in the room sat at a long table. The interpreter welcomed everyone on behalf of the government and airshow personnel, and then proceeded to go through the flying programme, starting with the Russians. She asked whether their display team, the Russian Knights, could display their aircraft twice a day – once in the morning and again in the afternoon.

The Russian general in charge immediately started shouting that they needed more time between their displays, more jet fuel and that they had to stop for one hour for lunch too, so they couldn't do what they were being asked to. The Chinese generals said nothing, but I could see that they were getting fed up.

When it came to our turn, the Chinese interpreter asked us the same question: could we fly for the press first thing every morning and then give both a morning and afternoon display? I waited for a while and then stood up and asked the interpreter to let the generals know how honoured we were to bring our team to China and display our wingwalking team, and that we would do whatever we were asked to with pleasure. I sat down and she started translating what I'd said, and at the end the top man smiled and thanked me in perfect English.

We had a wonderful time, with Coco always by our side arranging everything for us. The show drew in the biggest crowd that I had ever seen and our team were the real stars on TV every night. We were

Thanks to the persistence of Helen Tempest in sorting out the complicated logistics, we enjoyed a fantastic trip to China, displayed to large, appreciative crowds, and were treated like stars. Strange to think that it all came about because someone had seen our display in a videogame!

'The Goose' is a great new manoeuvre – performed while only wearing a safety strap.

> 'The soup was a bit of a surprise – when the ladle was pulled out, there was a whole chicken head in it. They also served goose feet and turtles, but we all mainly just had the rice.'

taken to a tea house, and we had our feet massaged in a small shop where people just walked in off the street and, when we were charged 50p for the massage, Coco complained that we'd overpaid and got us a refund.

The food was a bit of a problem for some of the team, especially one night when a banquet was held in our honour. The soup was a bit of a surprise – when the ladle was pulled out there was a whole chicken head in it. They also served goose feet and turtles, but we all mainly just had the rice.

Air traffic control could not speak any English so during our display our spare pilot Martin was our air traffic controller. We had finished our afternoon display and were turning downwind to land when Martin asked us to fly around the control tower because they wanted to see the girls. We then did that every day and a big crowd always came out on the balcony to watch. The crown really loved our team and after landing each day the girls were mobbed and asked to sign their names – even, once, on a baby's arm.

On the last day, Anne invited all our girls to go shopping with her and she bought them all beautiful Chinese dresses. When Anne asked Coco, who was by now one of the team, whether she would like a dress, Coco asked if she could have funds to buy books.

All in all, the whole event was a fantastic experience. It was very profitable and we made really good business friendships, like Sky Jiang, which we still have to this day and have since returned many times to display our team all over China. We tried to get Coco to visit us in the UK as a guest of AeroSuperBatics, but she was not allowed to travel.

When Utterly Butterly pulled out from supporting us, we needed to find a new sponsor quickly and we managed to get a media story about the team in *Marketing Monthly*. We were approached by the UK distributor of Guinot's skincare products and it immediately became obvious that they'd done their homework and knew everything about us – including the media coverage we'd got for both Cadbury and St Ivel, which was independently valued at around six million pounds per year. The company was owned by a Mr Robinson, who had inherited the British distributorship from his father. I soon discovered that he had a drink problem and that the company was managed and operated by a team of very hard-working, bright women.

They visited our set-up and I proposed a sponsorship deal and they explained that they would

A magical picture – a lot of hard work, training and skill goes into getting five aircraft and wingwalkers so perfectly synchronised.

In Guinot livery and flying over the desert in Al Ain in the United Arab Emirates.

also like us to manage a ground unit for them, which would promote their skincare products and sign up new clients at the shows. By the time they left, they had agreed to sponsor a two-aeroplane team. We were all so pleased because it secured the team's future and all our jobs for at least another three years.

I then got a telephone call from the CEO about two hours after they had left our meeting and I was terrified that she had rung to tell me that they had changed their minds and would not sign the contract. In fact, they asked me what I was going to do with my other two aeroplanes. Thinking on my feet I said that, although I didn't want to, I would have to find another sponsor for my other two aeroplanes. There was a moment's silence and then I was told that Guinot would take all four aeroplanes and double the money.

We did a good job for Guinot. They taught the whole team about their fantastic skincare products and we all had to attend various training courses. Their business was run really well and new clients for life were being signed up in our smart motorhome at all the shows. Everyone was happy and we were putting in the extra mile to do a first-class job, pushing all the media outlets and flying in a great many shows. We were within two weeks of signing up for another three years of sponsorship when the UK owner suffered a fall at work and later died in hospital.

It's fair to say that all hell broke loose. The owner of the UK business was expected to leave it to the staff who had been running the show very well for years, and I understand that Mr Guinot in France would have been very happy for the business to carry on with the UK distributorship in safe hands. However, Mr Robinson had gone to his solicitors a few weeks before he died and changed his will. He left a large percentage of his business to a lady friend who he had already bought an apartment for in the south of France, as well as a very smart new black Mini. I had met her before at various functions and she was very nice and good looking.

He left the balance of the shares to a local animal trust that he had driven past and noticed on his way to the solicitors...

The will was contested without success and Guinot France decided to do all their own sales and business in the UK. We lost the chance to renew our sponsorship with the French because they wanted to concentrate on sponsoring tennis. Never mind – we had great time while it lasted and I have many happy memories of our time working for Guinot.

Tim Senior at the controls of the Cri-Cri with Alan Plowman driving the Mitsubishi Shogun. Below: me starting the engines while perched on a ladder – no risk assessment back then!

Cri-Cri

Mitsubishi wanted to push the coverage around their Shogun SUV and I came up with the idea of having an aeroplane take off from the roof of the car. The smallest twin-engine aeroplane in the world available for me to purchase was a French-designed Colombian Cri-Cri aeroplane with two small single-cylinder 150cc engines. The pilot's cockpit was only big enough for one person to sit in, and they had the plastic fuel tank under their legs. It was a great little aeroplane and could perform simple aerobatic manoeuvres. The Cri-Cri was pushed up onto the roof on long ramps and there was a release mechanism that the plane was locked into.

The aeroplane was always flown into the air display venue while the Shogun made its own way by road. Both the car and aeroplane were parked on the flying, active side of the airfield, which was a great bonus because it was the only car allowed to be parked with the display aircraft.

The Cri-Cri's engine had to be started like a lawnmower, standing on a ladder with a cord wrapped around the pulley. The aeroplane was attached to the car and then taxied out to the runway just using the two high-revving engines for propulsion. The car and plane would line up on the runway and the car would accelerate to 70mph. On the pilot's command, the driver pulled the release cord and the aeroplane sprung into the air.

We designed a nice display sequence with the car and aeroplane flying in formation, and both doing opposition passes and finally taxiing together back to their parking space. Mitsubishi Motors loved the show and all the local dealers would sponsor each of their local events.

Piper Cub

I also built and designed a trailer from which the pilot could take off and land. It was more difficult than it seemed. None of us were able to land on the trailer until we worked out that the airwave coming off the front of the trailer needed a duck tail, which diverted the airflow away from the aeroplane wing.

We used to do a crazy flying act with the Cub bouncing off the trailer platform and the commentator building tension up saying, 'Will he make it this time?', as well as an opposition pass with the aeroplane zooming over the trailer platform at the last second. The trailer-top landing was sponsored by Kia Cars and the media called it the World's Smallest Runway. They liked the show so much that they had the Kia Sedona renamed as an aircraft carrier, rather than a people carrier!

Right and over page: just some of the impressive press shots for new sponsors Breitling – taken from the back of a Short Skyvan.

'The next day they would be coached out to the airfield and taken flying with the Breitling Jet Team to perform tandem parachutes, fly in aerobatic Pitts Specials, and taken wingwalking with us.'

When we lost the Guinot sponsorship, we needed to find another partner quickly. For many years (going right back to the Cadbury days), we were always contracted by Breitling SA in Switzerland to fly out to Buochs – the airfield where Pilatus Aircraft, the aeroplane manufacturer, was based. Breitling would take over the airfield for two weeks with dealers and VIP guests flown out from each country around the world every day. They were put up in the best hotel on Lake Lucerne, given a fantastic evening, and the next day they would be coached out to the airfield and taken flying with the Breitling Jet Team to perform tandem parachutes, fly in aerobatic Pitts Specials, and taken wingwalking with us.

It was hard work because we did lots of flights every day but we were really spoilt, with wonderful lunches and evenings off for ourselves and the other teams to generally have a good time on and around the lake.

My friend Derek Bell would turn up as the Ambassador for Bentley and give a talk in the evenings about his wins at the Le Mans 24 Hours. He won it five times, which is an incredible feat. He would give the guests a real blast during the day while we were flying up the nearby mountain and they normally came back in a state of partial shock, surprised how fast Derek would drive.

We looked forward to those two weeks a lot. It was a great change from our busy airshow programme, which was much more intense and stressful, refuelling every two hours at airports *en route* to our next destination and always having to check the weather.

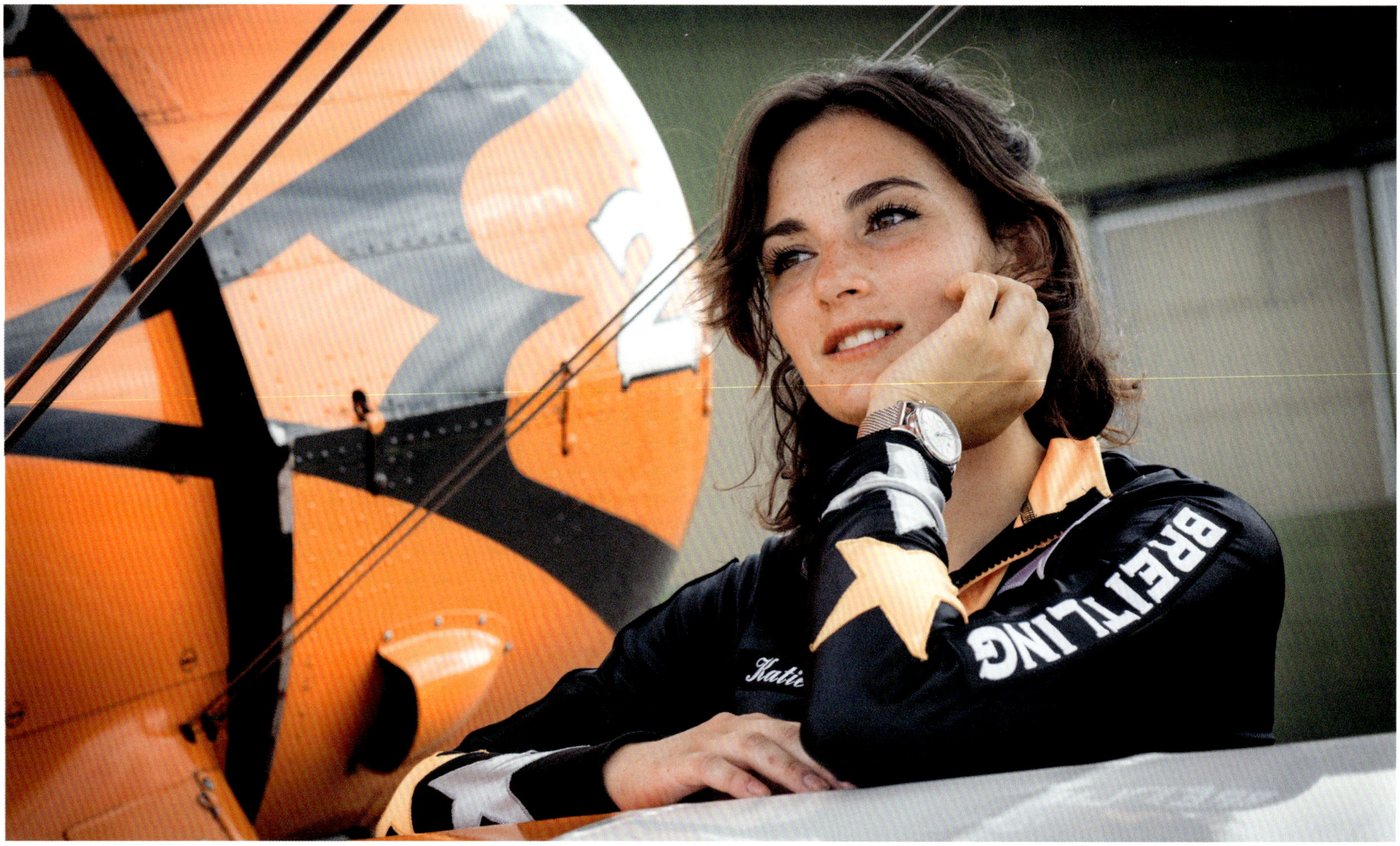
BREITLING
Katie

BREITLING

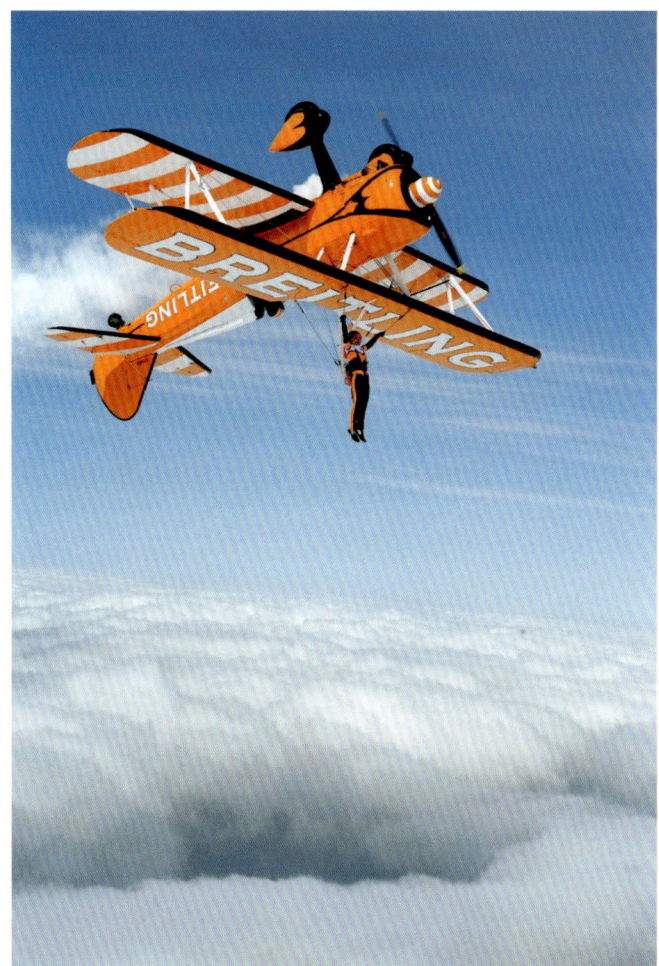

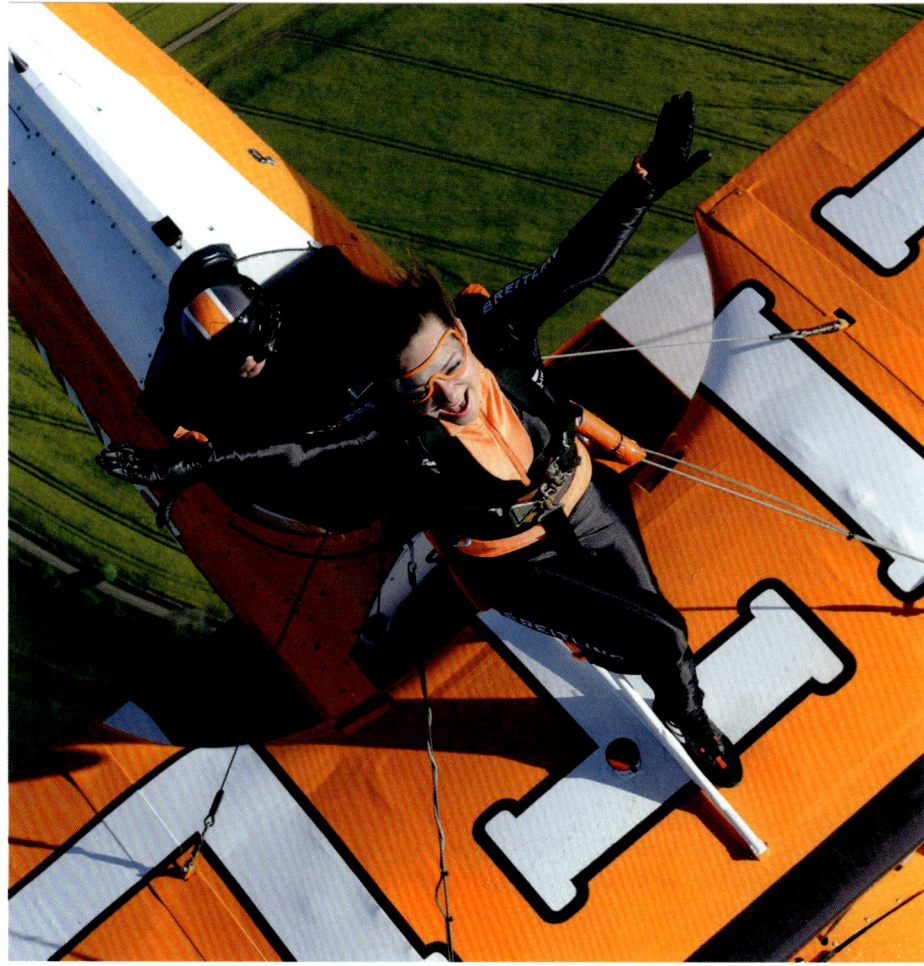

A considerable number of PR shots were also taken for Breitling – it certainly helps that our team is so photogenic!

I approached Breitling and agreed to a one-year sponsorship deal for just two aeroplanes and for much less than we had been getting. That first year went really well. Breitling were great to work with and the owner, Mr Schneider, was a down-to-earth man and I got on very well with him and the rest of the Breitling team. They were all truly passionate about aviation and they knew how to make the most of the teams that they sponsored. We were all in the Breitling Family.

I did what we always had done with our sponsors and gave an end-of-season report on all our activities and all the media and TV shows that we had been on. When I presented this to Breitling, they must have been very impressed, and I am sure that we were the only team doing this sort of presentation and also getting far more media coverage than any others. We had a visit to our base and airfield from Mr Schneider and his 'Mr Fix It' man Stefano Albinati, who organised all the team's activities and was a very switched-on bloke. I liked him very much as a person and also as someone to work with.

After the visit, Stefano came to see us again and said that since Mr Schneider and Breitling would like to carry on with our sponsorship, he'd like to know what my wishes were. This was a bit of a shock. I told him that I would like to run a four-aeroplane team so we could be at the big shows flying all four wingwalking aeroplanes together and, at other times, because we were so much in

Clockwise from left: in the United Arab Emirates and flying past Atlantis, The Palm in Dubai; displaying in Switzerland with 'jetman' Yves Rossy; the happy couple; on tour in Australia with the iconic Sydney Opera House in the background; Dave Barrell — number one man, team leader and 'Mr Reliable'.

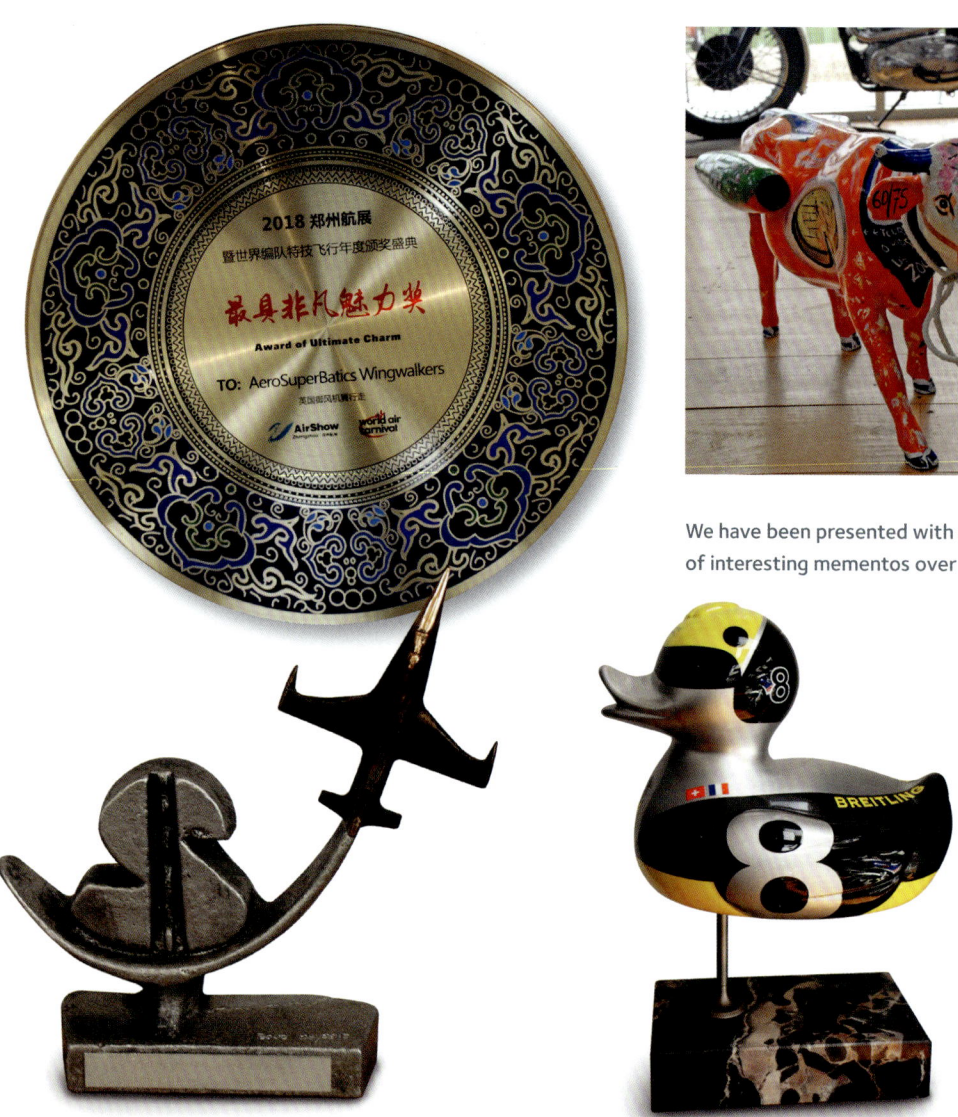

We have been presented with a variety of interesting mementos over the years!

demand, we could then run an A Team and a B Team and cover twice as many events. My wish was granted and I had an 18-month rolling contract with Breitling, working for a great company that produced very fine watches and instruments for professionals. We were all spoilt as far as watches were concerned, with the whole team getting a new watch every year.

I still keep in contact with Stefano and he always reminds me that his negotiations on behalf of Breitling ended up in him paying me too much and that unfortunately he was under my spell! I should mention here that we would negotiate an appearance fee with the show organisers for each and every event. These fees helped our sponsors because around a third of our operational costs were paid by those fees.

We had great time with Breitling displaying our wingwalking team all over the world, including Australia, Japan, India, China, UAE, Dubai, Bahrain, Oman, and every European country. We were kept very busy.

Mr Schneider then spoilt everything by selling the business to CVC and bringing in a new CEO who wanted to make his mark, so he pulled out of the aviation sponsorship, which was a shock to not only ourselves but also for the jet team and the many historic aircraft and World Champion pilots they supported. Whether this will prove to be a good move for the brand, only time will tell.

Nikolai Antoshkin

In 1995, a wonderful evening was spent with my good friend Micky Suffolk (the Earl of Suffolk and Berkshire). I had been displaying my wingwalking team at Farnborough and arrived back at Rendcomb when I received a phone call from Micky, who had been a VIP guest at the airshow. He told me that he had a Russian General with him, and asked if he could pop into my airfield to show the General our old aeroplanes on his way home.

Micky, who is a wonderful pilot, landed and out jumped the Russian General, a Russian display pilot and a charming Russian interpreter. Anne and I were asked back to Charlton Park later that evening for supper. When we arrived, the American Senator Stevens and his wife had also turned up.

Nikolai Antoshkin – a man who beat Chernobyl but succumbed to Covid – was such an interesting person. He was a Hero of the Soviet Union for his part in commanding the helicopters that dropped boron sand and clay, magnetite and lead on the burning open reactor to bury the fire and tamp down the radiation. He led from the front and flew many missions – his nickname was 'the Radioactive General'.

Supper became a very jolly affair, as all of Micky and Lady Suffolk's evenings tended to be. The wine flowed and I remember how Senator Stevens' wife mentioned how lovely was the silver bowl that was in the middle of the dining table. When she was told that it was a gift from Oliver Cromwell in around 1653, she found it hard to comprehend.

Toward the end of the meal, Micky remembered that he had some Russian Kümmel in the cellars and he went off to collect a bottle or two. Small glasses were produced and the evening was getting very merry indeed. Suddenly the General picked up a bottle of the Kümmel and started talking at full speed to his interpreter. He had noticed that the bottle's label had the crest of the last Tsar of Russia on it, which was, of course, before communism took over.

It turns out that the Tsar had sent over to the then-Lord Suffolk a stock of Kümmel as a gift. I have to say that this did not stop the General from enjoying numerous toasts of the liquid, which had been gifted from the dead Tsar. We all ended up dancing around the table and singing rude Russian pilots' songs.

A final memory is that the telephone rang and the person on the other end of the line said they were from MI5 or some Special Branch office because they had heard that a Russian General was a guest of his lordship. I think Micky told them to bugger off and put the phone down.

Flying past the Burj Khalifa skyscraper in Dubai – the tallest building in the world.

Clockwise from main: Eddie Jordan, David Coulthard and Jake Humphrey strapped in and ready to display at the Silverstone Grand Prix; sharing a joke with Eddie Jordan; a poster advertising one of our many displays; two admirers in the UAE.

Chapter eleven
HEROES

When I was displaying with my team on the American airbase in Iwakuni, near Hiroshima in Japan, I was introduced to a man called Masayuki, who was a Kamikaze pilot. He told me an amazing story about how fate had changed his life.

He was trained as a Kamikaze pilot having signed up to be a pilot for the Japanese Imperial Navy. At the age of 15, he earned his flying credentials and volunteered for a suicide squadron that was planning to attack US-occupied Okinawa in September 1945. A month before his mission, he returned to visit his family in Hiroshima for one last time. They celebrated him and what he was about to do for Japan. On 6 August, he boarded a train to return to his base on Kyushu.

Two hours later, a US B-29 Super Fortress bomber, named *Enola Gay*, dropped an atomic bomb on the city that killed Masayuki's family and destroyed everything he had ever known and loved. After the war, Masayuki spent months searching for word of his family before moving to Osaka, where he opened a shoeshine and noodle soup stand and tried to stay away from occupying American forces. That was until a young GI made a pass at Masayuki's fiancée. He fought the soldier and landed up in a US military jail, thinking that he would be killed. At the court martial, Masayuki told his side of the story to the judge and to his surprise the GI told the judge that he'd been drunk and it was not Masayuki's fault.

The GI and Masayuki became good lifelong friends and the GI was invited to their wedding. Later on, the soldier helped Masayuki join an exchange program to study in the US for five years. He was the guest speaker at the Marine Corps Ball in Iwakuni and he helps educate young Japanese students in the futility of war.

It was a real honour to talk to him and he is still with his childhood sweetheart.

My all-time superhero is, without question, Mr Glenn Curtiss. The simple reason for my admiration is that he was one of the first truly brave aviators and he combined my two greatest mechanical passions – motorcycling and early aviation. Glenn set the fastest speed ever on a V8 motorcycle he designed himself, and it was the development of this engine that led to the greatest mass-produced pre-1920 aircraft engine ever made: the V8 OX5 water-cooled Curtiss engine fitted to all early Curtiss Jennys.

When I saw that an original Jenny aircraft was for sale (which had a continual history and was barnstormed up to 1919), I just had to go over to the EAA Aviation Museum in Oshkosh, Wisconsin, to see this famous barnstorming aeroplane in the flesh. The big, stable, reliable Jenny was the first really

Above: with Masayuki Matsumuro, a trained Kamikaze pilot who went on to educate students in the futility of war. Right: Glenn Curtiss – a hero of mine and also passionate about both motorcycling and aviation.

Displaying my Curtiss Jenny at the Rendcomb Airshow. The aircraft was previously owned by Ray McWhorter (pictured top right).

'It was previously owned by Mr Ray McWhorter, a barnstormer from Iowa. Its last flight was in Mason City in Iowa on 11 August 1919, while carrying a wingwalker who was attempting to transfer to another Jenny.'

functional machine for wingwalking – along with the Avro 504 – during those early pioneering years of aviation.

Everyone asks what it's like to fly and, well, let me start at the beginning. As you walk up to the Jenny, your first impression is how big the aeroplane is. It has a 44ft wingspan, nearly half as much again as a Stearman, and although I am reasonably tall it's a big stretch getting into the cockpit. You put your left boot into a foothold, hold onto the side of the cockpit and pull yourself up as if you're mounting a horse. Then your right foot goes onto the seat and, as you try not to kick the side or sit on the turtledeck, which is not that bum-proof, you then lower yourself into what is a very large cockpit.

Once you're in the cockpit, the layout is very basic, as you would expect it to be in a 1912 design. There's a big slab of wood with a centre pivot, which is the rudder bar, a throttle, fuel cock (which is a large aluminium wheel), a high control stick, an rpm gauge, oil pressure, altimeter, and down by your right knee a booster magneto with a little wheel to turn.

The walk around and pre-flight checks also involve greasing the rocker gear, checking the water level in the radiator, checking the oil level via a pointer on the side of the all-aluminium crankcase, and all the other usual stuff. However, as the Jenny has miles and miles of cable runs, this all takes a long time, which does at least give you a chance to build up your courage before flying.

Now some facts and figures: the OX5 engine has a conservative rating of 90hp at 1,400rpm, the cylinders are cast iron with monel water jackets brazed to the outside, two banks of four cylinders set at 90 degrees in a V-configuration. The banks are slightly offset to allow the connecting rods to work side-by-side on the same crankshaft journal.

These engines were produced in huge numbers, about 12,500 of them, which meant around two engines for every airframe manufactured. These extra engines, after the Great War, were snapped up by the 1920s aircraft manufacturers such as Waco and Travelair. The big 8ft 4in prop on the Jenny needs a fair amount of effort to pull through a compression but, as long as you crank like mad on the booster magneto, the engine normally catches if you've remembered to flood the carburettor. Once it's going, a slow warm-up at around 600-800rpm is what you need.

Taxiing is similar to a Tiger Moth. You use engine bursts with large applications of rudder, line up for take-off (no mag check or the engine will stop), and full power – the rudder is very powerful and the tail comes up very quickly. After about 100 yards the Jenny is flying.

The climb-out is best achieved at 50-55mph, which is very flat, cruising at 60-65mph, and then it stalls at 38-40mph, while the rate of climb is around 200 to 300ft per minute depending on the load. Looking straight ahead, you can see the rocker arms dancing in the wind and the engine beats a steady and sure rhythm. Turns are initiated with the stick, but if they are too steep you need the opposite rudder to pick the wing up.

It's a very easy aeroplane to fly around in and feels very secure, with a good forward view. Looking over the side from the pilot's cockpit, you can hear the wind whistling in all those wires. The engine is very smooth with little noise heard in the cockpit.

In the Jenny, you could become unstuck in the tighter turns because you need a rudder to get the machine back on an even keel. The original pilot's notes specify not to take turns below 500ft but I've found that with a speed of 70mph it is all recoverable and good fun to fly.

The few air displays I did with the Jenny I really enjoyed, and it gave me a taste of how the 1920s barnstormers must have felt. Landing is a doddle. With an initial approach at 60mph, the speed bleeds off very quickly with all the drag during the round-out, and the big propeller provides a good blast over the tailplane even at low revs, which provides a good elevator control at low speeds. It stops after a few yards with the tailplane acting as a good anchor-type brake. The stick forces are heavy so you need to be constantly flying the aeroplane.

My ex-aeroplane registration number was 2525. It was previously owned by Mr Ray McWhorter, a barnstormer from Iowa. Its last flight was in Mason City in Iowa on 11 August 1919, while carrying a wingwalker who was attempting to transfer to another Jenny. They collided, and Ray survived the crash. He put the wrecked machine in a barn on his farm, where it remained until 1970.

There are only a handful of these wonderful aeroplanes flying today and I consider myself very lucky to have flown the old girl and to have become a member of the OX5 club. Ray McWhorter used to say that the greatest danger facing a barnstormer was not falling to death, but starvation.

When I started flying again, my first aeroplane was a French-built biplane called a Stampe. I used a clever legal scheme to keep the aeroplane very close to where I lived at RAF Kemble. At the time, in the late 1970s and 1980s, RAF Kemble was the home base for the Red Arrows and I got to know the team pretty well over the years, and I was often invited to join them at various functions in the officers' mess. I ended up becoming good friends with some of them and, when I moved up to flying my Zlin-50 aeroplane at shows, I would meet the team at events several times each season. When my wingwalking team got under way, we became a major attraction, mainly because we always had bright young girls as our wingwalkers, who were often the only female attraction in what was a very male environment.

The big show every year was The Royal

Helen strapping in Prince Faisal at Rendcomb Airfield. After the Royal International Air Tattoo, we spent the evening flying VIPs and heads of Air Forces from around the world.

Inspiration from the early 1900s as a wingwalker performs on a Curtiss Jenny biplane in the skies above New Jersey.

From top: pilot briefing in the Officers' Mess before the Rendcomb Airshow; flying Prince Michael of Kent at the post-RIAT party; Prince Michael and other guests at the post-RIAT dinner; one of our first ever airshows at Rendcomb.

International Airshow at Fairford, which was just down the road from Royal Flying Corps Rendcomb, our home airfield. Anne and I would lay on a very private party for selected guests each year. There were no spying eyes looking on and we would have amazing live music put on by Rick Fenn, a fantastic guitar player and member of 10cc, who was supported by the best of the best session players. The food arranged by Anne was always fabulous and the evenings could not have been more fun. The word soon got out and all the other aerobatic teams were very keen to get an invite.

I have been lucky enough over the years to go on various trips with the Red Arrows, including being allowed to be a backseat passenger during two public displays and a further three team practices. I have flown with four team leaders and three other team members. Anne was also given a ride with the team as a 'thank you' to her for all the hard work and arrangements she had made organising the Rendcomb parties. Being a qualified pilot herself, she was given the controls flying a Red Arrows Hawk around the skies over Lincolnshire.

I doubt any civilian has flown with the team during public displays as often as I have. Being a display pilot myself, as well as a display pilot examiner for the Civil Aviation Authority, allowed

Left: Anne outside the 'Hangar' marquees. Below: an impressive line-up of vintage aircraft at Rendcomb Airshow.

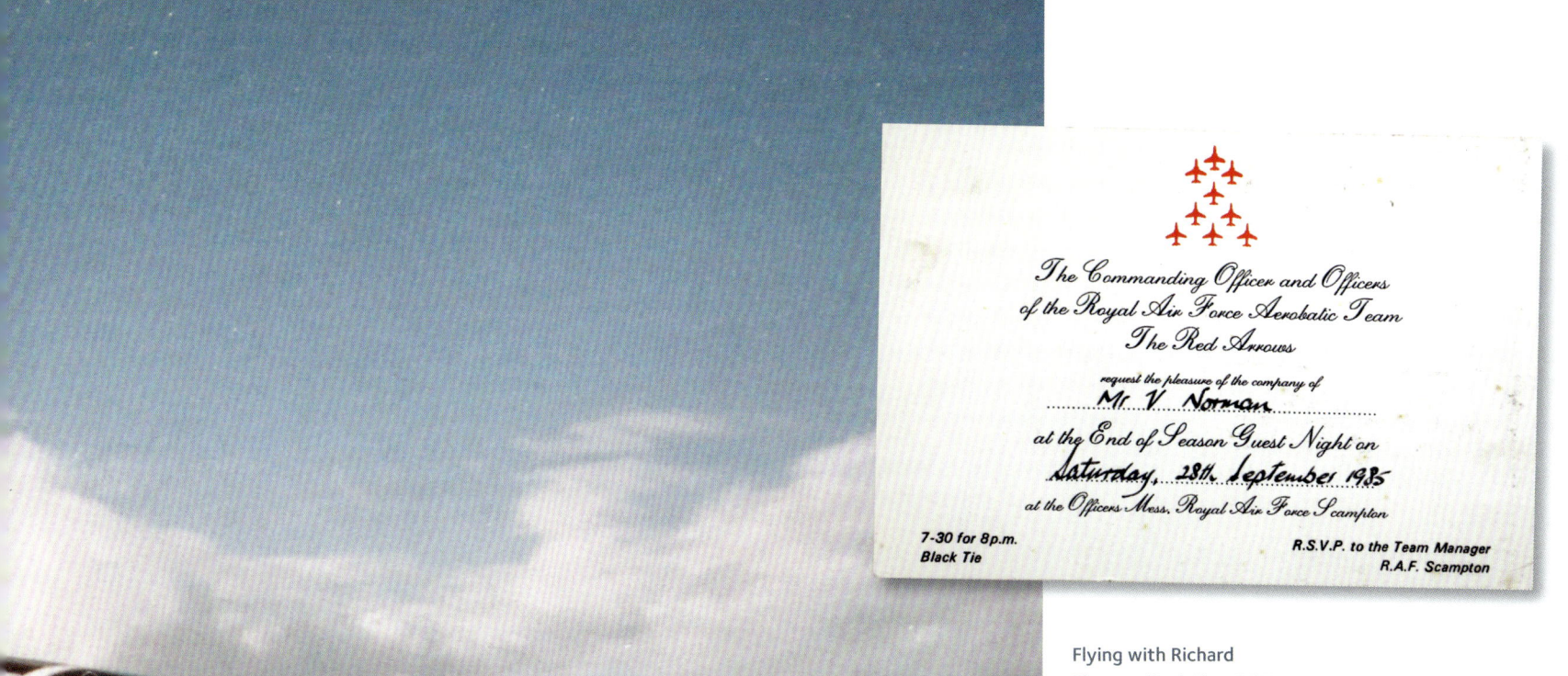

Flying with Richard Thomas (Red 1) at RAF Scampton in 1986 – a definite highlight from my career in aviation.

this to happen. I remember on one of my planned rides with the team, I had been asked to do a live commentary for Sky TV from the rear cockpit of the team leader's aircraft, RED 1, during a display flown by Squadron Leader Andy Offer at Biggin Hill. The team were going to land at the airfield the morning of the show and I was already there because I was also going to fly in the back seat, along with Nigel Lamb, commentating on the Fighter Collection Team, which was led by Ray Hanna, who was an ex-leader of the Red Arrows.

However, earlier on a vintage jet aircraft had damaged the first part of the runway by blowing off some of the tarmac surface and so the Red Arrows decided to arrive overhead directly into their display slot, meaning that I would not be able to fly with them. All was resolved, though; they instructed the Hercules aircraft that had brought the team's ground crew to the show to fly me to RAF Lyneham in Wiltshire and I had to be fitted out *en route* with flying uniform, boots, etc, in the aeroplane because time was critical.

This was a huge bonus because the team were giving a flyby display at RAF Brize Norton while flying across the country from Lyneham to Biggin, and Andy let me take the controls during both the flyby itself – with eight other jets formatting on me – and then in a loose formation all the way to Biggin. How lucky can you be? Of course, Andy then took control for the run-in to start the display but it was so very special.

NORMAN CONQUEST

Andy then became one of our team members after he had left the Reds and went from Red 1 to Utterly Butterly Yellow 4 – a bit of a downturn, but he so enjoyed flying one of our biplanes and I loved being with him.

Having watched all the world's teams, the Red Arrows are without doubt the best, and although I have seen them display more than 100 times during my 40 or so years doing air displays, I always watch their full display and it makes me and the whole crowd very proud to be British.

One year, while displaying our four-aircraft wingwalking show at The Royal International Air Tattoo (RIAT), both Andy and I got given a red flag for flying too low along the crowd-line in opposite directions after our final break. Apparently, one member of the flying control committee insisted on raising the bottom height of our display from our normal approved height of 30ft to 100ft. After much disagreement, I agreed and made a point of reading out all our bottom heights during the display. However, on that final break we ended up at our normal 30ft and the committee member got his chance to get his own back for all our disagreements. It was all pointless and no one was put in any danger, neither pilots nor members of the public.

Finally, I want to say a big THANK YOU to the Red Arrows.

In the back seat with Red 1 — I lifted up my helmet visor so I could prove that it was me!

I was honoured to fly Dominic Bruce into the Royal International Air Tattoo at RAF Fairford in 1995. Bruce made 17 escape attempts from various prisoner of war camps during WWII – including several from Colditz – and is pictured above with other officers, including Douglas Bader in the middle of the front row.

Chapter twelve
A DAY IN THE LIFE

Although there is a lot of work to be done on display days, there is still time to enjoy a post-show ice cream!

I will base this account of a typical flying display day on a busy weekend in the UK and Europe. One or two days before the event, the whole team would start preparing our wingwalking aeroplanes: engineering, checking the oil and getting enough bottles of oil ready to top up with over the weekend, making sure the fuel tank is completely full to give you two hours' flying time at cruise settings with 15 minutes spare before the engine stops, and of course double-checking everything.

One of the pilots would get the job of working out the programme for the weekend. This starts with whatever display slots the airshow organiser has given you and, if the team has multiple shows to do in any one day, then we'd have to negotiate with the display directors to make sure we had enough time to meet the schedule, including transit and refuelling stops. It takes around 45 minutes to land, refuel, and get airborne again. We use airfields that know us and are always very helpful in speeding up the whole process.

The wingwalkers do the actual refuelling – they sit on the top wing with the fuel hose and make sure that at least two or three gallons are put into the tank because, with our little range, we might well need it.

We always arrive get to the aeroplanes one hour before our take-off time. You don't want to be in a rush, and on arrival we agree a time to start the engines with enough leeway to warm up and taxi to the take-off runway. Early-morning departures can

be very cold in our open-cockpit biplanes and lots of layers are needed, which can be discarded as the day warms up. If it's raining, we just get wet. Some of those early-morning sunrise flights can be magical, with the wonderful feeling of freedom that you get from being up in the sky and rushing along at 500ft above the ground.

Then there was the added excitement of performing in front of 20,000 to 50,000 people and precision flying, trusting in your wingman and only flying a few feet apart, with the girls performing their own aerial routine, looking so graceful even though they are fighting g-force and winds up to 160mph.

We'd arrive at our first show, land and taxi to our parking slot. The first thing to do is refuel if needed and then the pilots go to a briefing, where all the teams sit down while the display director goes through the day's programme in detail, right down to arranging departure slots.

Meanwhile, the girls would have gone to see the commentator, spoken to the media and checked to see if any TV crews were at the show, then made sure that they were available to give interviews, as well as talking to the public. They'd write up a report after each weekend, which was sent to our sponsors.

A start-up time would be agreed, and again we'd get back to the aeroplanes one hour in advance so we could do a walk-through of our whole routine. We'd also decide what allowance we'd need to make for the wind to make sure that our display would stay positioned by the centre of the crowd rather than being blown off miles away.

The team would carry out the pre-display safety checks, the most important one being that the wingwalkers' safety harness and attachment wire is secured. The actual display is very much routine because we know all our manoeuvres and turns in detail, right down to when the leader calls for the aircraft's smoke to be turned on and off. The whole routine is like a dance in the sky and on stormy, rough, windy days it's really hard work, but on calm, smooth days it can run just like clockwork.

Our display lasts 15-17 minutes from take-off to landing, we taxi in close with the girls waving like mad to the crowd, and the area where we'd park always became a hive of activity with the team being applauded and the girls rushing over to sign autographs and chat to the public and media. We generate a lot of attention and our team is very much a family attraction with aeroplanes, girls, pilots, glamour, excitement – what more does anyone want?

We'd always have a debrief to pick up on what we could have done better. It's very much an open discussion and you say exactly what you think with a view to improving things next time or, sometimes, patting ourselves on the back and agreeing that the show was as good as it gets.

We'd agree the next meet time, refuel our aeroplanes, and normally go our own ways, meeting friends or getting coffee and lunch if we have time.

'The team would carry out the pre-display safety checks, the most important being that the wingwalkers' safety harness and attachment wire is secured.'

Sometimes we'd have a second show on the other side of the Channel and would have to file a flight plan to cross an international border and, of course, put on our life jackets.

We'd carry out the same routine and, at the end of the day, after refuelling for the last time and cleaning the aeroplanes, we'd put the cockpit covers on. If it's windy the aeroplanes are tied down and we can relax, get taken to our digs and enjoy the rest of the evening; eating, drinking and talking to friends in other teams.

Before bedtime, we agree what time to meet for breakfast and the whole routine starts again. When we finally get back to our home base, regardless of what time it is or how long the day has been, we refuel the aeroplanes, clean them and leave them ready for the next outing. It really is more than a job, it's a passion and love. How lucky can you be spending your time flying around in an old biplane, being in a team and getting paid for what you do? It is almost a unique job – we are the only professional wingwalking team in the world.

For me, display flying has to be one of the scariest things you can do and I never want to forget that fact. It's only by being afraid that you can start to think about what could go wrong and then work to the best of your ability to make the job safer. You have to go through all the 'what ifs' so you can placate your worries to an acceptable level.

> 'We get loads of applications from wingwalkers to join the team and the ones who say that they are not frightened of anything, we put in the bin.'

Does everyone have concerns or is it just me? I think they all do and they take an acceptable risk. Most of us, for example, will drive our car on a wet day at 70mph on a motorway, but for me that's also scary. Having been display flying for 43 years, I've had my scary moments but hopefully I have learnt from each and every one of them. It's the people with no fear and those who don't admit their mistakes who really worry me.

We get loads of applications from wingwalkers to join the team and the ones who say that they are not frightened of anything, we put in the bin. In all my years of doing this job, I have met a few pilots who would not admit their mistakes. I remember on one occasion getting a four-page letter from a pilot who had run out of fuel in one of our aeroplanes explaining in detail why it was not his fault (I don't think so!).

The most frightening moments I've had to endure have definitely been landing in the dark from a cross-country flight and not being able to see the runway, which taught me to always check sunset times and not to try to press on while it's still light, and losing control of my Stampe biplane in a stormy crosswind and wiping off the undercarriage. The lesson there was that I needed more training!

Flying around in a biplane built in the 1940s is a huge amount of fun. However, there are no mod-cons and no heating. Overseas flights to Ireland and Europe always meant lots of planning, with all the aviation maps spread out either on the floor of the office, and later on our long wooden tables. Then, when technology caught up, everything needed to be logged onto a satellite-navigation system.

Flying over the sea in a single-engined aircraft has its hazards and we were always careful to pick the shortest routes. You can easily get caught out with an unexpected change in the weather and we had to turn back or divert to a different airfield more than a few times, which also brings its own logistical problems when trying to get to an event on time. The old saying – time to spare, go by air – has a lot of truth in it.

On one of our many trips to Ireland, we set off in good weather and got caught up in low cloud as we coasted in over Scotland. Turning back meant returning across the sea and the map showed a glider site, so we were good to divert.

The glider site turned out to be a very narrow strip on the side of a steep hill, used as a winch-line launching site by the local glider club. What we thought was the runway was instead a boulder-strewn boggy field, and the actual runway was just a very narrow dirt strip alongside the neighbouring woodland. We missed all the rocks and boulders by sheer luck.

Luckily, there were some club members on site and we tied the aircraft down for the night and went off to find accommodation in the local town. When the weather cleared the next morning, we found ourselves in a stunning location, but not one we wanted to visit again by aircraft.

After encountering low cloud, we opted to divert to a glider site in Scotland, and although the conditions were less than ideal, we landed safely – narrowly missing a larger stone boulder.

Lessons learned

Monaco
Displaying in unbelievably bad weather and having to follow the coast from Nice to Monte Carlo even though the helicopters were grounded. Lesson learnt – don't be forced into something just to satisfy an ITV camera crew.

En route to Monaco
Flying blind in cloud with no instruments until I burst through the top of the clouds into brilliant sunshine. Following an aircraft above cloud, becoming IFR (Instrument Flying Rules), ending up CAVOK (Ceiling and Visibility OK) on top, getting lost and in French controlled airspace and being arrested on landing. Lesson learnt – don't fly if the weather is not VMC and don't try anything stupid, like following an IFR aircraft in formation in cloud.

Flying under the Severn Bridge
In bad weather, to maintain VFR [Visual Flight Rules] I learnt not to go IFR – but I also learnt not to fly again in bad weather. In formation, all three aircraft flew under the bridge and I told the CAA the next day, who then advised me that maybe I should not have been flying that day. How right were they?!

In fact, most of my scary moments have been weather related, so I hope I can now learn from that!

Maintenance
During my 43 years mucking about with old aeroplanes, I have learnt that maintenance, both normal and preventative, is the most important factor. But what have I done about it?

Well, I employ a first-rate engineer who is not frightened to spend my cash on new or overhauled parts. I go to the best engine rebuilder for our 985 cubic-inch-capacity Pratt & Whitney engine, and time has taught us that if some minor fault develops it always needs fixing, otherwise it will end up as a major snag or failure.

Stearman biplanes have dodgy brakes that can snatch, especially in wet weather, so we changed them for a disc brake set-up. Now there is no problem there.

Pre-flights are essential, but I also take the cowling off after each weekend to have a really good look around. You always have to look, check, and look again.

SSAC: Safety Standards Acknowledgement and Consent
That very long-winded title and scheme was adopted by the Civil Aviation Authority in the UK to cover various flying operators who wanted to fly passengers in historic aircraft (for instance, two-seater Spitfires); it also covers public wingwalking flights.

The scheme is based on two main issues. Firstly, you must inform your passenger of all the dangers, what exactly could go wrong, and how you could end up being injured or killed. Secondly, it made sure that the aircraft were maintained to a full public transport standard and that the pilots were able to fly to a very high standard.

In-flight warnings
A strong smell or vibration, even slight, means you should land ASAP. Don't press on to your next destination. I have had the engine in my An-2 explode in mid-air. Luckily, I was able to pull off a forced landing without any more damage to either myself, my wife, or my aeroplane.

But the scariest thing...
For me, the most frightening thing above all else was watching my children and my wife get their pilots' licences. And even worse than that was watching my son's first air display in an RF4, but it was also my proudest flying experience.

> 'A strong smell or vibration, even slight, means you should land ASAP. Don't press on to your next destination. I have had the engine in my An-2 explode in mid-air.'

Above: Rendcomb airfield from the air. Right: two of our current and wonderful wingwalkers – Kirsten Popjoy and Gemma Craig.

Looking resplendent against a clear, blue sky – our wingwalkers and pilots giving another show to remember. Left: AeroSuperBatics was recently the subject of an article in *FlyPast* and offered readers an insight into the world of display flying and wingwalking.

Above: our brilliant team posing with wingwalkers Kirsten and Gemma. Left: team leader and ex-Red Arrow Andy Cubin.

NORMAN CONQUEST 205

Chapter thirteen
AIRFIELDS AND HOUSES

Kemble Airfield

When I got back into flying and I was living at Hammerton House, I had nowhere to keep my newly purchased Stampe 1950s French biplane, and I had become good friends with Neil Wharton, a team member of the Red Arrows who lived nearby in Cirencester.

Neil was a real anti-establishment bloke and he said that he would see if I could keep my biplane at Kemble. They didn't keep any other civilian aircraft there, but he said that he'd see what he could do. Well, he discovered an RAF order, which I think was JSP 360. It was a very old document and it basically said that an officer could keep his horse on a base provided that the commanding officer gave his permission. Neil could not see why this shouldn't also work if an officer had an aeroplane.

So, this is what we did in the pub one night: I wrote on a beer matt that I had given a £1 share of my biplane to Neil, making him a part-owner. Neil then went to see his commanding officer to explain that he had a share in an old biplane with a local businessman and a Ferrari garage owner, and that he would like to keep the aeroplane at Kemble under the JSP 360 ruling. It was all agreed and the aeroplane ended up in a fantastic, heated hangar, which was used to service various RAF aircraft. Kemble was a maintenance unit airfield for the RAF.

I had to have a pass to be allowed on the airfield and after a while I also got a key for the hangar because at weekends no one worked in any of the maintenance buildings. It was run as a separate entity and the Red Arrows operated from a different part of the airfield.

I ended up keeping three aeroplanes at Kemble

> '**I used to give flying displays during all the Battle of Britain celebrations and also private displays when the commanding officer wanted his visitors to be entertained.**'

and it was a very happy relationship. I used to give flying displays during all the Battle of Britain celebrations and also private displays when the commanding officer wanted his visitors to be entertained. During the flying season, I would display at most of the RAF stations and I obtained permission to operate after hours, landing and taking off from the grass that was next to the runway and directly in front of the fire station, which was manned 24/7. I became very friendly with the firemen and would sometimes have my lunch and tea breaks with them on the turf since they were very bored most of the time.

Kemble was a maintenance unit, so all the aircraft engineering facilities were on the base and I got various small jobs done on my aeroplanes through the back door. There was one security officer, called Officer Flynn, who was very good at his job. He would check everyone's car boots and luckily he only ever stopped me once when I, of course, had nothing untoward in my car, but I knew that he was desperate to catch me out somehow.

Well, his chance came on a Sunday when I was refuelling my aeroplane from jerry cans in the hangar and he caught me red-handed. He told me that he was going to report me on Monday morning and that I would be in big trouble. He was so pleased at having got me at long last.

He was about to drive off when I suddenly remembered something that I had been told by the Squadron Leader, who was the senior air traffic controller and also a good friend of mine. I shouted, 'Officer Flynn, do you have to report me tomorrow?'

With a big smile on his face, he said that he had no choice since refuelling in the hangar was very dangerous and of course he was right. I said that I understood and that it was a very stupid thing to do and that I had no excuses, but as he was about to drive off I asked him if the police had managed to find out who had driven on the wet tarmac and left tyre marks all over it. I said that I knew the station commander was very annoyed about it all and had heard that he was determined for the police to find the culprit. I also knew that Officer Flynn had seen who'd done it and had agreed not to report the incident.

'I suppose,' I said, 'you'll also have to report that, even though it happened several weeks ago, since you know who the guilty person is.'

Flynn went bright red and drove off at 100mph, but needless to say I was not reported. That said, I had to be very careful and act by the letter of the law from then on.

When the airfield was sold, the RAF had to pack up shop. They made all of their civilian workforce redundant or offered them employment elsewhere. My aeroplane was the last to leave and I then moved my business to a smart new hangar at Staverton Airport in Gloucestershire.

Yugo Cars and Mitsubishi Motors liveried aircraft in the hangar at Staverton.

Staverton Airport

My operation was based here for several years and I had a very nice set-up in the new hangar, which I'd had built to my specifications. It also had a 25-year lease with very little outgoings. We had to fit in with air traffic control but we soon got them on our side, and during busy times at the weekend the refuellers would always sort us out first, and we would be given priority to both take-off and land because they knew we had a precise timeslot at whatever show we were going to.

The airfield could be very busy with circuit traffic at the weekends. In the early days of wingwalking, our girls used to take off and land strapped onto the aeroplanes and sometimes they would be standing on the wing for up to an hour and a half. One time, I was heading back to Gloucester and the air traffic controller told me that I was fifth in the queue to land. I could see that a small aeroplane had called that it was number one in the queue and ready to land and, as it was actually quite a long way out, I cut in front of it and called finals number one to land short finals. The controller got rather cross and told me to go around and overshoot but I ignored him since back then the service was an advisory service and not a full control service.

I landed right at the start of the runway and

Above: team photo outside the hangar at Staverton.
Right: waiting to fly with my formation pilot Brendan O'Brien.

turned off while the aircraft I'd cut up was still a long way on its finals. I parked up and the controller came storming down to tell me off and said that I would be reported to the Civil Aviation Authority. I told him that I could see that my wingwalker was very tired and cold and so, for her safety, I'd decided to land knowing that I could land clear without affecting the following aircraft's circuit. He went off in a rage.

Back at home that night, I discovered from Anne that I had in fact cut her up when she was about to land her aircraft during her first solo flight...

Hammerton House

When we moved from the farm, more than 40 years ago, we bought a typical Cotswold house that stood in 20 acres with two separate cottages. We sold one of the cottages after three years and got back half of what we had paid for the whole house. Property prices were rapidly going up at that time. I turned the garages and stables into a workshop and garage, and started my racing car restoration business there.

It was a great family home and Anne, of course, made it a wonderful place to live. All our three children had a very nice childhood being able to run about and play outside in the garden whenever they wanted. Anne had done a lovely job in the garden and she became very friendly with the well-known gardener Rosemary Verey and ended up running her gardening classes for her, as well as flying with her to visit her customers' gardens

Rendcomb Aerodrome Ltd

From the 1970s to the 2000s, my family home was Hammerton House near Cirencester. I flew every weekend and displayed at around 120 events every summer during the season, which started in May and ended in September. Between events, if I had time, I would land in a field near my house (called Aeroplane Field) and Anne used to come and collect me and take me home, which was about one and a half miles away, or she would sometimes bring all three children up to the field and we would have a picnic.

This field, in fact, was used by another Norman family (no relation) in the 1930s and their friends also used to land and have a picnic lunch. Torquil Norman, now Sir Torquil, also landed his Tiger Moth here and his house was even closer than mine, being just one field away. I can't remember where, but Torquil and I met and discovered that we both had a passion for aeroplanes and flying.

During the summer of 1990, I was flying from Staverton Airport, where I had my own hangar. I would drop off our three children – Zoe, Nina and Sam – at Cheltenham Ladies' College and Cheltenham Boys' Junior School and go onto the airport, which was all in all about 10 or 12 miles away.

One day Anne gave me an old book that she had picked up from a secondhand dealer in Cirencester about the First World War and, to my amazement, it mentioned a Royal Flying Corps Training Aerodrome just one and a half miles from my home. I rushed up to try to find it and recognised some First World War buildings that were surrounded by ploughed fields.

I was very excited and knocked on the door of the large farmhouse opposite the site. An elderly gentleman came to the door and asked me what I wanted in rather a stern voice. When I explained that I lived just over the valley in Hammerton House, he immediately said, 'Oh, so you're the pilot who flies low over the house every weekend!'

This was not a very good start. The farmer, Mr Farnsworth, asked me in and we went into his sitting room. I wanted to know about the Royal Flying Corps operating from his farm and so he told me how his father was approached by the Army to take over his land to turn it into one of the first Flying Corps training fields. He said that over 3,500 men and women worked there, all with the task of training pilots who were then sent over to France to join the action.

I was fascinated by all of this and I asked him if it would be possible to rent a small section of the field that could be used as a landing strip next to the one hut that was still standing, but which was in a very sad state. He said he would talk to his three sons and think about it.

I telephoned Torquil Norman that evening. He had no idea about the airfield and told me that I had to try and somehow do a deal and, if possible, purchase the historic aerodrome. I told him that I didn't have any spare cash and that I would have to

RFC Rendcomb

RFC Rendcomb was first opened in 1916 as part of the British aerial campaign in the First World War. By then, so many pilots had been lost on the Western Front that new training airfields had to be opened to train replacement aircrew. Rendcomb was built to meet this demand. It trained young pilots and received Bristol Fighters, and an aircraft and engine repair facility was later added.

Two former aviators who spent time at RFC Rendcomb were Lieutenant William Leefe Robinson VC (who, in September 1916, became the first person to shoot down a German Zeppelin over Britain) and Keith Park (later to become Air Chief Marshal and command RAF Fighter Command Group 11 during the Battle of Britain).

Aircrew training and the building-up of new squadrons at Rendcomb was a success, as is illustrated by the departure of 48 Squadron to the Western Front on 8 March 1917. All 18 members of the aircrew flew to Lympne in Kent, where they refuelled, crossed the Channel, and arrived at Bertangles Aerodrome (five miles north of Amiens) fully serviceable that same morning.

This so impressed the higher-ups that Major General Trenchard, the RFC Commander, reported to the War Office: 'I would like to point out that No. 48 Squadron arrived out here with 18 machines intact all on the same day before noon. This is the first squadron like this, and it was undoubtedly due to the excellent arrangements made and to the training of the Squadron.'

Once the war ended, the need for training pilots decreased. In 1921, RFC Rendcomb was closed and returned to the family who had tilled it for six generations.

The inside of the Pancho Barn all set up ready for a corporate day, my beautiful Gipsy Moth and Piper Cub aircraft helping to add to the atmosphere.

We have held many amazing and fun parties at Rendcomb, and my wingwalkers always come up with some great costume ideas.

NORMAN CONQUEST 213

214 NORMAN CONQUEST

Many of the Rendcomb parties have been for the Red Arrows and their guests. We always manage to put on a great evening and have some fantastic live music.

sell something to pay for my half. I also didn't know if the farmer would sell and, even if he would, I didn't know how much he would ask for, but Torquil told me that he would fund it if needed.

The next day, I visited Mr Farnsworth again and he told me that the field (which was around 70 acres) was an important bit of land since it was right in front of his house and farm buildings. He had spoken to his sons and partners, and they all wanted to go their own way and would consider a sale but they wanted top market price. I stuck my hand out and said that we'd buy it providing that we could get planning permission, and so an agreement was reached. I telephoned Torquil and told him that I had agreed to purchase the farm subject to planning. He asked how much, and when I told him, his immediate reaction was to say, 'Well done', although the price was probably double the normal farmland rate at the time.

Now the fun began. We submitted planning and just before the meeting a local property man and aviator told me that I should withdraw the application because he knew it would be rejected. He suggested that Torquil and I meet both the local parish councils and put our proposals to them, explaining that we would operate the airfield solely for our own use and only operate historic aircraft in the same way that car collectors build garages to store their old motors.

We had several meetings and I felt that half were on our side. I then arranged a meeting with the chief planning officer at the Cotswold District Parish Council and he said during the meeting that he would not give it his backing. He was worried that we might sell the field later on and that it could become a flying training school with aeroplanes droning around overhead all day every day.

I suggested the following, which I hoped would cancel out the planners' fears: 180 days' flying a year; 35 take-offs in any one day; no night flying; no microlights; no helicopters.

These restrictions allowed the chief planning officer to approve the application and we were full speed ahead. We built two blocks with four hangars in each block, so we had eight hangars in total; Torquil was to have one whole block while I had the other. Of course, I still had no funds so Torquil paid all the bills and I arranged all the building works, and researched every detail down to the grass-seed mixture used for historic aerodromes, which I had made up specially and sown.

I had already turned my good chum Nick Mason on to aviation and persuaded him to buy my hangar lease that I had at Staverton Airport. I had a tenant who wanted to take it over for his Spitfire and collection of old racing cars, and Nick was happy to put it into his portfolio. This, however, did not raise enough money for me to give Torquil my half of the costs. But then I also persuaded Nick to buy half of my share in Rendcomb, which gave him two of

The engine shed

A few years after we had bought and moved into the airfield, the AeroSuperBatics office was down in a small building in the middle of the airfield that we called the Officers' Mess. It soon became obvious that we were outgrowing the office and needed more room and privacy, rather than a building that was open to visitors and other shared owners of the airfield.

I approached the local farmer because there was a building just off the main road that bordered the airfield. It was falling down and, after doing some research, I discovered that this had been the power-generating room that housed two engines producing power to the workshops on the airfield, during the Royal Flying Corps days.

I managed to buy what was left of the building from the farmer and our local builder, Alan Plowman, did a first-class job rebuilding the whole place in keeping with Royal Flying Corps theme. It was a fantastic place to work. We could taxi our team's aeroplanes right up to the front door in between our training flights. Alan had various other jobs, which included driving a Mitsubishi Shogun with a Cri-Cri (the smallest twin-engined aeroplane in the world) perched on the roof. He also used to drive our Utterly Butterly display unit to the shows and hand out thousands of slices of bread with Utterly Butterly spread on it.

When I'd built a new office next to my new hanger in preparation for my retirement (whenever that's going to be), my son Sam bought the Engine Shed and got planning permission to convert it into his house.

The Engine Shed at Rendcomb served well as office space for AeroSuperBatics, but has since been converted into a house by my son Sam.

NORMAN CONQUEST 215

my four hangars, so I managed to pay Torquil and everyone was happy. Nick has made good use of his hangars and has his car workshops there, with three engineers working on his cars.

Torquil and I were so happy with our new purchase. It was the start of an amazing adventure. Over a period of time between 1990 and 2020, the owners of Rendcomb Aerodrome managed to end up owning a separate house each surrounding the airfield. I used my house, which was called the Engine Shed, as my office.

On the northern side of the airfield, there was an old disused quarry and a large brick wall, which had been the rifle range during the RFC days. I thought that if I could get planning permission to rebuild the rifle range and turn it into a smart VIP hangar, the building could be used not only to house aeroplanes but also for corporate parties and events. We were fed up with using marquees, which were rather basic.

So again I approached the local farmer and asked if it would be possible for me to purchase this section of land, which had a road running from the main road and included the quarry (with its own slurry pit full of cow shit). Down the end of a long track there was another farm building, but it was falling down with three walls and a tin roof – and not much else!

Anne suggested asking the farmer if he would also sell me this old building as part of a package deal when I negotiated to buy the rifle range, which we now call Pancho Barn (named after the famous Florence Lowe 'Pancho' Barnes, a wonderful American flyer in the 1920s). The farmer agreed to sell me both the rifle range and the disused building, luckily for not very much money.

We immediately started building Pancho Barn as a new corporate building. By chance, it also luckily

My small office next to Merkel Air has proven to be a very pleasant place to work and much of our planning is now done from here.

Merkel Air

I'm always thinking and planning ahead for my retirement. I managed to get planning permission to build a new purpose-built hangar on this bit of land that I owned, which I called Merkel Air. It gives me the opportunity to keep an aeroplane, a few old motorcycles and a couple of old cars all in one place. I also applied for planning for a small office next to Merkel Air. It has turned out to be a lovely place to work and my current AeroSuperBatics team (Lorraine, Dave, Kirsten, Gemma and Andy) run our public wingwalks and airshows from there. I have a great bunch of really hard-working team members at the moment who are all very motivated.

Every few years or so, we'd end up selecting new wingwalkers to join the company and the flow of new, young, bright people always brought fresh ideas and enthusiasm with them. We never liked seeing our wingwalkers go, but they would either get married and move away or have children. It's too risky for mums to fly in the airshows, and difficult to be away from home for long periods of time.

We get so many people wanting to join the team, and I think the word has got out that if you're a wingwalker you get to travel all over the world to different venues. It probably also helps that one has a good chance of meeting a nice pilot or aviation-minded person.

coincided with my daughter Nina's wedding. It was a great place to have a party. We had some wonderful events in that building that were great fun, and I eventually sold Pancho Barn to Nick Mason because he needed some more storage space.

I completely forgot about the farm building at the bottom of the road, which was called Rainbow Barn on the Ordnance Survey map. Sometime later, I tried to get planning permission to turn this building into a dwelling. The Cotswold District Parish Council planning inspector came and visited the building, and told me that it was obviously derelict and had no separate entrance to the road so they wouldn't be granting any planning permission.

I got a local builder in and we picked up and replaced all the Cotswold stones, rebuilding the walls that had fallen down, along with the tin roof and timbers (all terribly rotten and rusted), which we took off and replaced with new timbers and tin. I then went back to the farmer, who was now jolly pleased to see me because he was sure that he was going to sell me some more land, and I asked if I could have a 10m-wide strip of land from the main road to Rainbow Barn. He agreed to sell it to me for £6,000 an acre, which was a very high price at the time, especially since the drive was over 800 yards long, so it ended up costing me a bit of money.

I then got the planning inspector to visit the barn again. He asked if I'd rebuilt it and I said no, we'd just picked up the stones and put them back. I asked whether I could now have planning permission to turn it back into a house because there was both a separate entrance from the road to the building and an existing farm track running to the barn.

> 'The best thing about the place was its situation – totally secluded... the only drawback was all those noisy aeroplanes!'

I have to say the planner was very surprised at what I'd done and said I would have to submit formal plans, which I did. The planning was then refused again on the grounds that the track leading to the barn came within 11 metres of a badger set! So again I went back to the farmer and bought another 10m-wide strip of land and we diverted the road around the badger set. That badger set cost me another £6,000.

We finally got the planning permission for a two-bedroom cottage, but we kept adding extensions and finally ended up with a lovely home that Anne and I could move into after selling Hammerton House and downsizing. Of course, we realised that we had downsized too much and finally ended up with five bedrooms, four bathrooms and a grandchildren's dormitory, as well as two large kitchens and two sitting rooms – and in a separate building, a sunset shed, a walled vegetable garden and an old-fashioned greenhouse.

The best thing about the place was its situation – totally secluded, and from the garden you can't see a single property. The only drawback was all those noisy aeroplanes!

Chapter fourteen
MOTORCYCLES

The first motorcycle that I bought was the BSA Bantam I had when I was about 13 years old, which I used to tear around our garden on, cutting up the lawn. When I started taking it out on the road, I wore a crash helmet with a big scarf hiding my face in case the police saw me, but luckily I was never stopped. When I was 16, I persuaded Mum to let me have a 250cc Kawasaki, which was a two-stroke and really went well. The big thing was trying to top 100mph but I never managed it; 90mph was the fastest it would go.

In 1971, the Honda CB750 four-cylinder came out, which was an amazing bike, beautifully made, so fast, and looked fantastic. I took it to the farm when we lived there and used to chase hares in the water meadow with my children sitting on the back. I only recently sold it about 15 years ago to Nick Mason. I don't know if he still has it.

My great motorbiking friend Geoffrey St John, who died a couple of years ago, was a very good engineer and got me interested in vintage motorcycles. I have worked my way through a few, including the Land Speed Record-breaking AJSs, Vincents, Scotts, and various others. But it was the very early pre-1915 'Pioneer' bikes that I was really passionate about.

This came about because we would always visit our friends Alain and Alison de Cadenet in California after the airshow season had finished in Europe at the end of September. Alain and I would go out on a couple of his motorbikes, either Vincents or Ducatis, and head up to the hills, often stopping at the Rock Cafe for a coffee. On one occasion, Alain and I met Jay Leno at his garage and he took his aero-engined car with us as his outriders on the way to the Cafe.

We'd visit the local airfields and often ended up at Bud Ekins' place. Bud was Mr Motorbiker, such a lovely, fun guy – but he had to like you. He was, of course, a great friend and mentor to Steve McQueen. He taught Steve all about riding in the

The 1913 Flying Merkel: 998cc, 85mph, one gear, one brake and my favourite machine out of everything mechanical that I have ever owned.

Bud Ekins, famous for his friendship with Steve McQueen as well as his skill on two wheels, has been an inspiration to many. Meeting Ekins was a fantastic moment and we remained in touch. He eventually agreed to sell me his Flying Merkel, which I have used a number of times on the London to Brighton Pioneer Run (right).

'It was only after my many visits over a three-year period, chatting and talking to Bud, that he finally agreed to sell me the Merkel. Plus, I rather think he liked the fact that I was an airshow pilot.'

desert and Steve was selected to represent America in the six-day trials held behind the Iron Curtain in East Germany. Bud also did the car chase with McQueen during the making of *Bullitt* and he did the jump on the Triumph over the fence in *The Great Escape*. Bud told me that he was paid $1,250 for that stunt, which at the time was the most any stunt rider had ever been paid.

Bud also told me that when they started doing the motorbike chase in the film, the director asked Steve to slow down a bit because the stunt riders playing the Germans chasing him could not keep up. Steve was not happy to go slower because he wanted it to look like he was really trying to get away. In the end, they got rid of the other stunt riders and both Bud and Steve dressed up as Germans instead. They did the chase themselves without their faces showing and were edited in so it looked like they were chasing Steve.

Steve was not allowed to do the jump because if he got injured they'd have to stop filming. One evening after filming, Bud wanted to check the ramp they had dug in the field for the big jump. He decided to do the jump with no one looking except Steve, and it all went well – except that it was just too much for Steve, who jumped on his bike and charged down towards the ramp in the grass as it was getting dark and flew over the fence. It was kept quiet, but at least Steve was now happy.

The first time that I visited Bud with Alain, the place was full of motorcycles. I fell in love with his 1913 Flying Merkel, still in its 100-year-old original paint, and wanted to know everything about the bike. Bud told me that it was bought new by a wealthy man who lived in New Mexico and that he used it on the road until 1923, when it then ended up in his emerald mine, with its back wheel taken off, being used to power the electric lights.

Bud bought the bike and found the back wheel. In 1913, it was one of the fastest machines on the planet, capable of going nearly 100mph. It had a 1,000cc V-twin engine and just one gear with an Eclipse clutch that had to be slipped to get you going.

Flying Merkels went on to be the bike to have on

The Flying Merkel pictured with my 1912 Indian. The Merkel is without doubt the last thing I would ever part with if circumstances so dictated. It may not be the easiest machine to ride, but it is certainly the most enjoyable and thrilling.

Top: my 1967 Triumph TR6C – a classic British motorcycle.
Above: a replica of the Triumph on which Bud Ekins won the 1957 Big Bear Endurance Run.
Right: my Suzuki 750RR was featured in *Fast Bikes* magazine.

the half-mile, banked, wooden board tracks called motordromes that opened up in the USA. It was only after my many visits over a three-year period, chatting and talking to Bud, that he finally agreed to sell me the Merkel. Plus, I think he rather liked the fact that I was an airshow pilot flying 1940s Boeing Stearman aircraft with wingwalkers.

We rebuilt the engine and it's still in its original paint and goes like a rocket every year during the London to Brighton Pioneer Run. Merkel's advertising slogan was 'The Next Thing To Flying' and in 1913 it really was. Maybe that's what hooked me.

I've had a few bikes, not because I was collecting them or with any hope that I might earn a profit, but always just for the joy that I got from riding them and going on trips by myself or with friends.

I find the early bikes are a challenge to ride and that there is a lot to do. You have to adjust the carburettor fuel, air levers, the ignition advance and retard, and control the drip feed of oil to lubricate the engine's internals, most of which eventually ends up all over your clothes. Some have only one gear and a clutch that needs to be slipped when setting off at a slow speed, and others need to be paddled with your feet to get moving before engaging the engine. But I really love a mechanical challenge.

My bikes at the moment...
- 1913 Flying Merkel
- 1912 Indian 1,000cc twin
- 1912 Douglas (with two friends, we do the Pioneer Run on those bikes)
- 1931 Indian Scout, the favourite mount for Wall of Death riders
- 1950 Vincent Rapide
- 1950 Vincent Rapide (an ex-American red one – the American importer told Vincent he could not sell black bikes so all the bikes exported to the US were painted red)
- Replica Triumph that Bud Ekins rode to win the Big Bear
- Triumph Bonneville
- 1967 Triumph TR6
- Suzuki 750RR
- Buell
- Harley-Davidson 883

Suzuki 750RR

I used to race my Maserati and a few other cars at Donington Park circuit in the 1970s and 1980s. One day I was walking around Tom Wheatcroft's Donington Grand Prix Collection museum when I noticed this special Suzuki hiding in a corner. I discovered that it'd been used on the Friday evening before the 1986 UK vs USA Transatlantic Trophy races by Kevin Schwantz for a few laps around the circuit because he'd never raced at Donington before, and also never raced in the wet and it was pouring with rain.

Suzuki sent it because Schwantz's race bike hadn't turned up and Barry Sheene and Mick Grant managed to borrow Rutter's Suzuki. The rest is history. Schwantz won four out of eight races, falling in one race in the wet and finishing second in the others. It was a defining moment in the career of Kevin Schwantz, and Barry Sheene got him a wildcard ride in Grand Prix racing the same year.

My bike is a cracking one-off, being the homologation limited-edition 1986 bike.

Harley-Davidson 883

The Harley-Davidson dealership in the UK contacted AeroSuperBatics asking if they could bring all of their dealers to Rendcomb for wingwalking. They all turned up on very smart and new motorbikes, and had also brought the latest 883 Harley, which they were selling to the dealers as a race bike in a series that was going to take place at the British Sports Bike Championships.

At the end of the day, the boss of Harley-Davidson said how pleased they were with the event and, if I could get an invoice ready, he would pay the next day. His parting words were, 'Unless you want me to leave the race bike.' We called it all square, and that's how I got the 883.

Pioneer Run

The Pioneer Run is my favourite event of the year. It's organised by the Sunbeam Motorcycle Club and it's an event for pre-1915 veteran machines. The route starts from Tattenham Corner at Epsom Downs Racecourse and finishes at Madeira Drive in Brighton. There are usually around 400 entrants from all over the world, with the oldest machines built before 1905. My 1913 Flying Merkel is one of the fastest bikes on the run and although the event is not a race, it is jolly nice to overtake fellow competitors on the way. It will do 85mph and only has one (not very powerful) rear brake.

I also have a 1912 Indian and a 1912 Douglas, which I loan to a couple of friends so we can all enjoy the run together. The route takes us down Reigate Hill, which is very steep and, aside from using the brakes, I've also worn out more than one pair of boots using the soles as additional braking power!

The best part of the day is the relief of getting to Brighton in one piece without breaking down and then having fish and chips on the seafront, talking to mates, and looking and chatting about our machines – sheer joy.

Top: the 1912 Douglas is another motorcycle eligible for the London to Brighton Pioneer Run and I frequently lend it to friends so they can also take part. Left: adopting the necessary position atop my 1929 1,000cc AJS Land Speed Record attempt motorcycle – now part of the National Motorcycle Museum collection.

Desert conditions make for interesting riding – even when on a modern and well-equipped motorcycle such as my 2009 BMW 1250 GS. I will admit to falling off a number of times on the sand.

Around the Mediterranean

Our leader Nick Laing (who also owns an amazing VIP travel company called Steppes East) got us to the Mediterranean after 18 months of him doing all the planning and the rest of our gang doing very little (and in my case, nothing all). I knew I had to meet Nick at the Eurotunnel by 10:15am on the day of our departure. I knew we were hoping to go around the Mediterranean, but I had no idea what route we'd take. The team consisted of Nick Laing, Tim von Halle, Myles Sandy, Nick Hanbury-Williams, and Charlie Brocket. I was riding a BMW 1250 GS 2009, which is the one modern motorbike that I own.

I turned up early, as I always do (being well-trained in air-display timing, where if you missed your 15-minute slot you didn't get paid) and Nick, Myles and I headed down through France on our way to meet the others in Alicante. We got the overnight ferry to Oran in western Algeria and I had to share a cabin with Charlie, which made me feel sorry for his missus.

When we arrived in Algeria, we experienced the first of many three-to-five-hour waits to clear customs; paying for various licences and fees while the officers got as much cash as they could from us wealthy tourists. I don't blame them because they needed the money much more than we did.

We left on the first leg of 250 miles to Algiers via a scenic route along the coast. I remember beautiful rolling hills. We had a 12-car special forces police escort, maybe because of Lord Brocket's presence and the fact that a tourist had been shot a few weeks earlier. We were told that if our bike broke down we had to leave it and jump in a police vehicle, which was all a bit scary. We stopped in Tipaza to look at the Roman site, which was the first of many.

Our escort cleared the roads as we got near Algiers, forcing the locals to pull over while we raced through at dangerously high speed. That wasn't really what we wanted, and 12 hours after leaving Oran we finally arrived and were pleased to get off the bikes.

We spent a day looking around Algiers and walking through the Kasbah. Everything was run down. The next day, we set off towards Batna. The ride took us up through the hills, through twisting

Our trip around the Mediterranean was great fun and we rode through some amazing landscapes, pausing to cool off in the Dead Sea and partake in an all-over mud mask!

gorges, past the local Berbers going about their daily lives. I reminded myself that I must never complain about anything ever again.

We stopped at another Roman site in Timgad, which was impressive. Then we headed to the border and crossed into Tunisia, which was very clean and tidy with orderly rows of olive trees, clean loos, and no plastic bags. We visited Carthage, the birthplace of Hannibal. The roads were great because there was no traffic. We stopped at the amphitheatre of El Jem but it was hard to imagine that what went on there classified as entertainment.

It took several hours to cross the border into Libya and we were issued with Libyan numberplates and received more cash. Petrol was cheap at 17 pence per litre. We stopped at Sabratha, one of the three cities that made up the Roman Tripolitania. Mussolini addressed his troops there.

Tripoli was a bustling town with chic hotels, street stalls and friendly, smiling faces. The next day, we had a long trip of about 460 miles from western Libya to Ajdabiya in the east. There were lots of sheep, camels and goats walking over the road, and many Greek ruins. We left Apollonia and headed towards Tobruk, and the sky turned very dark and we were hit by a sandstorm. Our speed was reduced to below 30mph, with visibility down to 30 metres. All I could see was Nick's tail light so I had to remain close – Charlie was behind me but I could only just make out his headlight. The sides of the road disappeared and we were only kept on track by the odd car and lorry that passed us.

This went on for over two hours and our mouths were full of grit, our eyes were sore and the sand was everywhere. Suddenly, it stopped. We rode into a wall of steady rain and we could then see that our bikes were sandblasted with the windscreens opaque and all the flash chrome on Charlie's Harley scoured off. When we arrived at our overnight stop I got in the shower with my full riding kit on in an attempt to remove the sand. When morning came, we looked around the war memorials, both British and German. It was very sad that there were so many young who were killed.

We headed for the Egyptian border, where chaos erupted because of swine flu. We were escorted into a small room where we waited for a doctor, and masked, giggling girls took our temperatures. We then ended up going to nine different offices at the border and six hours later, minus another large payment, we were on our way to Marsa Matruh. The Egyptian roads were chaos and very dangerous, with cars in our outside lane coming towards us at speed.

We visited a small museum at El Alamein, which gives prominence to the Italians in the battle that occurred there. We headed south-east across the

'We left Apollonia and headed towards Tobruk, and the sky turned very dark and we were hit by a sandstorm. Our speed was reduced to below 30mph, with visibility down to 30 metres.'

desert towards Cairo and, as we got closer, we hit gridlocked traffic and Nick's bike got stuck in second gear, but we made it to our flash hotel because we all thought that we deserved a treat. That night, we had a full five-star evening meal and both Myles and I woke up to a severe dose of the runs, but we soldiered on with both us having to stop more than once and disappear into the bushes before being caught short.

The pyramids lived up to all expectations, as did our visit to the Cairo museum, which holds an amazing collection of artefacts, including the magnificent contents of Tutankhamen's tomb.

The next day, the Harley-Davidson Cairo Club turned up to wish us well and escort us on our way east, passing under the Suez Canal, where Anne had learnt to swim when her dad, Major George Hackett, was there after the war.

We rode into Sinai heading south. The centre of Sinai was very beautiful with sandhills sculpted into myriad shapes by the wind. We arrived at St Catherine's Monastery, which is the oldest monastery in the world and the site where Moses is meant to have seen the burning bush. It was a truly magical place and has left a lasting impression on me. In fact, for me the highlight of our whole trip was sitting and watching the evening sun as it lit up the holy place.

We cleared customs in Nuweiba, caught a ferry across the Red Sea and eventually arrived in Aqaba

'We were met by the leader of the Royal Jordanian Flying Falcons. I was friends with the team and had spent many days with them at various airshows in the UK and Europe.'

in Jordan. I kept thinking of Lawrence's attack from the desert.

We were met by the leader of the Royal Jordanian Flying Falcons. I was friends with the team and had spent many days with them at various airshows in the UK and Europe. We were rushed through customs and taken to our smart hotel, and the next morning we were collected and taken to their airfield as guests. We ate a wonderful Arabic breakfast with the team and were given our own private air display – what a treat! That afternoon we visited Petra, which dates from 2000 BC.

When we turned north, the whole atmosphere became very relaxed and enjoyable. There were no roadside cafes and, after a morning spent riding, we stopped by the side of the road where a fresh sheepskin was hanging and a basic barbecue was on the go. We ate our lamb sitting down in the sand Arabic-style. While we were eating, a car pulled up and the young girl who was looking after the sheep, watching them graze on any greenery they could find, spoke to the man. She then called out a name and one sheep walked over to her, which she sold to the driver, I guess to be eaten and killed that night. I was amazed and felt rather sad.

We headed towards Amman along a spectacular scenic road that's known as the King's Highway and suddenly dropped down to visit the Dead Sea. We caked ourselves in the filthy volcanic mud and floated about laughing at each other and acting like children, which for me and Charlie was pretty normal behaviour.

We left Amman via the Roman site at Jerash and headed to the Syrian border. Nick, our leader, said how we had developed natural riding habits over those first few weeks forged by our own individual characteristics. Namely, Nick led; Tim, who was Germanic, liked a precise order with a set distance between each bike; I was more used to formation flying, so sat very close to Nick's rear indicator and

Even our motorcycle journey wasn't without some aircraft content and we were fortunate to meet up with the Royal Jordanian Flying Falcons, who treated us to our own private display.

NORMAN CONQUEST 231

was in the same spot every time he looked in the mirror. Nick Hanbury-Williams and Myles both liked their own space and paid no attention to Tim's rules, while Charlie just went wherever he liked, joking with everyone.

The Syrian people we met were very friendly and we stayed in a lovely house in the middle of Damascus. The old town was a special place. Anne flew into Damascus and I was very pleased to collect her from the airport because I was really missing her. It was the longest that we'd ever been apart since we got married in 1967 – 42 years previously.

We spent a great couple of days together in Damascus and then rode 750 miles together across the Syrian desert to Aleppo. We got very hot because the outside temperature was over 40 degrees Celsius but we listened to Mark Knopfler, who is a friend and keen biker, playing *Telegraph Road* – it was just wonderful. We visited dead cities and provincial Roman towns with Anne, and I was sad when I dropped her off at the airport for her flight home.

We carried on through the Taurus Mountains of southern Turkey and spent two nights in Cappadocia, which is a beautiful place. Two days later we were in Istanbul and we visited all the sites there, including the Blue Mosque, where I really got shouted at for not taking off my shoes – a big mistake!

On the way back home, via Bulgaria and Serbia, we met very heavy-handed border thugs. Kosovo was full of new housing, which I guess was a result of the war. After 14 hours' riding and eight border check points, we crossed into Montenegro and then rode on to Dubrovnik.

We headed up the beautiful Dalmatian coast and stopped in Trieste. The next day, Charlie and I were keen to meet up with our wives and families in the south of France, where we both had holiday houses. We put our foot down or, rather, twisted our throttles and sped at much too high a speed into Italy and then France along the coast to our pads.

It was an amazing trip and, in total, it took 42 days. We crossed 17 countries and 24 border controls, took three ferries and rode 9,500 miles.

Another trip on two wheels – this time with Anne and the 'normal' gang. We rode from Las Vegas to Aspen in the mountains, returning across 'cowboy country'.

Chris-Craft Cobra speedboat

As I mentioned earlier, after one season my dad gave his 1955 Chris-Craft Cobra speedboat to his best friend Bill Larkin. Bill was the man behind Larkin's Peanuts, which were sold from the 1950s until the 1970s in every football stadium on match days. Bill was larger than life and always good fun to be around. I guess that's why my dad liked him so much.

When Bill was not very well before he died, I went to visit him and we had a nice talk about old times and he told me what fun he had with my dad. Anyway, at the end of his garden was the Chris-Craft and he said that I should take it because he wanted to give it to me. It was very kind of him, but having got it home I quickly realised that it was not in the best condition.

Over time, we got the big 331 cubic-inch Chrysler Hemi engine going and I decided to take it up to Lake Windermere and enter it for the last Windermere Motor Boat Racing Club speed event before the speed limit was imposed. We booked into a flash hotel on the lake and Anne, Zoe, Nina, and Sam all had a lovely time running the boat around. On the Friday, the racing club held the speed trials and Zoe, my elder daughter, came on the boat as my crew. It went really well and we ended up winning the speed trial.

The next day was the race and the course was five laps around the lake. Along with the boys in front of the clubhouse, there was a very big crowd watching – I suppose because it was the last race meeting and so marked the end of a series of amazing water speed records set at Windermere.

As the fastest boat, I was the last to start in the handicap race and I had to make up a full lap on the slower boats. This time Nina, my youngest daughter, was my crew member. We set off at a real pace and, although the lake was rough and the boat was taking a pounding, we were catching and passing the other racers all the time. Then, on the second or third lap there was a bang and we started sinking fast when we were a good 200 yards from the shore, right in front of the clubhouse.

The race was red flagged and the rescue Zodiac came rushing over to get us off the boat. I steered towards the shore and got Nina to sit on the front of the boat so she would not get caught on anything if the boat went down. The rescue crew tried to get us to abandon the ship but, although we were sinking, I kept it afloat by going around 5mph. I got close to the shore and Nina leaped off to safety and dry land, then I closed the throttle and sunk right in front of the clubhouse and all the spectators. I swam ashore to claps from the crowd and Anne came over to check we were all OK and gave me some dry clothes to get into.

A plank had popped because the screws holding the bottom of the boat together had become hardened over the years from being in salt water. Another rebuild and several years went by, and with the help of Bob (a retired aircraft engineer and a keen boatman who lived on his small sailing boats, one near Poole and the other in Spain) we managed to get the Cobra looking really good and running again.

Anne and I decided we would give it one last fling and we towed the boat down to Lake Maggiore in northern Italy as the ASDEC (Associazione Scafi d'Epoca e Classici) were holding a rally for vintage and classic boats. We stayed with a couple of friends in a wonderful hotel and spent a few days travelling around the lake visiting restaurants. We decided, however, that we'd sell the boat because it was so costly in terms of both time and cash, and that with the funds I would buy a new car.

My dad's Chris-Craft Cobra was given back to me by Bill Larkin, but required a lot of work. Once seaworthy, we entered it into a speed event on Lake Windermere, but a 'popped' plank cut our weekend short.

Chapter fifteen
INTO THE FUTURE

Royal Air Force 614 Squadron is a general support squadron with a variety of personnel to support defence at home and overseas. The Squadron was reformed in Cardiff after a 57-year absence to provide a hub for reservists in the region. It recruits from South Wales and the surrounding area. The Squadron has a fantastic Second World War record, operating in a variety of roles including bombing, pathfinding, and dropping supplies to partisans in the Balkans. Later on, from 1946 to 1957, it was reformed as a fighter unit flying Spitfires and de Havilland Vampires.

Her Majesty The Queen appointed me Honorary Air Commodore to the Squadron, which I was very proud to accept. I have really enjoyed being involved and helping out anywhere that I can. My squadron was employed to help testing during the coronavirus pandemic and they have done a fantastic job.

Reservists play an important role for the Royal Air Force – they represent around 20 percent of our fighting force and can be deployed at short notice wherever they might be needed. It not only saves the country money but also makes for a very flexible Air Force.

Anne had been with her father, Major George Hackett, to the garden party at Buckingham Palace before, but I had never been. Anne and I were very excited because it was shortly after I had been appointed Honorary Air Commodore of 614 Squadron and it was a chance to dress up in my RAF uniform.

We arrived at the palace very early on a lovely summer's day and there was already a very long queue because it there'd been a terrorist attack on a soldier not that long before. Anyone in a uniform was told to enter via a special gate and queue-jump, in case another uniformed person was being targeted.

I was selected to be one of the 10 people to talk to Prince Phillip. When it was my turn, he was well briefed and asked me whether I was still flying. I asked him if he remembered flying a very small Volkswagen-powered, home-built, single-seater aeroplane that was part of the Tiger Club display team. He remembered it very well and told me how much he enjoyed his flight.

I then told him that the next time the aeroplane flew, the engine stopped and it landed in a farmer's field. He was very amused by this and we carried on chatting for some time before he was gently advised that there were others waiting to talk to him and moved on.

Anne and I had a lovely day in the gardens and seeing the Queen at close quarters was great. She looked fantastic and the day made me even more proud to be British, and made me realise how important the Royal Family are to our country.

When my operation moved from Staverton to Rendcomb in the early 1990s, myself and Sir Torquil Norman, along with Nick Mason, felt it would be a good idea to have a very small flying display at our airfield. We could ask friends and local residents to come and watch our aircraft and friends' aircraft during a flying demonstration.

From memory, that first event was a bit of a washout because it never stopped raining and the airfield became very waterlogged. However, the event went on and (although not ideal) everyone had a jolly good time.

While we were sponsored by St Ivel to promote Utterly Butterly, we held a garden party for aerial stunts and fun entertainment, which took place on Sunday 1 July 2001 at Rendcomb. AeroSuperBatics was celebrating its 20th anniversary as Europe's premier airshow company. The event was also to benefit the Children's Leukaemia Trust and Cirencester Housing for Young People, and we had over 500

Being appointed Honorary Air Commodore to 614 Squadron by Her Majesty The Queen was a great honour.

Below: one of many posters produced for displays put on at Rendcomb Airfield. Bottom: Anne and I next to the Curtiss Jenny.

children and their helpers from various special educational needs schools visiting the show.

We were lucky that the Red Arrows agreed to display and the flying programme included the best of the best of the airshow world performing in the UK and Europe during this time. The Royal Navy bought their Fairey Swordfish biplane and one of the crew who took part during their display was Sir George Martin – famous, of course, for his production and studio work with the Beatles.

The whole day was packed with fun flying. There was a motorbike stunt team re-enacting *The Great Escape*, the smallest twin-engined aircraft in the world, and finally a baker's dozen of daring ladies showed their dedication to the charity by letting a Stearman aircraft fly past and remove their skirts! All their skirts were attached by Velcro and linked together with a string that the aeroplane tugged with a hook as it went by.

Anne's father, Major George Hackett, was a wartime soldier in the Grenadier Guards and his theatre of war included action in Dunkirk, El Alamein and Italy. When the charity Help for Heroes started, Anne was very keen to get involved and she became the Healthy Heroes Representative for Gloucestershire. She put in an enormous amount of work and was totally dedicated to raising money for the charity. We put on two charity airshow events and, with huge support from our friends and companies who knew us, we managed to raise more than £90,000.

The last event we put on, in 2018, was supported by our team sponsors Breitling in Switzerland. It was a private event planned for only 800 guests. I had become an ambassador for the Royal Air Force Association, which is a charity that supports RAF families. We believe every generation owes a debt of gratitude to the RAF and their families, and I was really proud that our event raised more than £60,000 for the Royal Air Force Association. I have seen first-hand how much help they continue to give to people who need either financial help or (just as important) someone to talk to.

Again, all our friends turned up and purchased tickets for the day and they were treated to fantastic flying and a wonderful lunch. During the day, we were also involved with filming for *The Grand Tour* programme, with Richard Hammond taking to the skies while strapped to the wing of one of our Stearmans.

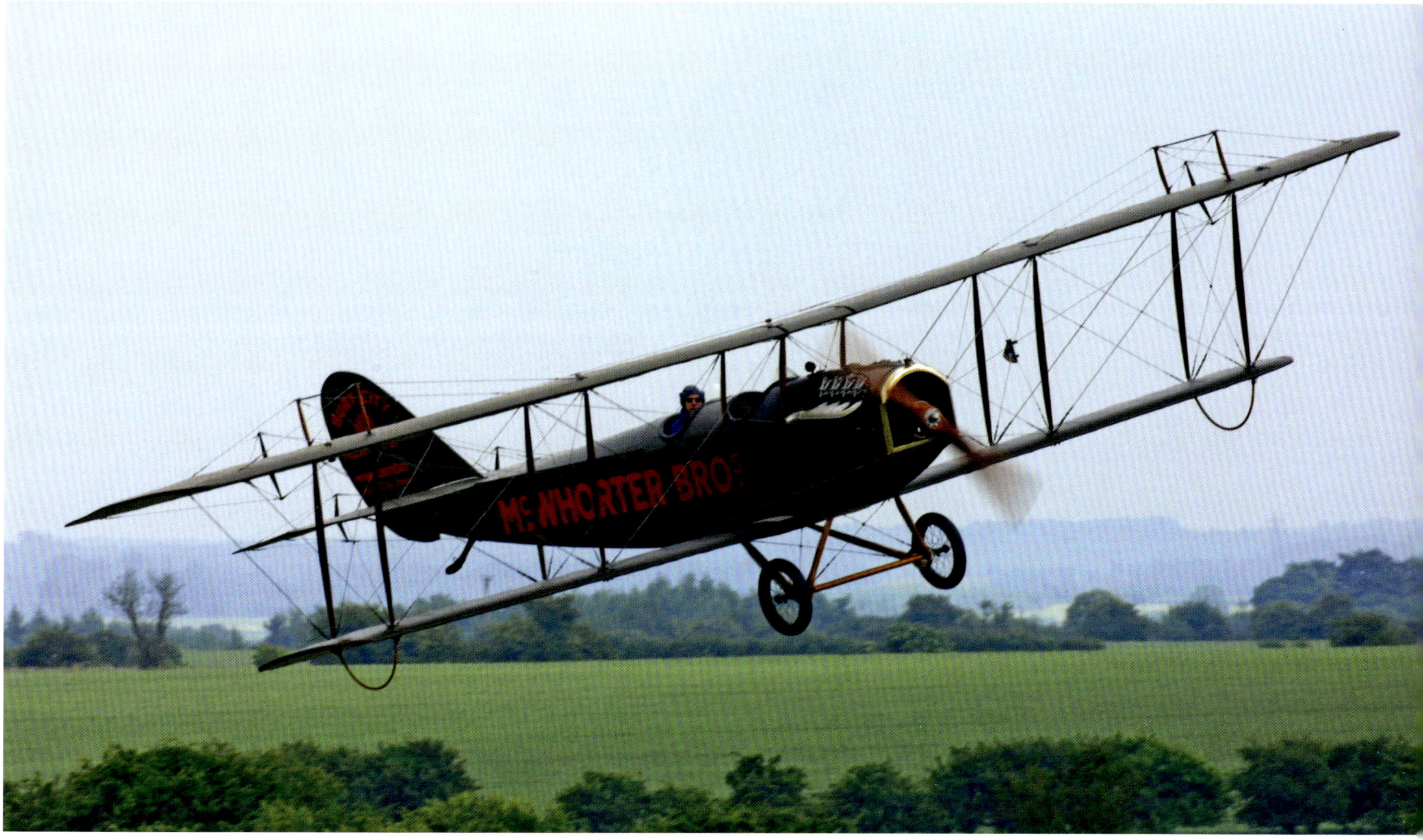

Our Royal Air Forces Association events have raised important funds for this wonderful charity as well as providing supporters with an excellent day of flying displays.

POST OFFICE
TELEGRAM

From. The RAF Association

Date of event. 7th June 2020

To.

AIR COMMODORE AND MRS VICTOR NORMAN REQUEST PLEASURE OF YOUR COMPANY AT RENDCOMB AERODROME CIRENCESTER STOP + FEAR BATTLE OF BRITAIN IMMINENT STOP + JOIN US ON SUNDAY SEVENTH JUNE 2020 FOR SPIFFING AERIAL PAGEANT AND LUNCHEON STOP +

TICKETS:
£150 (ADULT), £75 (CHILD 5-12YRS), FREE (CHILD UNDER 5) STOP +

ADVANCE BOOKINGS ONLY
rsvp@rafa.org.uk OR 0800 018 2361 STOP +

Please note access on the day is by advance ticket only. Early booking is advised as tickets are limited. Organised by RAFATRAD Ltd, a wholly-owned subsidiary of the Royal Air Forces Association (Registered Charity 226686 (England and Wales) SCO37673 (Scotland). RAFATRAD Ltd is incorporated in England and Wales under Company Registered Number 3455255. Registered office: Atlas House, 41 Wembley Road, Leicester, Leicestershire LE3 1UT. VAT No: 222 4642 92.

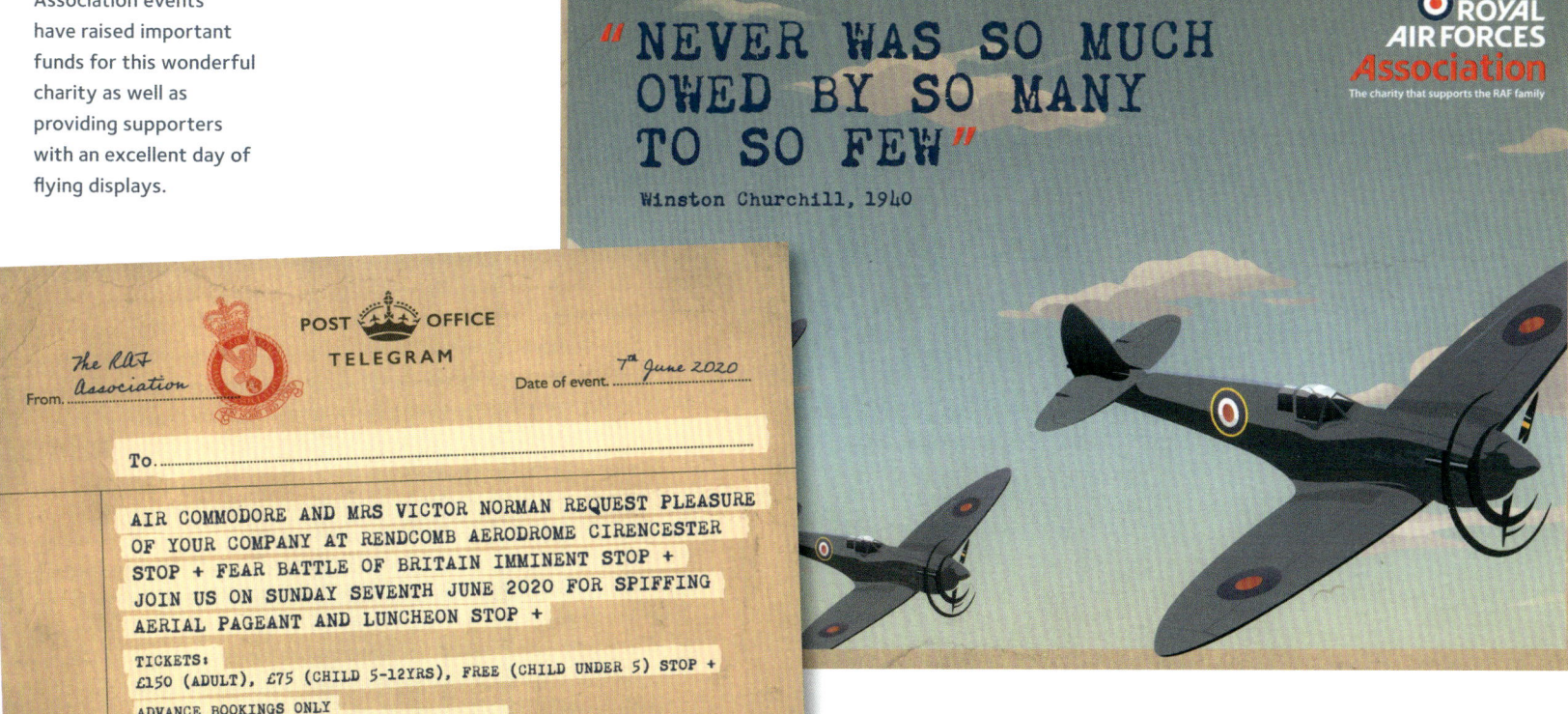

Richard Hammond put on a brave face during a wingwalk for the filming of an episode of *The Grand Tour*.
Below right: our wingwalkers are always happy to come and help out with our RAFA airshows at Rendcomb.

Rendcomb air show events

Rendcomb display
Sunday 12 September 1993
The Most Amazing Show on Earth
Sunday 1 June 1997
The Greatest Show on Earth
Sunday 1 July 2001
Evening display
16 June 2007
Heroes Airshow (Help for Heroes)
14 September 2008
Bugles at Dusk (Help for Heroes)
23 May 2010
Evening with Georgie Fame
14 May 2011 (for Help for Heroes)
Breitling Heroes Airshow
11 May 2014 (for Help for Heroes)
RAF Association Air Show
3 June 2018

> '"He said that if I ever saw his son do anything in his life that you know would have made me proud, you must promise to give him my watch." Roy then took the watch off and gave it to me.'

Whenever my father came home for a few days, or sometimes just a day, from the ages of three to six years old, I would be there waiting for him to arrive. After lunch, he would go into our TV room and sit in the big chair and I would go and sit on his knee and have a cuddle. When he was fed up with me or he wanted to talk on the phone, he put me down on the floor and took off his gold watch, which was very heavy and I could play with it for hours – I was fascinated by it.

I thought nothing about it until around 1965-'66, when I started flying from Stapleford Airfield. I was still in my teens and a friend of my dad's, Roy Stephens, who had an engineering business in Stratford and was also a flyer with his own twin-engined Piper Comanche (a quick little four-seater aircraft), sometimes used to take me and Anne to Le Touquet for lunch. He was very kind to us, and he loved talking about when my dad was alive and what they used to get up to.

We always went to Flavio, which was next to the Westminster Hotel and opposite my dad's old villa. I noticed that Roy was wearing a gold watch and I asked him if it was my dad's. He said it was. I really wanted to have the watch, but Roy told me that it was a very lucky watch and that it had bought my dad (and now him) good luck so he would never part with it. Roy idolised my dad.

Every time we met, I asked him if I could have the watch but the answer was always the same. Eventually Roy's younger brother, Ray, learned the business and took over Roy's engineering firm. It became very successful and Ray threw a big party at his house, which was near Stapleford Airfield, and he got hold of me and asked if I could do an aerobatics display for him. I quoted my usual fee, which at the time was £500, but said that I would give him the friendly price of £350. He said that was great, and told me to bring black tie and get Anne to come along to the party after the show. He said that his driver would collect me in the Bentley.

The display went really well and, after doing the aerobatics at height in a very exact and safe manner, I came down very low and brought the pace up in and out of the trees, which I knew Ray would love. I was collected from the airfield and went into the large marquee and got a standing ovation.

During the dinner, which started with a huge pot of caviar for each person, Ray's brother Roy came over and sat next to me. I had not seen him for years because he'd retired and moved to Spain. He showed me his wrist and said, 'I'm still wearing your father's watch.'

I really didn't want to get into a conversation about it but Roy said, 'I will now tell you a story about your dad's watch. You know that I was very fond of him and so I asked him before he died if I could buy his watch. He told me that it was not for sale but that he would give me the watch on one condition. He said that if I ever saw his son do anything in his life that you know would have made me proud, you must promise to give him my watch.'

The Royal Air Squadron

In 1997, I was invited to join what was then the Air Squadron by my great friend and flying chum Micky Suffolk, the Earl of Suffolk and Berkshire. I was thrilled to be asked to become a member. The Squadron was founded by a group of friends that included the shipping magnate Anthony Cayzer, the owner of the *Times* Hugh Astor, one of the Queen's stockbrokers Peter Vanneck, and Douglas Bader. There are now around 130 members and our Honorary Air Commodore is HRH Prince Philip, Duke of Edinburgh. To summarise, the Squadron's aims are:

- Membership by election
- Camaraderie
- Exuberant flying
- Light-hearted amateur aviation maintained at the highest professional standards
- Fine dining
- Style

Recent major trips include:
1992 Russia
1997 Pakistan and the Himalayas
2000 USA and Alaska
2003 South Africa
2005 Norway and Spitzbergen
2010 Menorca
2011 Jordan
2012 Gibraltar
2013 Ukraine
2014 Venice
2015 Sweden and Estonia
2015 Elba to Waterloo
2016 Britain tour

We've had numerous other UK and European trips and, best of all, fly-ins to members' strips. The membership is really made up of fun people who have a true love for aviation, and I feel proud to be a member.

We are fortunate to call the Dysons friends and to have spent many enjoyable hours in their company – be it on their yacht or looking around the fabulous Garden of Ninfa in Italy.

Sir James and Lady Deidre Dyson

These are two of not only the most gifted but also kindest people who Anne and I can call friends. I can't remember exactly when we first met, but James and I built up a rapport very quickly around aviation and aeroplanes, and hearing him talk about engineering and mechanical things fascinated me.

I offered to do a wingwalking flying display at James' 60th-birthday party as a gift from Anne, and I knew that it would be a very private affair. Dodington House is in a most wonderful setting, the house looking down onto a series of lakes set in a valley, with very mature trees lining the entry and exit to the lakes. I went to do a recce a few days before the event and also to check out a possible landing area just above the house in a field that was mostly flat.

I could see that to get low over the lakes was going to be a challenge rather like the Dambusters' approach to the Eder. However, I was not going to be shot at – until possibly the week after by the Civil Aviation Authority for low flying.

Martyn and I were sitting in our Stearman biplanes waiting for a 10-minute signal. We started and warmed up our 450hp radial engines and took off from the field and climbed away from the house. I decided that we would sneak up behind the house, which was where drinks were being served, and arrive low-level over the roof at high speed, smoke on, with our wingwalkers starting their own choreographed routine. Our display went very well and I must admit that we did rather beat the place up, flying in and out of the trees, which was great fun – proper barnstorming.

Anne and I have had great fun with Deirdre and James. They are both so gifted and Deirdre's carpet designs are fantastic. We have spent time together in Norway and Italy, looking around the wonderful Garden of Ninfa, which, with its small river flowing through the garden, must be the most romantic landscape garden anywhere.

James recently purchased RAF Hullavington, which I am very excited about, being local. It has an interesting wartime history and the World Aerobatic Championships were held there in 1970 – an American stunt pilot, Art Scholl, battled with the Russians in a bitterly close contest. As mentioned elsewhere, Art and his wife Judy later helped me by building a special rig for my Stearman aircraft, enabling AeroSuperBatics to give wingwalking rides.

Roy then took the watch off and gave it to me.

I gave the watch to my son Sam when he was 18 years old and became the youngest qualified display pilot in the UK. I told him that he could now do everything that I could, but was probably better than me.

I met David Gilmour through Nick Mason and got to know him much better after the Pink Floyd split in 1985. Those concerts without Roger Waters were just as good or better, and David was doing all the singing and carrying the whole show on his shoulders, night after night.

David became interested in old cars, and the flying bug really grabbed him too. I sold him various vintage aircraft and he became a very good pilot. He is one of those talented people who can do anything really well if they put their mind to it. He is a superman and a very nice man. Anne and I spent some time with him and his first wife Ginger and their adorable children, and we did go to his wedding party when he got married to Polly, who is also charming. I've lost count of how many children are now in the Gilmour family!

We met Roger Waters when the Floyd were in the South of France recording during the year the band took out for tax reasons. He was renting a nice house and we would go round there for very casual, laid-back lunches with our children. Roger was very competitive and we would have swimming races and table-tennis competitions and everything was turned into a challenge to see who was the best.

During the recording of the album *The Final Cut*,

I ended up selling this 220hp Continental-engined Stearman to Pink Floyd's David Gilmour.

Gilmour in his P-51 Mustang – his lyrics to Pink Floyd's *Learning to Fly* perfectly summed up his passion for taking to the air.

I am always happy to get involved with a new project, and here we played host to rockers Status Quo as they filmed for a forthcoming video. The entire band, including frontmen Rick Parfitt and Francis Rossi (right) were taken wingwalking, and in true rock style there was a fantastic party held in the Pancho Barn afterwards!

I got a phone call, I think from Nick, who asked if we could get our local church at North Cerney to ring the bells. Anne arranged for this to happen and a recording was made. At the same time we drove down to the main road and recorded our car's windscreen wipers.

I was then asked if I could arrange for the recording engineer to go up in a four-engined Lancaster bomber. I explained I didn't think this was possible but said that I would get back to them. During this time, I was very good friends with one of the Red Arrows, Neil Wharton, and his wife Sara and I asked Neil to see if anything could be arranged.

A few days later, Neil telephoned me and said he could organise a trip in one of the Royal Air Force's four-engined Shackleton bombers that operated from Scotland, going on seven-hour flights to secure our air space from the Russians. All was arranged and the sound man had a new quadraphonic sound system that the Floyd were experimenting with. The flight was booked and the soundman got on a train with all his stuff, heading for the airbase. We then heard that he was, in fact, an Argentinian and we were then at war with Argentina. Neil told him to say he was Italian if asked. In fact, he never was and he went on a reconnaissance flight for seven hours hunting for Russians and got some really good recordings.

Following this success, Roger asked if we could get the sound of a bomb going off. Neil was never one to say no, so he came up with a cunning plan. Every week on a Monday or Tuesday, the pilots of the Red Arrows would go up on their own, not in formation, to hone their flying skills even more. Neil arranged for the Argentinian sound man to be set up with his recording equipment in a remote field in Devon and to start recording at 9:45am precisely. Neil climbed his Red Arrow Hawk up to 20,000ft and dived down towards the sound man and pulled out at the last minute – it sounded exactly like a bomb falling!

Roger was very pleased with the results and on the record sleeve there is a note: 'Special thanks to Neil Wharton'. No one knew who Neil was, including the Royal Air Force.

I have already mentioned that Anne and I met at a Rolling Stones concert in 1964, which took place at the local swimming pool. A friend of ours is an amazing lighting designer and engineer and he has done all the lights at concerts for both Pink Floyd and the Stones, as well as hundreds of other gigs. He knew our story about meeting at that early Stones show and we were invited to go and see the band perform at Madison Square Garden.

We were very excited, of course, and although we had seen them live at Wembley, to be invited to America and given VIP tickets was going to be special.

On the evening of the show we were asked to join the band's guests and their families for a meal

backstage, which was great fun. I ended up sitting next to this charming, older, very smartly dressed, blue-rinsed lady, who I discovered was Keith Richards' mum. We got chatting and she told me that she was staying with Keith down the road in his apartment and she proudly told me how wonderful Keith was because he cooked her a full English breakfast every morning. She burst out laughing and then told me that the only trouble was that it was served up around 4pm every afternoon, when he usually got up.

We had great seats and being up close to the band and seeing them perform was just fantastic.

Gary Numan is another musician with an appetite for flying and together with Norman Lees formed the Radial Pair, displaying at air shows in the early 1990s.

Family is so important and we are blessed with our lovely children, pictured here through various stages of their lives.

I could write so much about our three children. They have turned out to be wonderful adults with families of their own. The best part of it is that we all enjoy each other's company and spend most of our family holidays together as a large group of around 16.

All of them – Zoe, Nina and Sam – have achieved so much and Anne and I love them dearly. We are very proud of them all and we never stop showing off to our friends about how great they all are.

We are again so lucky with our grandchildren. They come in all ages and sizes, and each one of them is special and a great character. Diana, Tiger, Flame, Rose, Jasmine, Alfie, George and Eliza all bring us such pleasure and joy and they are a very close-knit gang. They laugh a lot about Anne and I, and they are always playing games together.

Son Sam made his way into the *Guinness World Records* book as the youngest wingwalker, with his dad at the controls.

More family photographs. We are a close-knit family and share our lives with our wonderful children and now grandchildren.

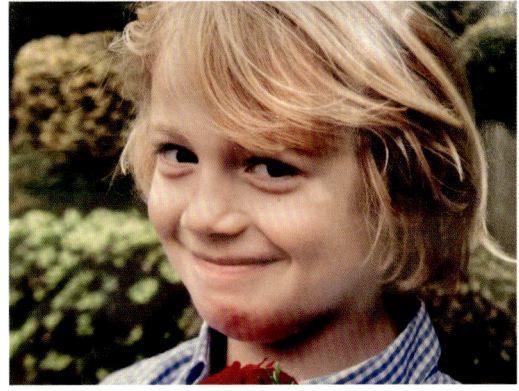

'Anne was unbelievable during the whole ordeal… she put up with me being very scared, frightened, selfish and bad-tempered.'

In September 2014, I was getting breathless and having trouble walking up hills, and was just generally lacking in energy. I visited my GP, who is also a friend, and after doing various tests and having an X-ray to check my lungs (which were fine), my blood test results showed that I was anaemic. I was sent to a blood specialist and after many unpleasant tests I was diagnosed with having stage 4 mantle cell lymphoma.

I was with my youngest daughter, Nina, when the doctor told me and we both burst out crying. I asked how long I had and he looked it up on his computer, putting in my age and various other details, and said about four years.

Nina, who used to run her own VIP concierge company in London and knew how to find doctors and specialists for her clients, found out that the top specialist in London for this type of cancer was a Dr Robert Marcus, who worked with private patients in Harley Street at the London Oncology Centre, Wellington Hospital and Kings College Hospital. She telephoned his secretary and asked if her dad could come and see him but there was a two-week wait.

I was, and still am, in the Royal Air Squadron and I was friendly with a lovely lady called Dr Margaret Spittle, who was a cancer specialist herself. My daughter telephoned her because she also had a practice in Harley Street and Dr Spittle confirmed that Dr Marcus was the top specialist,

and told Nina that she would see what she could do. Within the hour, Nina was told that I had an appointment for the next day.

The whole family came, of course: Anne, Zoe, Nina, and Sam. Dr Marcus was a bit surprised at how many of us were there but he was charming, very straightforward, and didn't mind being quizzed by my daughters, who had done their own research on my type of cancer and on all the new drugs that were being tested. We all really liked Dr Marcus and he had me in to be tested all over again to confirm exactly what stage my cancer was at and what needed to be done.

I won't bore you with all the treatments but I had high-dose chemotherapy every couple of weeks and then a maintenance drug programme that lasted four years. I quickly became cancer-free and in remission, which I still am five and half years later.

Anne was unbelievable during the whole ordeal. She drove me up and down from Gloucestershire to London, stayed with me during my treatments, and rushed me into hospital a couple of times when I got a dangerous fever. She put up with me being very scared, frightened, selfish and bad-tempered. On top of this, we were building a large extension on our house and Anne was dealing with all the 101 questions I had for six months while I was mainly staying in London with my daughter. Thank you, Nina and James.

What does the future hold? I will never know, but my hope is that Anne and I stay healthy enough to enjoy our lives together. Being a close-knit family is important and spending time with our children and grandchildren and doing things with them is nearly always a joy.

I hope when the coronavirus pandemic ends or when we can live our lives without fear of getting it, that we will be able to travel around freely – flying to places piloting ourselves, and riding on one of my motorcycles with Anne not falling asleep on the pillion. Or, if she does, with me pinching her leg to wake her up.

I want to keep flying for as long as the powers that be allow me – and maybe even a little bit longer – and to keep enjoying trips in an old Porsche.

How lucky have I been to lead the life that I have had, with the girl I love, never having a proper job or working for anyone and doing all the things that I love. What a lucky bugger!

An evening shot of Anne and I, having just landed after a flight in the 1916 Curtiss Jenny.

POEM BY VIC FOR ANNE

With my head on the pillow and my thoughts far away,
It's not very long before they wander your way,
Your love and devotion is strong and so sure,
But my trouble is darling I always want more.

But this is the moment to start being real,
And grab with both hands a wonderful deal,
Both hugs and big kisses are here to be got,
I must just go out there and grab the whole lot.

You're gorgeous, you're sexy and romantic as well,
The list never ending and we somehow do gel,
Vic stop for a moment, think about all this,
I'm a real lucky blighter, Anne give us a kiss.

ROYAL AIR FORCES ASSOCIATION

Being Honorary Air Commodore of 614 Squadron provides me with valuable opportunities to learn in greater depth about today's RAF. I feel privileged that, when meeting people on RAF stations and at events, I get to understand some of the responsibilities they shoulder on a daily basis. Despite the challenging situations they often face, I am always incredibly impressed by their professionalism and their resilience. I have huge respect for anyone who has served in the RAF, and their families.

It was during the course of my 614 Squadron duties that I first became aware of the important work of the Royal Air Forces Association (RAF Association) – a national charity that supports the whole of the RAF community. Founded over 90 years ago, the Association provides practical, emotional and financial support for all generations of RAF personnel and their family members.

The charity relies entirely on donations from individuals, companies and charitable trusts in order to be a good friend to tens of thousands of members of the RAF community every year. I was very keen to start lending a hand and, in 2016, I began donating charity wingwalks to help raise funds. Since then, Anne and I have met some fascinating and courageous people who have been sponsored by their family and friends to wingwalk to raise money for the RAF Association, as well as many people we have helped support as a result.

Among them is former WAAF officer Bryony Fuller, a grandmother who lives in Wiltshire. Bryony was one of the first female officer cadets to go through the RAF College at Cranwell. What she learnt at college has inspired her throughout her life, especially after a devastating fall. Running down the stairs one morning in 2008, Bryony missed a step and fell. She was not discovered for 30 hours and sustained serious spinal injuries that mean she has since relied on a wheelchair to get around.

Bryony was determined to help the Association as thanks for the help they have given her, and has now completed two wingwalks with our team to raise vital funds for the charity. She is an incredible individual and a huge inspiration, and it was a joy for Anne and I to be part of this by helping Bryony fulfil her ambition to take to the skies.

Keen to do even more to help, I was absolutely thrilled when I was invited to become an RAF Association Ambassador. In 2018, Anne and I, supported by our brilliant AeroSuperBatics team, staged the first Rendcomb Airshow fundraiser for the RAF Association. In true Rendcomb style, it was an unforgettable party involving all our best friends and, even better, it meant that we could help support the vital befriending service recently launched by the Association. The charity's 'Connections for Life' service trains volunteers to provide veterans and those they leave behind with face-to-face and telephone friendship, to help them feel less isolated and lonely, and to keep their connection with their local communities.

The money we raised through the airshow helped the Association to train more than 400 volunteers, who in turn supported 421 lonely and isolated people that year alone. I am now proud to be a volunteer for the service as well.

Anne and I are looking forward to playing an important role in helping the RAF community for many years to come, through our support to the RAF Association. If you want to join us, we'd love to have you on board – just email enquiries@rafa.org.uk or call 0800 018 2361 for more information.

AFTERWORD #1
JEREMY CLARKSON

I'm often asked if I will ever write an autobiography and the simple answer is, 'No, because I can't really remember anything I've ever done. It's all just a blur.' There are a few things that are still in sharp focus, though. Dropping a laser-guided bomb on something in North Carolina. Landing on the *Dwight D Eisenhower*. Most of the weekly calls to say that Richard Hammond had become upside-down again. And the flight I once took in the back seat of Vic's stunt plane.

In my mind it was a Zlin, which means it probably wasn't. I am a man who is largely untroubled by motion sickness. I thought I was immune. Vic demonstrated in less than 30 seconds that I am not. And then, having shown me that food in my body could go up as well as down, he went on to show me that I could retch up not just what I'd eaten that day, but everything I'd eaten, ever.

I do not remember how long the flight lasted but I do recall that when we landed, my face was the exact same colour as a piece of photocopying paper and that I did not fully recover for several days.

Still, I did get my own back in the end. I employed his daughter on *The Grand Tour* and have spent the last five years making her life as difficult as possible.

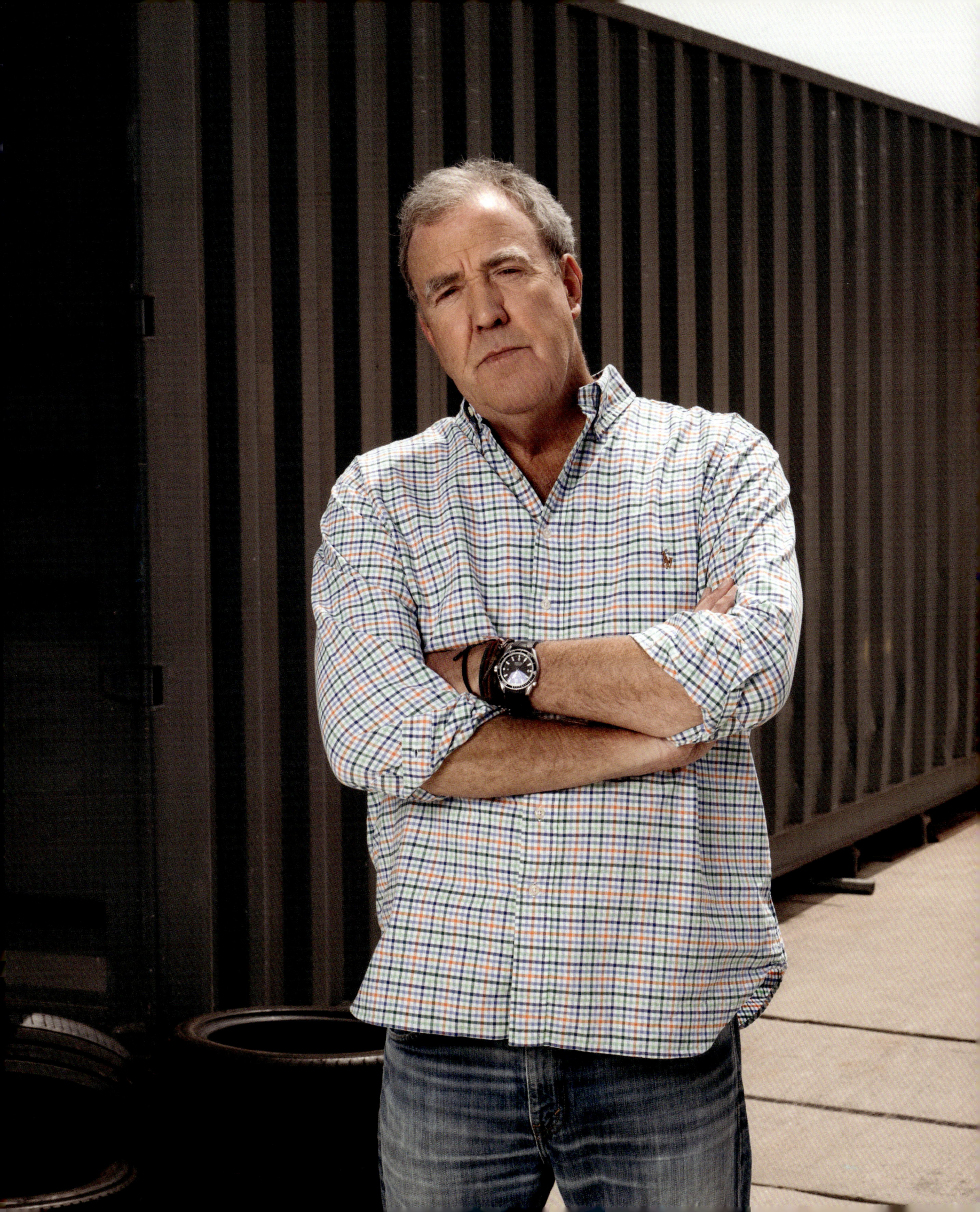

AFTERWORD #2
NICK MASON

Dearest Vic

Firstly, thank you.

You've provided enhancements to my life that even 50 years in a rock and roll band failed to provide, and you've been one of the greatest financial advisors it's been my privilege to listen to.

It might have been all too easy to fritter those royalties away on VAT, income tax and dull old pension funds, but you rose to the challenge and, undaunted by the fact that I was frightened by flying, helped me not only buy lots of aeroplanes, but also a share in the airfield to go with them – possibly the most expensive therapy ever, but worth every penny!

All of this has given me enormous amounts of fun and satisfaction, plus the odd fright and many happy hours just sitting about, talking about what to do next – usually preceded by the phrase 'It's not dear...' followed by a mesmerising description of something I never knew I needed until that moment.

My wardrobe has been enhanced by your success with AeroSuperBatics. I have a wide range of Crunchie, Utterly Butterly, Guinot and Breitling hats, t-shirts and bags, butter (oops, I mean I can't believe it's not...) dishes, mugs, jackets, watches, scarves and model aircraft that makes me a style icon in North London.

And that's not all. You arrived in my life with a fabulous family and some extraordinary friends (no names, no pack drill). You've been a good friend to me, but also to all my children, and the fact that they all love you indicates a far better assessment of your personality than relying on mine.

Lots & lots of love,
Y.P.S.C.
Nick

AFTERWORD #3
ANDY OFFER

I do think I have done a lot of interesting things in my life. I am fortunate enough to have commanded a frontline Harrier Squadron in war, as well as flying in and leading the Royal Air Force Aerobatic Team – the Red Arrows. I have been to many countries with some fantastic people and seen things that sometimes I want to forget.

I had a 20-year-plus career in the Royal Air Force and first flew with Vic in the back seat of my Red Arrow as he commentated at the Biggin Hill Airshow, and while Vic shared a zeal for aviation there was something else. He is passionate, interesting and, importantly, interested in you. It immediately dawned on me he was like the rest of us Air Force aviators, and I really liked him.

My career continued and I went to Staff College, which for a pilot, while educational, is somewhat dull. My new mate Vic suggested I come and fly with him in his wingwalking team at Rendcomb Airfield. Well, let the fun begin. I was flying in a four-aircraft civil display team: same skills, different disciplines, amazing people, limited training and bags of laughs.

I knew I liked Vic but during this period I became, and still am, full of respect for him. He was an excellent pilot, he loved aviation and all the people around him, he led from the front, and in a non-military way he commanded the respect of all.

I am so happy that I had the opportunity to share so many experiences and laughs with Vic. I only wish we had the time to do it all again.

APPENDICES

APPENDIX 1

AeroSuperBatics – staff history

P – Pilot   W – Wingwalker   O – Office   S – Sponsor   D – Driver   G – Ground Crew   M – Merchandise Unit

YEAR	TEAM		NAME
1981–86	Colt Cars		Vic Norman
		O	Emma Heardman
		O	Ros Thilthorpe
1987	Yugo Cars	P	Bob Thompson
		W	Lesley Gale
		S	Malcolm Fairs
1988	Yugo Cars	P	Paul Noble
		W	Helen Tempest (1988-93, 1995-96, 1997-2006)
		O	Ros Thilthorpe
1989	Yugo Cars	P	John Adams
1990	Crunchie	P	Brendan O'Brien
		P	Vic Norman
		W	Caroline Pridham
		S	Richard Frost (1990-98)
		S	Adrian Cox
	SEAT	P	Vic Norman
		O	Helen Green
	Vladivar Yak Pair		Paul Bonhomme & Richard Goode, Vic, Harpo
1991	Crunchie	P	Mike Dentith (1991-2006)
		P	Matthew Hill (1991-94)
		W	Sara Cubitt (1991-94)
		S	Simon Davis
		S	Mark Nelson
		O	Brian Russell
1992	Crunchie	W	Taff Hunter (part-time but did several shows 1992-98)
		W	Tracey Lynch (part-time)
1993	Crunchie	S	Stewart Wilson
		S	Alan Chadwick
1994	Crunchie	W	Mandy Pantell
		P	Robin Bowes (1994-95) RIP 1995
		S	Lewis Jones (went onto London Rubber Co)
1995	Crunchie	S	Peter Poole
		W	Rachel Taggart (Harris – part-time but did several shows)
		W	Tanya Gaze (1995-96 & 1998)
		W	Leyla Ahmet (part-time 1995-96)
		O	Jodi Cumberlin (Crush – 1995-97)
		O	Cherine Harrison (& part-time WW)
	St Ivel AN2	P	Jez Cooke (RIP 2019)
		O	Jessica Naish
		S	Adrian Cox
	Crunchie	S	Julia Parkhouse

YEAR	TEAM		NAME
	St Ivel AN2	S	Katherine Hale (1996 & 1997)
		P	Andy Wyatt (1996 & 1999)
		P	John Harper
			Alan Plowman – driver for roadshow (1996, 1998-2002)
	Crunchie	W	Sara Mozayeni (1997 & 1999)
		W	Andreya Wharry
		W/O	Rachel Huxford (1997-end 2000)
		S	Paul Weddepohl
	Crunchie	S	Chris Houlton (now Carlsberg)
		P	Tony Richards
	St Ivel AN2	O	Mandy Castle
		O	Lisa Farnsworth (& sampling unit 1998-99)
			Darren Rumley
		S	Wendy Masson
		S	Claire Fitzgerrald
		W	Annabel Howard (part-time)
		M	Angie Draycott – sampling unit manager
		M	Darren Rumley – tastometer supervisor
	Mitsubishi	P	Tim Senior
		D	Keith Davis
		S	Colin Peirce (1998 & 1999)
		S	Philip Price (1998-2000)
		S	Nick Spratley (1998-2001)
		S	Ed Bowen-Jones (1998-2001) RIP
		S	Tara
		S	David Miles (1998-2001)
		S	Di Towse (1998-2001)
	Utterly Butterly	S	Adrian Cox
		S	Tony Lucas (1999-2001)
		S	Wendy Masson (1999-2001)
		S	Kelly Weaver
		S	Claire Knott
		W	Juliette Pendleton
		O	Helen Holness (1999 – end 2000, then part-time 2001)
		O	Penny – book keeper
	Mitsubishi	P	Dave Evans
		D	Rob Greville
	Utterly Butterly	S	Alison Buck
		S	Claire Knott
		S	Caroline Baker
		W	Lisa Hampstead

YEAR	TEAM		NAME
		W	Rebecca Hachenburg
		M	Patrick Jones
	Shape	S	Dave Hall
		S	Vicky Kipling
		S	Nina Leijerstam
		S	Liz Griffiths
		S	Hanna
		O	Chris Francis – skydiving team
		O	Andy Bennett – skydiving team
		O	Liz Danby – skydiving team
		O	Ivan – skydiving team
		O	Fran Shashkova – skydiving team
		O	Gary Watson – skydiving team
	Shape Sampling Team		Laura Bouvenizer, Sally Westmacott, Hailey Mason & Mike Matthews
	Kia	S	Mark Quinn
		S	Gary Elliot
		S	David Wilson-Green
		S	Paul Carter
		P	Martyn Carrington – 2020
	ASB	O	Rhiannon Nugent (& Shape)
			Rachel McMillan – chef (2000-2003)
			Keith Rockman – BBQ king (2000 & 2001)
			Maurice Cowling (book keeper)
	Utterly Butterly	W	Lorna Cookson
		W	Rachel Cookson
		S	Michael Gun
		S	Ceri Bennett
	Kia Cars	S	Guy Jones
	Utterly Butterly	W	Marie Duguid – 2004
		W	Sophie Sharpe (RIP 2018)
		S	Karen Smith
		S	Ceri Bennett
		S	Jane Holdsworth
		M	Sara Mozayeni (commentator)
		M	Rob Greville
		M	Kirstyn Kennaugh
		M	Ian Hibbs / Kevin Holness
2003		W	Elisa Mason
		W	Kirsty Joly – 2004 and then part-time
		P	Andy Offer – 2005
		S	Karen Smith
		G/M	Clive Bond – 2004 (and beyond)
		G/M	Debs Pearson (commentator) – 2004
2004		W	Poppy & Libby Dover (part-time)

YEAR	TEAM		NAME
		S	Emma Dews
			Mark Lane – airfield maintenance
2005		O	Debbie Boston / Jess Jenkins (Rhi maternity leave)
		S	Emma Dews then Charlotte Bagchi
		S	Paul Davies
		W	Poppy & Libby Dover
		W	Bethan Jennings & Lucy Foster (part-time)
2006		S	Charlotte Bagchi / Mark Nelson (ex-Crunchie)
		W	Lucy Foster
		W	Sarah Tanner
		P	Andy Wyatt
		O	Kat Nicoll (Helen's maternity leave)
2007	Guinot	W	Lucy Foster
		W&O	Sarah Tanner
		W	Danielle Hughes
		M&W	Hannah Mitchell
		W	Lorraine Sadler (part-time)
		P	David Barrell
		P	Steve Hicks (part-time)
2009		W	Dannielle Hughes
		W	Stella Gould
		P	Al Hoy (part-time)
2010	Breitling	W	Danielle Hughes
		W	Stella Gould
2011		O	Sally Cook (part-time book keeper)
2012		W	Freya Paterson
2013		W	Nikita Salmon (part-time) – 2017
2014		W	Charlotte (Lottie)
		W	Emily Gould
2015		W	Nikita Salmon
		W	Lydia (part-time)
2016		W	Stephanie Pansier
		W	Florence Rollerston-Smith
		W	Maria Quintin
2017		W	Katie Hobbs
		W	Gina Marshall
		P	Brian Cornes (part-time)
		P	Nick Barnard (part-time)
2018	No sponsor	O	Lorraine Wright – to present
		W	Kirsten Popjoy – to present
		W	Gemma Craig – to present
		P	Andy Cubin (part-time) – to present
2020		P	Steve Noujaim (part-time)

Engineering
Burt Leverett
Tony
Will
Rupert Waisey
Paul Barrett
Smithy (Mark Smith, RIP 2020)
Callum Hunter
Oli Crossthwaite
Carl Bamforth
Nick
Tony Wilkinson
Andy Brereton
Les Lucas RIP
Terry Blackwell – painter (RIP)
Dennis Richings – painter
Clive Bond
Matthew Boddington
Mel Perry
Gordon McDill – CAA engineer for overseas trips
Ben Cooper
Andy McLuskie – CAA engineer for overseas trips

Others
Philip Castle – artist
Henk – sign-writer
Richard Baldwin – sign-writer
Ashton Coleman-Smith
Simon Ward
Yves Rossy
Gill Rowe
Melvyn Hiscock (RIP 2021)
Richard Dongray
Doug 'the plank'

Team photographers
Alain Ernoult
Duncan Cubitt
Chris Bennett
John Dibbs
Jeff Bloxham
Katsuhiko Tokunaga
Paul Johnson
Karle Darge
Darren Harber
Marc de Tienda
Glenn Stanley
Alberto
Jim Clarke
Michael Jorgensen
Phil Walley
Andy Cubin

Team video
Steve Meakin
Your Digital Memories
Planes TV

Overseas airshows
Qionghui Jiang (Sky Jiang) – China airshows

APPENDIX 2

World records and other firsts
Longest wingwalk Helen Tempest in 1988 (2 hours 40 minutes), Roy Castle in 1990 (3 hours 30 minutes)
Baton pass 3 feet long **Shortest baton pass** 1 foot long
Hand-hold Helen Tempest and Sara Cubitt
Youngest wingwalker Sam Norman (age nine), Tiger Brewer (age eight), Rose and Flame
Oldest wingwalker Dizzy Seals and Tom Lacey
First wedding on the wing (and second)
First formation wingwalk 2-ship, 3-ship, 4-ship, 5-ship
World's only formation wingwalking team
World's largest crumpet Utterly Butterly PR. Chef: Nick Mason and Whiddets Bakery in Cirencester
Skydiver walking along the bottom wing and hanging between two aircraft Simon Ward and Yves Rossy
First human flag in the UK (flown at Biggin Hill Airshow for the Queen's Jubilee)

Countries we have displayed in
The whole of the UK
Ireland
France
Italy
Holland
Belgium
Portugal
Luxembourg
Czech Republic
Austria
China
Australia
India
United Arab Emirates: Al Ain and Dubai
Bahrain
Oman
Switzerland
Channel Islands
Japan
Philippines
Kuwait

Sponsors – date order
Lonsdale Cars
Colt Car Company
Yugo Cars
SEAT
Vladivar Vodka
Car Magazine/Super Car Classics
Cadbury's Crunchie
Hype
St Ivel Utterly Butterly
Mitsubishi Motors
Red Zebra – Mitsubishi secondhand dealership
St Ivel Shape
Kia Cars
QBE
Guinot
Shell
Breitling

TV shows and other PR
Blue Peter
You Bet
Don't Try This At Home
National and local TV & radio
Jack Osborne: Adrenaline Junkie
GMTV
Big Breakfast
Really Wild Show
You'll Never Believe It
Family Fortunes
Robbie Coltraine's B Road Britain
Top Gear
News Round
Famous and Fearless
BBC Radio 4 *Woman's Hour*
Pulling Power
Daily Telegraph
Daily Star
The Times
Daily Mail
The Sun
The People
The Help Squad – Banner tow (wingwalker search day), Sara Cutitt
Crime Watch
Good Morning TV
Tartan Army – For Zoe
Go Getters
Disney Adventure
The Mirror
The Big Breakfast – Channel 4
Esquire magazine 31/8/95
Marie Claire magazine 1997
What Ever You Want TV
How Do They Do That – American TV – Simon Ward aircraft transfer
Vogue magazine
Telegraph
Big Brother
FHM magazine 20/03/2003
Emmerdale 20/01/2006
Jim'll Fix It 14/12/2006
Formula 1 GP Silverstone – three presenters on the wing
Question of Sport
CBBC *Dare Devil*
Blue Peter
Sky Discovery Channel 19/08/2014 – baton pass
The Grand Tour 03/06/2018
Birdman Rally

VIP wingwalkers

NAME	FLIGHT DETAILS/NOTES	DATE
Roy Castle	World record – longest wingwalk (Gatwick Airport to France)	
Linda Lusardi		
Bear Grills		29/8/02
Dizzy Seals	World record – oldest wingwalker	
Charlie Dymock	National Meals on Wheels Day	
Richard Branson		
Jack Osborne	*Jack Osborne: Adrenaline Junkie*	
Chris Packham	*The Really Wild Show*	
Davina McCall	Shape Skydiving Team PR	
Keith Chegwin	Super nervous!	
Richard Hammond	*The Grand Tour* (at 2018 Rendcomb Airshow)	
Kris Akabusi	World record baton pass for *Record Breakers*	
Sir James Dyson		
Dubai Princess		
Eddie Jordan	British Grand Prix	05/07/2012
Bucks Fizz		
Elon Musk		
Status Quo	For their new music video filmed at Rendcomb	
Bill Murray	At Airshow press day	
Rick Fenn		
Cheryl Baker	*Record Breakers*	
Chuckle Brothers		
Robbie Coltrane	Flew inside	
Carol Vorderman		
David Coulthard	British Grand Prix	05/07/2012
Jake Humphrey	British Grand Prix	05/07/2012
Georgie Fame		24/04/2013
Beth Tweddle	2012 Olympic medallist (Breitling book)	
Aled Jones	*Daily Mail* – Conquers his fear of heights	21/09/2018
Fleur East	Pronamel Stronger than Ever campaign	19/11/2020
Matt Tebbutt	RAF Association charity day (*Saturday Kitchen* TV show)	

Saturday Kitchen's Matt Tebbutt proves his mettle.

APPENDIX 3

Aircraft flown (from my logbook)

AIRCRAFT TYPE	DATE	NOTES
Aircoupe		First flying lesson and first solo
Cherokee		
Bolkow		
Stampe		
Zlin 50L		
Pitts S2A	26/07/1983	
Beech Staggerwing	05/06/1990	
Pace Spirit		
PA18 SuperCub	06/04/1989	
PA28R		
Pitts S1	26/07/1988	
Chipmunk	11/07/1984	
Comanche Single		
Devon	10/07/1985	
Zlin 526	Oct 85	
Fiesler Storch	Dec 85	
Hawk	20/03/1986	Flight with the Red Arrows
Gypsy Moth	19/07/1986	Belonging to Hamish Moffat
Stearman 220hp	24/07/1986	G-THEA belonging to Lindsay Walton
Stearman 450hp	19/11/1986	Belonging to Ray Hanna
Rollason Beta	12/04/1987	G-AWHW
Stearman 450hp	23/05/1987	N54922
Yak 50	18/04/1988	
Stearman 220hp	06/05/1988	N435V
Piper J3 Cub	14/06/1988	
CASA 1131E	03/02/1989	
Ryan PT22		
Hornet Moth	10/07/1989	
Grob 115	02/08/1989	
Sia Marchetti SF260c	13/10/1989	
Sukhoi SU26M	16/10/1989	
WACO UPF7	16/11/1989	
PC7 Pilatus	25/08/1990	With the Martini Team (Jacques Bothlin)
Zlin 142	11/10/1990	At Moravan in Czech Republic
Bonanza F33	20/08/1991	
Cessna 180	09/09/1991	Torquil Norman's aircraft
Fokker Triplane	12/09/1991	Robin Bowes' aircraft at Rendcomb
Robin DR400	02/10/1991	To Czech to collect Zlin G-1001
Cessna 210	04/02/1992	King City
Tiger Moth	14/08/1992	Rendcomb to Woburn
Yak 52		At Rendcomb
Antonov An-2	26/06/1993	05/10/1994
Fornier RF4	10/4/95	At Rendcomb
Extra 200	23/05/1997	Collect aircraft from the factory EDLD
Super Decathlon		For trailer-top landing display
RF-4		G-IVEL
Curtiss Jenny JN4D	02/07/1999	G-ECAB
Broussard		G-YYYY
YAK 18T	05/07/1999	
Cessna 152	29/03/1994	
Jaguar	24/04/1996	
Gipsy Moth	11/06/1996	G-AAOR
WACO 1934		
Piper Dakota		
Firefly		Tiger Airways
ASK 13		2-seat glider
Beechcraft Bonanza		G-ATSR
VANS RV7		G-DMBO

APPENDIX 4

Scan the following QR codes to access video content

Breitling 2011

Breitlings over Sydney harbour

Rose and Flame – youngest wingwalkers

Breitling 2010

Guinot 5-ship display

Utterly Butterly 3-ship

Poppy and Libby – wingwalking twins

Tiger Brewer – youngest wingwalker

Yves Rossy hangs between the wings

Wingwalk for the RAF Association

Breitling wingwalkers over Dubai

Danielle – My Life in Motion

Shell Oil

Vic talks about RFC Rendcomb

2018 Breitling video

2015 Breitling wingwalkers in Japan

Wingwalkers – 360° video

272 NORMAN CONQUEST